FLASHBACK

FLASHBACK

A Soldier's Story

Charles Richardson

Charles Richardson

WILLIAM KIMBER · LONDON

First published in 1985 by
WILLIAM KIMBER & CO. LIMITED
100 Jermyn Street, London, SW1Y 6EE

ISBN 0–7183–0567–1

Typeset by Grove Graphics, Tring
and printed in Great Britain by
Redwood Burn Limited, Trowbridge, Wiltshire

To my wife

Contents

List of Illustrations

ILLUSTRATIONS IN THE TEXT

Acknowledgements

The genesis of this book lay in a collection of letters which, unknown to me, my mother had kept during the years I spent abroad from 1931 to 1946. Our children recently dipped into them and the pressure on me mounted to 'write it down'. Having done so I was encouraged to proceed more seriously by Sir Denis Hamilton, and his son Nigel, author of *Monty*. I am greatly indebted to both of them for their permission to use material from the *Monty* biography, and to Hamish Hamilton Ltd, their publishers, for their consent.

General Sir Michael Gow, my ADC of 1946 and lifelong friend, read an early typescript and gave me much sound advice, for which I am most grateful to him.

My thanks are due also to Viscount Montgomery for permission, readily given, to publish certain of his father's writings.

My vivid but random recollections of the headquarters of SOE in Cairo in 1941 have been disciplined by re-reading *SOE: 1940–46* by M. R. D. Foot, *Baker Street Irregular* by Bickham Sweet-Escott and *Greek Entanglement*, the account by my friend Brigadier 'Eddie' Myers of his historic achievement as leader of the Greek guerilla bands.

My recollections of two days spent at the Nuremberg War Criminal trials were likewise brought into perspective by *Nuremberg* by Airey Neave.

I am grateful also to Messrs Chatto & Windus for permission to quote from *My First War* by Sir Basil Bartlett, and to Messrs David Higham Associates for permission to quote from *Operation Victory* by Sir Frederick de Guingand.

My thanks are due to my friend Mrs Daniells for so quickly and accurately typing the first draft and to my wife for her patience and encouragement in typing the innumerable amendments which followed. Mrs Amy Myers of William Kimber Ltd accepted the resulting patchwork without a murmur and to my great surprise produced therefrom a legible proof. For her professional help and wise advice I am particularly grateful.

C.R.

CHAPTER ONE

Origins

'What is war?'

'It's what happens when one country fights another – usually horrible for both.'

To the sophisticated five-year-old boy of today, nurtured on television, this might seem a naïve conversation of seventy years ago between me and my father. I remember it well: it was July 1914 and the Archduke Francis Ferdinand had just been murdered at Serajevo. 'There will be war,' said my father, a lieutenant-colonel in the Royal Garrison Artillery.

But even amongst professional soldiers, there were few who foresaw the scale of events that lay ahead, and the appalling carnage that was to follow.

Except for the South African War, which many had regarded as an unnecessary conflict in a remote colony, and the recurrent small-scale operations on the NW Frontier of India and in Burma, peace had reigned for nearly sixty years. Nevertheless in 1914 Britain, as always in her history, intervened to prevent the domination of Europe by an aggressive power, and sent her well-trained professional army, small by continental standards, to stand with France and Belgium against the German onslaught. To many the international crisis, triggered off by an assasssination in remote Serbia, had seemed obscure. Memories of war had faded from the nation's mind. It would be awakened only by a series of disasters, and the victory in 1918 would be achieved only by an enormous sacrifice of lives.

Only twenty-one years later, in 1939, the situation would be repeated: a British Expeditionary Force, smaller than before and inadequately trained and equipped, would once again be sent across the Channel to stem an invasion of the Low Countries and France by the Nazi *blitzkrieg*. Once again a heavy price would be paid for our unpreparedness.

In 1914 my father, who had retired the year before, had rented a small house in Devon after he had returned from Mauritius, a 'non-family' station, due to endemic malaria. To fill in those two years of absence, my mother had taken my sister and me to live cheaply in French Switzerland. Those were halcyon days : tobogganing in the Alpine sunshine and picnics amongst the spring flowers. I always felt it was a shame to have to sit down on a dozen wild narcissus before eating my ham roll. With no effort on my part, I became bi-lingual in French and English.

My father's family came from Springfield, Lurgan, County Down; they were in the linen business. Amongst those mentioned in the family tree which starts in 1728 is a Mary Gamble, a great-great grandmother known in her day as 'the fair maid of Derry', a description which I find difficult to reconcile with her portrait over my desk ! Against the more recent Richardsons is appended a terse note : 'The men of this generation were all addicted to drink.'

This failing may have contributed to the early death of my grand-father Charles Richardson at the age of fifty-one. His widow, who married at the age of seventeen, was then received with her five children into the rectory of her father William Reeves. Thereafter this 'eminent divine' exerted a profound influence on the family. Of the three boys, two were to be soldiers and one a mining engineer in Canada. All were to be given a first-class education, in England or Scotland. Emma, one of the two daughters, went to Cheltenham Ladies College and married a rich husband from Johannesburg. We regarded her in later life as an opinionated blue-stocking, and were enticed to her luncheon table only by the prospect of a tolerable crême brulée.

The Rector, William Reeves, an archaeologist of international repute as well as a doctor of medicine and of divinity, became Bishop of Down and Connor, and in 1891 President of the Royal Irish Academy. Today, nearly a hundred years after his interment at Armagh Cathedral, two of his admonitions from the pulpit seem relevant to the contending factions in his beloved Ireland :

'Error can never promote religion, no more than ignorance can generate devotion.'

'When once a man of education shuts his eyes to facts and suffers love of country or any other predilection to suppress his love of truth, he should be outlawed . . .'*

* From *The Life of the Right Rev. William Reeves, D.D.,* by Lady Ferguson (Longman Green & Co., 1893).

My mother was English, for which I have always been grateful: a little of the Irish temperament goes a long way. Her father, Richard Paul Wingrove, spent his early life as a merchant in India, and during the Mutiny served as a volunteer in the force which formed the defence of Calcutta. Later he became a much respected company promoter in the City of London. Like many at that time his fortunes varied: my mother could remember sumptuous days with frequent parties and rides with her father in Rotten Row, followed by periods when her mother seemed desperately short of housekeeping money.

As in most Victorian families, my mother's brothers dispersed to seek their fortunes in the further parts of the Empire : there were Wingroves in India, Shanghai, Australia and on the West African Coast.

It must have been in one of the periods of financial stringency, that my mother, with a sister and cousin, decided to train as a secretary. With the cousin she went out to Johannesburg and at Durban, then a favourite overseas station of the British Army, she met my father; they were married in Colombo.

The early military careers of my father and his brother had both been marked by incidents attributable to the Irish temperament. My father was the first rebel: in the Cadets' ledger of the Royal Military Academy, Woolwich dated 1880 appears the following entry against his name and two others: 'Rusticated for one term for taking part in an improper combination against authority.'

This was mutiny, and the Duke of Cambridge had much to say on the subject, when he visited the Academy in 1881: he spoke sternly of certain irregularities which, if not very serious, had been such as to incur his displeasure. He said that he was at a loss to understand how young men claiming to be gentlemen could disgrace themselves by ungentlemanly behaviour. Without discipline, they were worse than useless, for they could not expect men to obey them if they did not understand obedience themselves. Discipline was the first principle of a soldier's life: without it an army was but an idle mob, not only useless but dangerous.

My father, who died when I was twenty, never mentioned this incident to me; but the story goes that he with his two accomplices threw the head cadet of his term into a very 'unsavoury' tank. I understand that the system in those days was that the boy who passed in top became ipso facto the Head Cadet, with disciplinary responsibilities. I can well believe that in many cases, either through intellectual arrogance or late development, the top boy might be quite unsuitable. Forty-five years later, I was spared this fate by the existence of 'Under Officers', selected for their leadership qualities. Though top boy myself, I was a late developer, and left the Royal Military Academy in 1928 as a cadet corporal, the lowest form of life.

In 1881 my father, rusticated for one term, had arrived back at his widowed mother's house in the same week as had brother Arthur, expelled from Haileybury for having a bottle of whisky under the floorboards. Arthur, however, had another outburst at the battle of the Somme : the story goes that he seized command of the brigade having decided that his brigade commander was incompetent, won the battle and was awarded an immediate DSO. Shortly afterwards he refused to confirm the death sentence on a young soldier for cowardice, and was immediately retired for the second time. At the age of sixty-two he took to flying, and piloted his own aircraft.

In 1915, by which time my father had succeeded in getting back to active service in France, we lacked a permanent home, but finally came to rest in Granny Wingrove's house in Hampstead. It was a convenient refuge for us while the war lasted. Besides Granny there were two others in the house : our 'unfavourite' aunt Beatrice, an intelligent spinster who was private secretary to the Marquis of Bute, and Granny's 'companion' Miss Abbey, known to all as 'Sabby'. She was one of those devoted gentlefolk, whom our grandparents seemed able to pick up from some desperate environment of poverty and bind uncomplainingly to their family circle with everlasting bonds. She was beyond the age to contribute much in the way of housework, but was mistress of the cats which lived in the basement : their daily needs, in every sense of the word, were administered by Sabby, whose sense of smell fortunately had long since atrophied.

The air raids, by Zeppelin, figure prominently in my recollections of that period. I even saw one descend, an immense flaming torch, over London. By modern standards the damage was infinitesimal, but the noise, due to an anti-aircraft battery close by on Primrose Hill, appeared stupendous to a nine-year-old. My uncle Staveley Wingrove, a senior executive in the Westminster Bank, Lothbury, became an air raid warden, and used to visit us during the raids, entering with his shiny

(Left) William Reeves, Bishop of Down & Connor, who brought up the Richardson family after their father's early death in 1871. *(Right)* My mother with her two children, Nancy and Charles, in 1911.

My father Colonel Charles William Richardson, OBE with his Adjutant in France in 1917.

Author aged four in Switzerland, 1912.

blue waterproof cape and policeman's torch, obviously enjoying every moment of it!

Granny and Sabby and my mother took it all in their stride, but in 1918 there was a fortnight when every night we were disturbed. Granny, in her eighties, would mount the stairs, knock on my mother's door and quietly announce: 'Eva, they've come!' We then assembled in the drawing room where my sister and I were treated to port and biscuits, while sitting under the Bluthner grand piano for greater safety!

It was then that my mother, though undaunted, decided that the succession of broken nights had gone on long enough, and might affect our schooling; so we packed our suitcases and took a bus to Victoria Station intending to move to the south coast which surprisingly was regarded as a refuge. The booking office clerk said:

'You haven't a hope, mum, half London is there already.'

'What do you suggest?' said my mother.

'You might try Dorking, but you'll be lucky to find a bed.'

So off we went. We tried every hotel: at the town hall people were sleeping on billiard tables. Dusk was falling, so I suggested that we leave our suitcases wherever we could, and make one last foray. We popped into the nearest 'semi-detached', explained our predicament and left the cases. Another hour spent in quartering the town produced no result. We returned to the semi-detached and, swallowing our pride, asked for shelter. The old couple were momentarily aghast; they then said they had a spare room at the top of the house with one double bed; we could have a look at it. Sleeping all three of us in that one large bed, there passed a fortnight of great happiness. The old boy, who would have fitted well into 'Dad's Army', occupied his time by throwing dummy hand grenades in his tiny garden, and tried to teach me. They were a wonderfully kind old pair and, after we returned to London, insisted that we should return for 'a proper visit'. This we did.

Occasionally our father arrived on leave from France, sometimes bearing a sack of French beet sugar. Food and rations were plentiful in Le Havre, and he thought we were having a thin time. Perhaps we were?

During our 'nomadic' period in World War I, I was sent successively to three preparatory schools and eventually reached St Ronans, then in West Worthing. Under Headmaster Stanley Harris, a 'Corinthian' who had gained four international caps at soccer and captained England, I spent four happy years. He was the most genuine and dedicated Christian I have ever met. In 1922 when I left, we got four scholarships : mine was to Wellington.

My father had by now decided I was to be a soldier : I did not dispute it. Later he said I was to be a sapper. As he was a gunner, I asked him why. He replied :

'If you get tired of the Army, or more likely the Army gets tired of you, as a sapper you can always turn your hand to something else.'

This advice still holds good.

Wellington on the whole was enjoyable, particularly at the end, but it was in some ways a strange place. The headmaster, F. B. Malim, was somewhat equivocal about the Army. Rumour had it that in his estimation a career on the Stock Exchange was the only one that rated below the Army. He certainly took the view that an intelligent boy entering the Army would be 'wasted'. He said as much to my father, causing a considerable rumpus ! When I left for the Army with the Wellesley Exhibition, the head of the school went on the Stock Exchange ! I did all the right things becoming head of my Dormitory, and a school prefect and playing rugger very badly for the Dormitory. To me cricket was a closed book, but eventually I was allowed to play tennis on two courts recently constructed in the wilderness : tennis players at that time were definitely 'below the salt'. In the Corps, I reached the rank of sergeant. My report from the Commanding Officer read : 'Could become a useful officer if he learned to assert himself.'

'The Shop' at Woolwich in 1926 was a peculiar institution. Then, as now, cadets from the Empire and overseas countries attended. Although the termination of the Empire lay only thirty years ahead, relations with the peoples of our dependencies were often conducted with the brash self-confidence of Victorian England in her heyday. I remember in particular two cadets from Iraq : one I think disappeared after a few weeks but the other, Sharkawi by name, stayed to the end. His family doubtless were of immense importance in Baghdad, but we treated him as a soft, insignificant fellow-cadet with no noticeable vices. The drill sergeant from the Grenadier Guards, resenting no doubt the obvious lack of precision in Sharkawi's drill movements, decided to try to 'make a man of him'. The first treatment was ridicule :

'Now then, Mr Shark Ahoy,' he would scream across the parade ground. 'You seem to have only one arm, sir! What have you done with the other one?'

And so with variations, some of them very funny, the baiting went on. I have often wondered whether these antics might have had some influence on subsequent events in the Persian Gulf. If this cadet ever rose to a position of power and influence in his own country, he might well have contributed to anti-British feeling and thus helped to promote the nationalisation of the Anglo-Persian Oil Company. Twenty years later to counter that event I was involved in mobilising Middle East Land Forces for the invasion of Iran, which fortunately never took place.

The civilian instructors, with one or two exceptions, were not inspiring and the academic standard was low. But the military instructors were good. Even if, like 'Cam' Nicholson, their mathematics might be shaky, their personalities were splendid. At one artillery session, Major Cam Nicholson got into a tangle, trying to prove by some laborious non-mathematical dodge a formula hallowed in artillery circles. He gave it up and turned to me:

'You show them then, Richardson.'

'It's quite simple: it's just a case of $Arc = R\emptyset$,' said the clever little mathematician.

After some further explanations, Cam Nicholson accepted my arrogant offering without demur. Surprisingly, throughout his distinguished career rising to Adjutant General, our relationship remained immensely cordial: he gave me a great opportunity at a very significant moment. He was a splendid general, beloved by all.

Another who stays vividly in my memory was Major Eustace Tickell, later to become Major-General Sir Eustace Tickell. He was my company commander and thus in a tutorial capacity; a sapper himself he seemed to think it in no way strange that a sapper cadet should contribute to the RMA Magazine, not the usual article on fishing or skiing, but a thesis reconciling Christian doctrine with *The Origin of Species*. No wonder that I left as a corporal, though armed with the King's Medal for the cadet best-qualified in military subjects.

Amongst those I left behind, in the term below us was Cadet Dick Keenlyside. He was a good cricketer and an accomplished musician. Our paths crossed throughout the war and we remained friends for life. His sense of the ridiculous, and his astringent sense of humour, too astringent perhaps for some of his superiors, were to me a great source of entertainment.

When I came on leave from 'The Shop', life at home still in Granny's house, was far from spacious, and not devoid of problems. The 'un-favourite aunt' and my father engaged in guerilla activity, touched off sometimes by genuine misunderstandings arising from his initiatives, such as installing electric light in our part of the house without consulting her or her mother, and planting a heavy crop of potatoes in the garden, or in *her* garden as she would have it. Horticulturally, and he was a great gardener, he was absolutely right : the garden badly needed 'clean-ing'. We were much hampered by lack of money, living as we were in 1927 on a lieutenant-colonel's 1913 pension.

During those lean years while my sister and I were being educated, our mother did much to supplement our father's pension by reviving her previous skills. She became secretary to various wealthy ladies, who ran small but respectable charities; from these she drew salaries that were not insignificant. In all those years, well into old age, she was to us a greatly loved companion.

After 'The Shop' there followed a period of training as a young officer at Chatham, the headquarters of the Royal Engineers, and two years at Clare College, Cambridge, in which we were expected to get an honours degree in the Mechanical Sciences Tripos. We were well taught at Chatham by sapper officers and others. Notable amongst the others was Captain E. E. Dorman-Smith, MC, Royal Northumberland Fusiliers, who was our instructor in tactics. A distinguished record in World War I, attested by a Military Cross, combined with an exceptionally fertile mind livened by Irish blarney made 'Chink', as he was called, a compulsive figure to young officers. In his exercises, ending with a sandwich lunch, a pint of beer and much gossip at the 'Leathern Bottle', dull conventional thinking was anathema; always he searched for some new thing. It was only much later that I realised it was unimportant to him whether 'the new thing' was practicable or not. Our two lives were strangely linked until a day in 1942, at our darkest hour in North Africa, when Winston Churchill removed him from Eighth Army.

On the sapper side, I particularly enjoyed the realistic tests, involving some appropriate engineering study, which we carried out in small teams over an intense, continuous period of three days. As sapper subalterns we were particularly fortunate to be sent to Cambridge.

Only ten years had elapsed since the end of World War I, yet someone in the War Office had taken this imaginative far-sighted decision. The entry system was strange : although in principle we were intended to go there, each of us individually had to apply to a college to be accepted. My family had no academic connections, but fortunately the 'blue stocking' aunt came up trumps. In her archaeological exertions in Palestine with Sir Flinders Petrie, she had met an Antarctic explorer called Raymond Priestley, who at that time was a Fellow of Clare, and later became Vice-Chancellor of Birmingham University; through him I was admitted to that small and very select institution. He had been a Royal Engineer in World War I, employed in Telegraph units, and had written the official history of the organisation which later developed into the Royal Corps of Signals.

Priestley was very good to me at Clare. We were at least two years older than the other freshmen, and joined the engineering course in its second year and, in my case, lived out of college until the final year. Perhaps for those reasons I did not take full advantage of the opportunities for friendship that I might have done. However, out of twenty-six sappers four of us gained First Class Honours; Clare College, in addition, gave me an Exhibition. I told Henry Thirkill, the Senior Tutor, who afterwards became a great Master of Clare and a revered university figure, that I could not accept it, as the War Office paid for my tuition. He said :

'You can use it. You take it, and ask no questions.'

I took it. My life was broadening in scope, and I could certainly use it. I was beginning to hear the call of India.

CHAPTER TWO

Indian Adventure

One of the prizes given me at the Royal Military Academy, Woolwich was Sir Walter Lawrence's *The India We Served** published in 1928, the year I was commissioned. It recounted vividly the attractive life of a member of the Indian Civil Service from 1879 to 1927. In his preface the author wrote: 'Some may think that the dreamland of Queen Victoria has gone for ever, and that the old relations between the Indians and the Sahibs are fast passing into myth and memories: even so, they reflect credit on both, and may be recorded.'

This book excited my curiosity, particularly as my father had been stationed in Colombo, and had often told me of the beauty of Ceylon. There was considerable competition to volunteer for India, and after four years of 'higher education', we were more than ready to start some soldiering; where better than in the Indian Army to which we could be seconded? Their units were kept up to strength ready to take part in active operations on the North-West Frontier. This was in marked contrast to the British Army, weak at that time both in men and equipment.

Although my father had died in 1928, my widowed mother never by word, hint or glance made the slightest protest as, lightheartedly, I prepared to say goodbye to her and my sister in 1931. For our last evening together, I obtained seats for Noel Coward's *Cavalcade* at Drury Lane, and we found that King George V and Queen Mary were in the Royal Box. It was an emotional evening: John Mills as the young subaltern going off to the 1914 war, and saying farewell to his mother at the realistically staged Victoria Station, and at the end of the show the audience fervently singing 'God Save the King' – these were themes which were not entirely irrelevant to my situation. Next morning I went by train to Tilbury, and with three other sapper lieutenants of the same

---

* Cassell & Co. Ltd.

vintage embarked on the troopship *Somersetshire* for our five-year tour. I was to find that Sir Walter Lawrence's dreamland had not gone for ever; only with the greatest difficulty was I to tear myself away from the spell of India after seven eventful years.

The sea voyage took three weeks but was most enjoyable. I played bridge, and enjoyed the troopship's library. Malta's Grand Harbour always makes a considerable impact when first entered, particularly as on this occasion the battleship *Queen Elizabeth* was anchored there. I little expected that on my next visit, ten years later in 1941, I would enter in the battleship *Valiant* as a wartime passenger to Alexandria.

The squalor of Bombay was horrifying; could I have known that forty years later it would be even worse, I might have been filled with despair. However the scene at Kirkee near Poona with British military organisation behind it was in great contrast.

Royal Engineer lieutenants in those days were seconded to one of the Indian Corps of 'Sappers and Miners'. These corps, the Royal Bombay Sappers and Miners, King George V's Bengal Sappers and Miners, and Queen Victoria's Own Madras Sappers and Miners, were the successors of the old Presidency Armies of the East India Company which had established settlements at Bombay, Calcutta and Madras. On joining any one of them, it was made very clear to you that you had joined the best; internecine rivalry was conducted at a high pitch on the polo field and, more seriously, in winning distinction in operations from the frontier stations (Kohat, Wana, Razmak, Quetta, etc.), which were allotted to them.

When forty years later, the then CGS of the British Army, locked in an Army Board debate about the disbandment of the Argylls, saw fit to remark that I, a sapper, could hardly appreciate the tribal rivalries which motivated the British infantry, I was able to assure him that I had been brought up surrounded by the most extreme manifestations of tribalism that anyone could experience.

Tribalism, of a different sort, was also manifested in the organisation of each Sapper and Miner's Corps. Except for Madras which was homogeneous, the other two were recruited from different races; thus the Royal BO's, as we were known, had Punjabi Muslims, Sikhs also from the Punjab, and Mahrattas from the region of Bombay. Racially, each was as different as Italians from Norwegians; and the recruiting policy, post-mutiny, was based firmly on the principle of 'divide and rule'.

With another sapper, a good half-miler, I was attached for six months to the Royal BO's, and thus entered a new and attractive world. We were worked hard, both in carrying out realistic training on engineer projects, and on combat training in readiness for a summons to a frontier operation. The need to take seriously the tactical aspect of such training was brought home by the untimely death in action of a friend of mine, a young subaltern, who had been ambushed by Pathans in a notorious locality on the NW Frontier.

We newcomers were allotted positions of authority on arrival, but one soon learnt that in reality we were apprentices still. Academically we were pupils under our Indian 'Munshi' to learn Urdu, and practically we were under the watchful eye of a subedar-major with thirty or more years of service, a row of medal ribbons from World War I, and a mature personality of such tact and generosity that the memory of that experience has remained with me for ever. It was a good inoculation against the disease of racialism.

My first task in 1931 was a shaming and well-publicised failure. There was to be a tactical exercise without troops twelve miles from our headquarters at Kirkee. My job on a moonlight night was to conduct six mules with the aid of an intelligent havildar, and arrive at 7 a.m. at the rendezvous. Maps, compasses, torches and water bottles were duly assembled, and with my pony and four mules we set forth across country with great confidence. By 1 a.m. we were totally lost, and at dawn my shameful error was exposed. We arrived two hours late for the exercise and were duly reproved not only by the Commandant, a friendly lieutenant-colonel, but also by the 'senior subaltern' who was not only very senior but fully conscious of it. I realised, not for the first time, that a first-class honours degree in engineering was no safeguard against failure in these mundane but critical activities, and resolved to apply myself in future more diligently to the simplest of military arts.

As officers we were mounted for ceremonial parades. For the annual Proclamation Parade on New Year's Day, instituted after the Mutiny by Queen Victoria regardless of the likely alcoholic repercussions, I was able to borrow a pony which, while objecting to the *feu de joie*, remained with me on Poona race course, unlike our Commandant who was carted at a fast gallop back to barracks seven miles away!

At the end of six months I was mortified to learn that the Royal BO's required my services no longer. It was said that there was only one vacancy and this was to be filled by the half-miler. I saw the logic of this, as he had already distinguished himself in regimental athletics, and this was an important asset in the relationship between the young British officer and the equally young and athletic Indian soldier. For me they said a vacancy might occur in future, but I suspected that this statement was designed to 'soften the blow', and I viewed the future with scepticism.

My disappointment increased when I learnt I was to go to Bombay as Assistant Garrison Engineer in the Military Engineering Services, an organisation charged with the building and works services of the Army and staffed predominantly by Indian civilians with British officers in the higher echelons. On arrival in Bombay, which I had briefly glimpsed six months before, I was met by an elderly and obese British warrant officer and driven to a one-time lunatic asylum, Back Bay House, a small and seemingly moribund officers' mess. It was by the sea and received the full benefits of the monsoon; fungi grew nightly in one's shoes and one's clothes were perpetually damp.

Bombay then, and I suspect even now, was a city of glaring contrasts: appalling poverty and squalor on the one hand, and, on the other, wealth on a princely scale possessed by senior British 'boxwallahs' and some of their Indian counterparts, particularly the Parsees. Thus the social life, for which a white face was the essential passport, was financially well beyond the pocket of an impecunious sapper lieutenant or even captain, as I found myself surprisingly to have become. The work, maintenance of some particularly unattractive old barracks, was extremely dull. I began to wonder what had happened to the 'dreamland of Queen Victoria' and felt I must search for some method of escape.

I have always been amazingly fortunate throughout my forty-three years of Army service and, after six weeks of depression and dismay, my luck changed. An RE major 'up country' in Mhow, Central India, had been admitted to hospital with a nervous breakdown, and I was summoned to take his place. There the 'dreamland' appeared in all its rosy colours. The work, management of large contracts for new projects, was stimulating and voluminous. There had been four occupants of my chair in the last four months and there was a fair state of chaos. I had very little idea of what I was doing and was left to my own devices. It was soon apparent that my Indian subordinates also had 'devices' designed to serve their own interests; containing these within reasonable bounds of financial propriety became a lively challenge.

The social life of the Mhow brigade was interesting and varied. I was lodged in a large well-found Regimental Mess; it is often the lot of the sapper, always a rare bird and thin on the ground, to lodge with other regiments. But there were plenty of young active officers concentrating seemingly on hunting, shooting, fishing, polo and 'poodlefaking'* without apparent damage to their professional careers. It was particularly fortunate for me that the brigade major was a sapper, Major Woolner; he and his wife took me under their wing, and were still counted amongst my greatest friends fifty years later.

I was kept busy, much of the time in the office, coping with the output of twelve *babus*† who, as a profession, have never been loth to put pen to paper; but there were also inspections of various engineer projects, and much sporting activity, all of which in the superb climate added a pleasant variant. Meanwhile I lived at a standard which I reported to my mother as 'luxurious', mentioning dining 'al fresco' with shaded lights, noiseless servants and a seven course dinner, including mango fool!

The Indian countryside was full of interest and in many areas breathtakingly beautiful. Flowering trees and shrubs of vivid red and purple, water in abundance and lush vegetation on all sides met the eye. The lost city of Mandu was a favourite picnic spot; although the jungle had forcibly crept in, the beauty of its temples and minarets was unforgettable.

After two months of signing away the Government of India's rupees with lighthearted abandon and undoubtedly enriching a number of Indian contractors, I was disappointed to hear that the neurotic major was about to resume his own seat, and I was to go as Garrison Engineer to Nasirabad in Rajputana. There appeared to be greater permanence

---

* To a recent enquirer I defined this word as 'unproductive social intercourse with the female sex'.

† The Urdu word for clerk; but also used in those days pejoratively for any Indian civilian.

in this plan, so I bought from a brother officer for a song an ancient Wolseley car of 1925 vintage. It had certainly been built to last, but the large lumps of steel incorporated in it sadly diminished its performance across country, a requirement which any officer's car had to meet in those days in India. However, with happy optimism, I set off down the Great Trunk Road back to Bombay to collect my belongings.

The journey was 370 miles; an average of twenty miles in the hour was a creditable achievement taking account of the clouds of dust arising from the water-bound macadam road (no tarmac in those days), and the well-known performance of the bullock-cart drivers; these would leave the navigation to their animals and go happily to sleep by day and with no lamps by night. 'Nothing on earth would wake them,' I wrote home; 'if by any chance they do wake, they make frantic snatches at the bullocks' tails and the two pieces of rope by which the whole ensemble is controlled.'

After sixty-five miles on the first day, I arrived with my bearer at a dak bungalow at 8 p.m., where entertainment was provided by a 1930 *Tatler* and a 1916 *Scientific American*. The next day I nearly ran out of petrol, a serious hazard as normally one passed only one car per day. However an ancient Morris-Cowley at the roadside with a conspicuous petrol tin on the running board provided the answer. The owner was a *babu,* and he was stuck with a slipping clutch. Filling up my tank with his petrol, I took him in tow and we set forth to reach the nearest railway station fifty miles away. En route we jointly crossed the River Tapti by a rickety ferry, and then said a comradely farewell. After a few more days and nights of adventurous motoring, I reached Bombay.

I packed my belongings quickly, put my car on the train and started on the journey to Nasirabad, 500 miles away. The train route was circuitous and took four days, much of it across 'the Great Indian Desert' where the temperature both by day and night was abominable. However, rail travel for the Sahib had its compensations : a large compartment with bunk bed, shower and toilet, an icebox with whisky and soda under the seat and one's bearer within call. There was no question of the train moving off until the Sahibs were ready; should the Sahib require hot water for shaving at a station, the train would be immobilised while the Sahib's bearer drew boiling water from a convenient valve on the locomotive while the engine driver assisted respectfully. That this process might sometimes delay the progress of a thousand Indian passengers, many of them travelling on the carriage roofs, was regarded as entirely irrelevant.

Nasirabad was a two-battalion station with a gunner battery and one sapper. It was close to Ajmer where was situated the famous Mayo College for princes, and on all sides were various princely states. In each a Maharaja, guided on a light rein by the Viceroy and with financial advice from a resident British 'Diwan', ruled autocratically.

In Nasirabad I found that the Garrison Engineer was a solo performer; my predecessor, a promoted warrant officer, had left under a cloud, having succumbed to the effects of massive beer drinking in a shade temperature of 105 degrees fahrenheit. The day after my arrival in 1931, I was summoned by the Garrison Commander who addressed me as follows:

'Captain Richardson, I am told that the garrison has only ten days' water left in our wells. What are you going to do about it?'

I played for time. 'I haven't assessed the situation yet, sir,' I said. 'May I report to you again tomorrow morning?' I was then permitted to withdraw.

At my office I found an able British staff sergeant also in his twenties, who was my sole link with the local situation and acted as my technical assistant. He explained that the water came from wells fifty feet deep. The station had had innumerable water crises, particularly when the monsoon was late, as was forecast that year. A programme of well-boring had been started, with the assistance of the accredited water diviner of the Bombay Government. I scented a whiff of scepticism here.

'What progress have you made?' I asked.

'Very little,' he said. 'We have dug in one place to seventy feet and it's as dry as a bone.'

'How do I answer the Garrison Commander's question?'

'There's nothing we can do to produce water in ten days, sir,' he answered.

'Where is the nearest reliable supply?' I asked.

'Neemuch, 150 miles away,' he replied.

The next morning, expecting dire trouble, I told the Colonel that an emergency plan must be produced immediately to evacuate the entire garrison to Neemuch. To my surprise he accepted this advice without a murmur, and plans were put in hand. Fortunately for me, the monsoon was not late; it arrived when we had two days' water left.

My next problem concerned the modernisation of thirty bungalows. These bungalows housed the officers and their families and were nearly a hundred years old. The walls were of mud brick, often three feet thick, and the roofs were of thatch with white-washed 'ceiling-cloths' beneath them. The roof space was the favoured home of cobras and wild cats. If during a dinner party the owner heard a suspicious noise he would look upwards and, depending on the profile of the sagging ceiling-cloth, announce 'probably a cobra: we know there's one up there', or 'It's only a cat; it keeps the snakes away.'

During the modernisation process I had a free hand to adapt the existing rooms and could demolish or rebuild as my architectural fancy dictated. The equivalent of £1,000 per bungalow* was allocated.

As young officers at Chatham we had been briefly instructed in architecture. The senior instructor had been a lugubrious colonel, who later gained distinction in the war rising to major-general. I have never forgotten a particular gem in his aesthetic advice: 'I implore you, gentlemen, do not make the "soil" pipe the principal feature of your front elevation.' By contrast, the instructor in electrical and mechanical engineering, Major 'Bill' Fryer, had been far from lugubrious. He was a wonderful teacher with a dynamic, extrovert personality and a splendid sense of humour. Later, he had a distinguished career in the war.

The bungalow project interested me greatly; as the only sapper officer in the garrison (and no superior came near me for a year) I was beguiled by the attentions I received from the senior ladies of the station, who desired various modifications to suit their personal whims. I wrote to my mother:

The Colonel's bungalow, which is now slowly rising from the ruins of the old, comprises two fine reception rooms, a study, four bedrooms, two dressing rooms, six bathrooms (i.e. a concrete floor and one cold tap) and a separate kitchen block. The Colonel is very excited and has made some helpful suggestions. 'An interesting event' is shortly expected, and he is very concerned as to where the pram should stand.

As a variant to these architectural problems, I was also responsible for the power station, which used to 'blow up' frequently. The power station

* Equivalent to £30,000 today.

was run by a qualified Hindu engineer. He was quite young, rather soft, and had enormous brown eyes. When the station was plunged into darkness twice in one week, I had to remonstrate with him and I feared he was going to burst into tears. I explained to him that the total black-out was not of great importance, but if it happened too frequently the *izzat** of the Royal Engineers, of which he rightly considered himself a part, would be irretrievably damaged. He blew his nose, wiped his eyes, and took it to heart; thereafter breakdowns occurred on average only once in two months.

Over the water supply, I had high ambitions to be the man who would solve Nasirabad's century-old problem once and for all. The plan before I arrived was to excavate further wells, by pick and shovel assisted by Indian women carrying the inevitable baskets of earth on their heads. The accredited water diviner, who had received a very substantial fee, had marked his chosen spot, forecasting potable water at sixty feet, and then retired to a manor in Gloucestershire. When informed by telegram that at seventy feet the well was bone dry, he wired back, 'Dig to one hundred feet' and drew another fee. After weeks of heavy labour I inspected the site : dry as a bone !

My staff sergeant and I then decided to introduce 'modern technology' in the shape of a well-boring rig. 'Where to start ?' we wondered. The answer, strangely enough, lay with the RAMC colonel commanding the hospital, who was convinced of his own powers with the hazel rod and had persuaded the Engineer-in-Chief in Simla to the same conclusion. I discovered to my surprise that I had to agree a fee with him every time he ventured forth; he assured me that his arcane powers had now been increased by the use of two corset bones joined with a piece of sealing wax.

We duly surveyed likely areas and he chose a site, unhygienically close to a village pond. The machine was erected and with high hearts we started to drill. Fifty feet : nothing doing. So it went on until we were nearing 140 feet. The staff sergeant put down his compressed air pipe and out gushed the water, greyish certainly, but genuine *pani*† and a great deal of it. That moment was one of the biggest thrills of my four years' service, but I did not feel called upon to drink the stuff. The next step was to have a sample tested at the hospital. Within twenty-

* Urdu for reputation.
† Urdu for water.

four hours the report came back 'Quite undrinkable': 'Bacillus this, and bacillus that in massive quantities'. We started again.

Fortunately I did not know then that within three months I would leave Nasirabad. We found no water; thirty-eight years later, while staying in nearby Jaipur, my hosts of the Indian Army assured me that the problem of Nasirabad's water supply 'had not yet been solved'.

One of the beauty spots which I had to visit on duty was Mount Abu, a convalescent station for British troops suffering from the hot weather. It was 4,000 feet high, and a place of pilgrimage for devout Indians as it contained a very beautiful Buddhist temple, built in AD 1021 of elaborately carved marble. My Indian overseer assured me it was a 'very worth-seeing place'! The ancient Wolseley took me there, over two hundred miles away, with a night's break in a *dak* bungalow. I wrote home that the country was rather like Switzerland.

My official duties were not arduous and were soon finished; I then explored the temple set on a hill with a splendid view. There were many *sadhus* living in caves having 'renounced the world', and I asked to meet the head man, the Mahatma. We sat facing each other in the temple on the marble floor polished by the feet of nine centuries of pilgrims. He was a benevolent old man wearing very little, but quite clean; he greeted me in Hindi, so I knew that my Urdu would be ineffective; but conversation did not seem to be called for. He besought me with gestures to relax, and we sat smiling at each other for a long quarter of an hour. Then, in faltering English, he explained his philosophy: 'Do good to others in order to obtain happiness.' I nodded in agreement. On leaving, I was disappointed that I felt no uplift of the soul.

My most vivid recollections of this eventful year are of 'off duty' moments. I was very fortunate that in the Gunner Mess into which I, as the sole sapper, was warmly welcomed, there were two officers slightly older than me who taught me more about enjoying life in the Army than anyone since that time. One was Captain Ted Fernyhough the 'battery captain' who seemed to me to be the dynamo not only of the battery but of the whole station, and the other was an RAMC captain, Robert Spicer, a keen sportsman, a delightful person and a highly competent physician cum emergency surgeon. The battery was commanded by Major 'Mossy' Marshall, whose life was saved by Robert Spicer after a serious pig-sticking accident.

Ted involved me in the pig-sticking and horse-riding activities of the station, both of which were excellent and cheap. We shot sand-grouse, snipe, quail and duck. A party of three or four would set off in the late afternoon to any likely waterhole in the sparse countryside surrounding us. No permission was sought from the local peasantry who, eking out a primitive existence, scratching away at a stony patch with a wooden plough or diverting a trickle of water from one channel to another by piling up mud with their hands, seemed pleased to see us. We had a regular *shikari*, a thin little man of uncertain age and inadequate teeth, who was keen as mustard. He was glad to be retained with an annual pittance, with perhaps an extra tip of a few annas* for an exceptional day; no doubt he 'oiled the wheels' with the local farmers. The Rajputs of Rajputana were splendid, tough, independent people, and a few were large landowners living in some state, not unlike an English landowner in the eighteenth century. We called on one such *Thakur* who had been particularly helpful over the shooting, and were regaled with a most potent drink of which I was highly suspicious, made from fermented carrots, which our host tossed away with no visible ill-effects. Any day he could have walked into a club in St James's Street and been warmly received as a member of the 'establishment'.

There were many princely states not far from Nasirabad, and the Maharaja of Jaipur took a particular interest in us, and was most friendly. He had himself passed through the Royal Military Academy, Woolwich, knew England well and was a popular figure in London. He occasionally came to Nasirabad to attend our gymkhana race meetings, which to him must have appeared very rough and ready. It seemed to me that everyone knew the winner before the race started! For the Christmas break of 1932, which like most festivals in India, Muslim, Hindu or Christian, was an extensive holiday of ten days, he agreed at Ted's suggestion to allow us to camp in Jaipur State to shoot duck and engage in pig-sticking. The area of about twenty square miles was reserved for the Maharaja's own use and the pig, present in large numbers, were reserved for pig-sticking. In addition there was a large lake harbouring duck and geese, which had not been shot for twenty years.

Some ten of us, led by the dynamic Ted, arrived at the camp site with our bearers to find that the Mess Staff of the RA Mess had already 'got

---

* One sixteenth of a rupee, which in those days were thirteen to the pound.

Boring for water in Nasirabad, India. Success at last!

(Below, left) En route to Chitral in the Hindu Kush 1936. Lt Col Smyth VC, our Force Commander, on radio. (Right) Our last camp before marching to the Lowarai Pass at 10,000 feet and entering Chitral. (Bottom right) Our reinforced concrete cantilevered cliff gallery on the track to the Lowarai Pass.

(Above) With the Chitral Ski Club at Madaglasht (10,000 feet) Capt 'Coco' Cumberlege RA with author (with eyeshade).

(Top left) In Chitral, which borders on Gilgit, polo is the national game; every village has its team. (Centre left) The Chitral Garrison polo team with Jackie Smyth in overcoat; author on left.

At Kirkee, Poona, thirty years later: my second and last farewell to my Mahratta Sappers, retired veterans of World War II.

things going'. We had no tents, as the days were spent in blazing sun-shine to be followed by starlit nights near to freezing, but with no risk of rain.

The horses for pig-sticking were troop horses of the Royal Artillery which throughout India could usually be hired for seven rupees eight annas per month and were known as 'seven-eighters'. This payment equivalent to about 6op covered fodder, groom and insurance. The Mahajara's 'pig preserve' consisted of a number of hills covered in dense thorn trees and with large granite outcrops and unexpected ravines; the whole was surrounded by extensive fields of sugar cane. Not a soul was there but ourselves. We were organised by Ted into two 'heats', one of four riders and one of two; one heat to take the hills and drive the pig into the open, while the other – my own – was to pursue and kill the pig. About a hundred beaters arrived, only too happy to earn a few pence for the day. I was far from effective, and found myself too frequently galloping, spear aloft, into a thorn tree. But the whole opera-tion was intensely exciting. It was not run in Kadir Cup style, but what it lacked in skill was compensated by the cheerful camaraderie of young men in their middle twenties, and the physical well-being from hard exertion in such perfect surroundings.

After less than a year of this particular dreamland, I heard to my surprise that the Royal Bombay Sappers and Miners wanted me back. I was not to go to Kirkee, the depot near Poona, but to Quetta in Baluchistan.

Before packing up to go, early in 1933, Robert Spicer of the RAMC said he had been invited by a nearby Maharaja to stay with him for two weeks, and would I like to join him? I accepted at once. Off we set by road to the Indian State. His Highness the Maharaja had been through the College of Princes at Ajmer: he was sophisticated, spoke perfect English, and was about the same age as we were. He had interested himself in our life at Nasirabad, and Robert had been able to help him on some medical problem.

The Maharaja, although entitled to a salute of only eleven guns, maintained an establishment which seemed to lack nothing: a large palace, rows of stables and innumerable motor cars. We were warmly welcomed and, that evening, His Highness assured us that in addition to duck shooting he very much hoped we should each get a panther before we left.

At dinner we met the Diwan, an Englishman retired from Government service; he managed the State revenues of which a substantial amount was reserved for the Maharaja's use. He seemed a very straightforward, guileless official, but was not always popular with his young master. The other character at the dinner table was an officer summoned from Delhi to advise on an epidemic amongst the Maharaja's polo ponies. It seemed to us that he had other irons in the fire : seizing every opportunity, he would criticise the Diwan's rigorous policy of retrenchment, and advise our young host that the time was ripe to improve the amenities of the palace. As impotent spectators of this oriental conspiracy, we learnt later that the Diwan had successfully defeated it. The expert on polo ponies returned downcast to Delhi; the Diwan was not as simple as he looked.

One evening His Highness's *shikari* arrived at the palace to say that there had been a natural kill in a village twenty miles away. Immediately cars in profusion drove up, assistant *shikaris* seemed to spring from the bushes, and off we went in a cloud of dust. At the village there was a bullock, looking after ten hours very dead with its belly devoured. 'A tiger,' said one of the crowd of villagers. 'Impossible,' said the head *shikari*. After much wagging of heads, the verdict was given : 'Two panthers'. To me this seemed highly improbable; but unversed in these matters, and a guest to boot, who was I to speak? HH invited Robert to sit up in a *machan** that night. We left Robert to his task and returned to the palace to await events. At about 9 p.m. a telephone message arrived : 'One panther shot'. At the village amidst rejoicing peasants there was Robert down from his tree, with a dead male panther at his feet. HH and his retinue studied the scene from all angles with much vocal encouragement from the locals. Cigarettes and bonfires were lit, the headman of the village and the elders stamped all round the corpse.

I was then invited to sit up the next night for the female panther. I viewed this with scepticism. Robert had seen no female, but she might have been lurking shyly under cover while goading her partner to his duty. But if there were a female in the vicinity would she not be scared away by all the signs and smells of human activity which no one, not even His Highness, attempted to control?

But 'mine not to reason why', so the next evening I was installed in the

---

* A platform constructed in a tree overlooking the 'kill'.

same machan with a lad holding a torch by my side. Tired perhaps by the drama and junketings of the last forty-eight hours, I dozed off. Some time later the lad nudged me, and in the dim light of the moon I saw something quite large feeding on the kill. I thought my loud heart-beats must frighten the animal away, but got ready to fire, and signalled to the lad to turn on the torch. There she was, very composed, licking her chops and blithely ignoring the torchlight. I fired and she rolled over. Quivering with excitement, I descended and viewed the trophy.

His Highness, with princely generosity, insisted on having both skins mounted for us by the expert taxidermist in Bombay. The bill would have been considerable.

On reaching Nasirabad I realised with a shock that my sojourn in that 'Never Never Land' was over. Orders to report to Quetta in Baluchistan in six weeks' time lay on my desk. Such changes of job were no penalty for a young bachelor and provided an opportunity to take leave. I decided to visit Agra and Delhi, and view the Taj Mahal as a conventional tourist. I visited Lutyen's masterpiece, the Viceroy's House in New Delhi, and was tremendously impressed by its majestic beauty. It was well known that Lady Willingdon had a strong preference in the general decor for 'imperial' purple which, rumour said, had been extended even to the toilet paper. I admired the specially woven purple carpet in the drawing room which appeared to be the size of a tennis court, but was not given the opportunity to verify the 'privy' rumour. The council chamber, august and beautiful, seemed to be an embodiment in marble of the permanence of the 'British Raj'. Certainly the Imperial tradition was still an accepted and potent influence amongst British officers, and to a less extent amongst the British commercial community, although we had little contact with them.

Yet political change was in the air. For over a hundred years a small proportion of the millions in India had profited from British-inspired higher education; it was evident even to a young officer that independence must eventually follow. The Round Table Conference on the Indian Constitution had ended in December 1932 and I had studied the White Paper of March 1933. The first Indian officer with a King's Commission (as opposed to the Viceroy's commission) arrived at the Royal Bombay Sappers and Miners Depot before I left India in 1938. By contrast we not infrequently had Mr Gandhi in Poona jail, to be visited regularly by the orderly officer to ensure that he was not being improperly treated by the Indian Police. In 1934 the onset of independence still appeared to be reassuringly remote. Our relationship with our Indian soldiers, whose Viceroy's commissioned officers had fought alongside British units with outstanding valour in World War I, was warm and comradely. Their educational progress, their social standing and the success of their careers was almost exclusively due to the British connection, but the relationship was devoid of patronage. They were fighting men of great experience who had learnt their skills not from books but in the crucible of war. However, in our attitude to the great mass of Indians outside the Army and particularly to those in the cities, the prejudice of the 'Imperial master-race' was often apparent.

After Agra and Delhi I visited Jaipur, and Udaipur, where a Viceroy's visit was expected. Udaipur was certainly an unforgettable feature of the Indian 'dreamland'. At sunset, the white marble palaces in the placid blue lake were tinged with gold. However, as so often in India, mundane practicalities intruded. A visit by a Viceroy demanded an abnormal application of 'spit and polish'. Hence the spell of this ethereal scene was rudely shattered by the noise of countless coolies busily tipping red gravel on the black mud, and strenuously whitewashing everything in sight.

Baluchistan, my next destination, a primitive arid province of what is today Pakistan, lies on the border with Afghanistan. Quetta, situated at 6,000 feet, guards the entry from Kandahar into the rich plains of the Punjab. It was a large military station, with an Indian division located there to resist any incursion from Afghanistan or the Frontier areas. I was to be second-in-command of a Divisional Headquarters Company RE. In contrast to my solo performance in Bombay and Nasirabad, I was now surrounded by brother officers, and was part of a team. The military scene was much more sophisticated, and I began to learn something of the roles of infantry, tanks and artillery. The countryside might have been constructed solely for military manoeuvres: vast spaces of marginal agriculture, over which military requirements took precedence, and a satisfactory number of dominating hills to intrigue the budding tacticians. The Staff College was in an agreeable residential area on the outskirts, where a certain Colonel Montgomery was making his mark. Dick Keenlyside, my friend from Woolwich days, attended one of his lectures and was amazed to hear him announce 'when I am Commander-in-Chief of the Allied Armies in the next war . . .' The war, in fact, was only six years away, but its shadow had hardly begun to fall upon us. Our interest lay more in the actual operations which sporadically occurred on the North-West Frontier, and in which deeds of gallantry sometimes gained a much-coveted Military Cross.

It was perhaps the existence of these Frontier operations that caused my commanding officer, an elderly pedantic colonel, to refuse an application from myself and another sapper friend Captain John Cowley to spend three weeks' leave in Afghanistan motoring to Kandahar, about 200 miles away, thence to Kabul and returning via the Khyber Pass and Peshawar. I did not take at all kindly to his refusal, and stood in his office with folded arms cross-examining him on his reasons. That year he reported on me as 'truculent'. All my life, I have regretted that missed opportunity. The colonel, I later noted, never rose to any heights.

In spring and summer we trained with the division. With winter came the snow, and we concentrated on trade training. Here I learnt to admire the natural mechanical talent of the Indian sapper. We had built a new workshop and in it we decided to install an ancient derelict diesel engine. Our Indian sergeant, a Muslim from the Punjab frequently addressed respectfully as '*mistri-ji*',* tended the monster for weeks, while old parts were assembled and new parts made. Thanks to him, eventually after loud explosions the great flywheel started to turn. His reputation as an expert in advanced technology soared to great heights, and he was delighted.

The Quetta Hunt was a popular well-organised affair. As usual we hunted jackal, which were plentiful. The country provided excitement in the form of water courses, streams, banks and *karezes*, which were deep dry water courses often fifty feet deep and fifty yards wide. The nearly vertical descent had to be negotiated by whatever rough tracks might exist. My pony, which I had bought for a song from Captain 'Splosh' Jones, a brother sapper, used to gallop and jump as well as any; but I soon came to the conclusion that he was a psychiatric case. Whenever the hounds checked at the edge of a precipitous *kareze* he would 'come over queer', start to tremble and proceed rapidly backwards often towards the very edge of the ravine. I had to develop a technique of

---

* An English translation might be 'Honourable craftsman'.

keeping him 'interested' every time there was a check, and happily his suicidal tendencies gradually diminished.

Thirty years later I was to follow in General Sir Charles Jones' footsteps as C-in-C Northern Command, Master General of the Ordnance and on retirement, Chief Royal Engineer. Revisiting Quetta in 1963, I said to our excellent Pakistani host :

'Colonel, you would not believe it, but out of that row of five single officers' quarters there eventually emerged two members of the British Army Board.'

With a twinkle in his eye he replied, 'Sir, it must have been the climate !'

I had now been in India two and a half years, filled with a variety of experience, and it was time to take leave home in the middle of my five-year posting. This coincided with the tragic earthquake in Quetta. The greatest destruction and loss of life occurred away from the cantonment area, so the loss of British lives was mercifully small. The toll among the Indian inhabitants was catastrophic. Sappers were a godsend in such an emergency, and John Cowley, later to become Lt-Gen Sir John Cowley, who was also housed in the 'Single Officers' Quarters', was awarded the Albert Medal, now converted to the George Cross, for rescuing lepers from the ruins of the hospital.

On my return to India it was to Kirkee rather than Quetta that I went as second-in-command of a field company. Skirmishes on the frontier were frequent and this kept us on our toes, but many still thought that a war with Germany was unlikely. While staying in my mother's flat in London, I had listened on her radio to Hitler at a Nuremberg rally; to me it seemed inevitable that this manic leader, with millions of tough young Germans enthralled behind him, would bring ultimate disaster. My intelligent company commander argued to the contrary and I was unable to convince him. However such speculations produced no ripples on our cheerful active lives. I took part in manoeuvres with the Royal Deccan Horse, a very ebullient regiment commanded by a wild Irishman, whose main interest was polo. Not unnaturally the horses of the regiment were selected with polo as the main objective, although officially they were to provide mobility in warlike operations. The wild Irishman, no longer interested in furthering his career, throughout the manoeuvres exercised enormous ingenuity, devoted exclusively to tripping up the

Directing Staff and Umpires. The Indian Army abounded in such colourful characters.

For our social life, devoid of radio and TV, cocktail parties, some of them dreary, were the rule. We decided to organise a Mess party that was different. It eventually took the form of a satirical 'pageant', based on Mussolini's Abyssinian War. We all regarded him as a comic figure, and looked upon the Italian Army's operations in areas where British Colonial power had been dominant as impertinent and amoral.

Major Bill Fryer and his wife were the leading spirits. The cast included the Emperor of Abyssinia with his court, and Marshal Badoglio with his generals. Mussolini had recently been reported haranguing his victorious soldiers : this classic role fell to me, and much improvisation was necessary.

The party ended at 2 a.m. with the entire cast being thrown into the swimming pool – whether by way of tribute or objection was never established. But our most senior guest, a general with his lady left early.

Six years later I was to find myself 'liberating' Tripolitania from Italian imperialists. Some of us at that time viewed with misgivings the destruction of Mussolini's colonial achievement and the substitution of Arab independence. Colonel Gaddafi was still to come.

At the end of the year I was surprised to hear that I was to take thirty sappers of the Royal BOs to Chitral in the Hindu Kush. A sapper detachment together with an Indian infantry battalion and a mountain battery RA had been located there since 1895 when the Government of India, fearful of Russian-inspired subversion after a 'Palace feud' had resulted in the murder of the then ruler of Chitral, sent a military expedition to pacify the local tribesmen and maintain a British garrison.

The independent state of Chitral, still under the rule of the 'Mehtar' whom the Government of India had installed, lay at 6,000 feet, surrounded by mountains rising to Tirich Mir, the fourth highest in the world. Indian soldiers, who had so far wintered there, had all been from the North : Muslims from the Punjab, Sikhs, etc. I was ordered to take Mahrattas, dark little men who came from the regions south of Bombay at sea level. I presumed the reasoning behind this was that the Mahrattas, a tough martial race which had fought Wellington's armies with some success in the nineteenth century, should not be deprived of the opportunity of serving in this unusual environment. So off we set by train in September 1936, thirty Mahrattas under Captain Richardson with his Jemadar, Ramchandar Sinde.

We left at midnight. Some capricious staff officer in Simla had planned for us to stop at every station on our 1,700 mile journey, so it was not until five days later that we found ourselves at daybreak moving slowly towards what seemed an impenetrable barrier of mountain.

On either side of the line, green crops stood head-high, in vivid contrast to the parched plains which had stretched endlessly along our route. Such luxuriance was due to the Swat Canal, which pierced the mountain barrier of the Malakand from north to south, and carried a plentiful water supply towards the plains below.

Our route crossed the states of Swat and Dir and was flanked by the Mohmand country on the west. The rulers of these states received subsidies and assistance from the Indian Government, and in return were called upon to arrange for the safe passage of a convoy every two years. The relief of the garrison was the occasion for sending up new supplies of ammunition and money for the State Treasury, and was regarded by the more enterprising hotheads of the districts as an opportunity not only for private gain but also for blackening their rivals' reputation by planning incidents in neighbouring territory. Thus the relief march was conducted as a warlike operation.

In 1936 a motor road from Dargai had been made as far as Dir, and for the first time this stage was to be carried out by lorry, with the exception of two platoons which were to be interchanged by air direct to Drosh in Chitral.

Our convoy joined its escort of light tanks and armoured cars, and final arrangements for air co-operation were completed. The next day we moved off at dawn, climbed the winding road to Malakand, with the ancient Buddhist road beneath us, and then descended into the valley of the Swat river, where Alexander's armies had marched and conquered two thousand years before. Intricately carved sculptures were still being unearthed by the peasants' wooden ploughs, dramatic evidence of the Grecian skills inherited by those he left behind.

Our march was long and seemed uneventful. Afterwards I learned that one or two long-range shots were fired by snipers, more to sustain their reputation than of any malice aforethought. I was unaware of this, but was later gratified to find that I had earned my first campaign medal!

That night we camped at Dir. As darkness fell, pinpoints of fire lit up the surrounding hills, where the Nawab's levies were on guard to protect the camp. By day, the enclosed bowl in which the camp was sited was too hot for comfort, but by night a sharp wind blew down from the Lowarai Pass, where peaks of 14,000 feet still had snow on their northern slopes.

Early the next morning, the loads from the lorries were handed over to the donkey drivers who, with great deliberation and an apparent incomprehension of all orders and entreaties, divided them into curious shapes and sizes, added large stones here and there as makeweights, rolled them in unconvincing nets and finally balanced them precariously on their small and uncomplaining donkeys.

It was only fifteen miles and six hundred feet to the top of the pass, but, as the donkey transport set the pace, we had to camp below the top on terraces built upon the steep sides of the valley. It was September, and the troops but a few days back had been sweating in the plains of Central India and the Deccan. So their surprise was complete when at three o'clock, before we reached camp, the sun gave place to an icy wind and before long hailstones as big as peas were falling amongst us. The tents had not been pitched before a torrent of icy black water swept down the terraces, swamping the cooking places, overturning the piled rifles and all but carrying away the boxes of ammunition and money. The storm stopped as suddenly as it had begun, but it was now too late for the sun to penetrate into the narrow valley. We settled for the night in our sodden tents.

The next day's march was steep but the track was good. On our left, a mountain stream cascaded down amongst large boulders; and from it channels were led to irrigate the lower slopes of the hills. These were cunningly terraced, so that every available patch of soil might yield its crop of maize to support the meagre existence of the hill-folk, whose squat wooden huts clung precariously to the mountainside.

As we climbed, the valley widened and great outcrops of rock showed up between the trees, and finally, on rounding a bend, the saddle came into view at ten thousand feet. Friends from the garrison at Drosh greeted us at the top, and we looked down for the first time upon the great valley of Chitral, dark green against the snow-topped mountains. This dramatic scene was in strong contrast to every landscape I had seen in my first five years in India; it stirred my childhood's memories of the Alps and thus was doubly welcome.

That night we camped beneath the deodars. The sun, filtering through the lofty branches, lit up patches on the mountainside, and soon the dry air made good the damage of the previous night. This welcome at Chitral's first camping ground was repeated by all her people and lasted until the day, eighteen months later, when I ski-ed down the Lowarai Pass for the last time.

Before going to Chitral we had heard much of the variety of its out-door amusements. Shooting of all kinds, ski-ing, skating and polo were the main occupations, with hockey, tennis, squash and swimming to fill in the odd moments. No motor vehicle had ever entered Chitral; so we were horse-borne both for business and pleasure. This was a splendid feature of our lives, contributing greatly both to physical fitness and enjoyment.

We had not long to wait before the first chikor shoot of the season took place. I set off at a brisk canter up the valley of the Chitral river with Captain 'Coco' Cumberlege, Royal Artillery, smoking a vile 'Burma' cheroot at my side. We reached some rocky slopes with sheer cliffs above us and with the river flowing down the gorge beneath us. Soon the first cries of the beaters were heard about a mile away. Then suddenly the first birds came flying over very fast. A few veered towards the cliffs, only to be turned by the 'stops', who stood gesticulating and waving their coats high up on the rocky ledges. A few bold spirits crossed the river, but most of the coveys came straight and fast; and the novices amongst us, accustomed only to 'walking up' these difficult birds, found our barrels getting hot, and empty cases piling up inside the butt, with little to show for them.

November and December passed, and soon the first reports came in from the ski hut, which had been built by my sapper predecessors at 10,000 feet, and thirty-three miles away. It was traditional to walk this in a day. They said the snow was late; only three feet had fallen, and the great boulders still showed above the valley floor. So we decided to go skating instead. His Highness the Mehtar placed at our disposal his bungalow at Garm Chashma – the 'Aix les Bains' of Chitral. There, a rink was prepared; rice fields under the shadow of a mountain were flooded, dams built and paths cleared under the stern eye of the Chitrali 'Revenue Officer'.

This picturesque character was worthy of the most far-fetched romances of the film world. Tall, aquiline and dignified, he had the perfect manners of a bygone age, relieved by a streak of sardonic humour, which, in matters such as horse-coping or Government contracts, sometimes led him from the path of orthodox finance. On this occasion, he spared no pains to make our visit a success. Our three-day journey became a triumphal procession : at every halt the local notables presented cold game, walnuts and pomegranates. It would be misleading not to mention that Ian Scott, the Assistant Political Agent, headed our party and dispensed largesse proportionate to the welcome received. For him this was a prelude to a distinguished career in the Foreign Service, culminating in a knighthood.

So, weary but well-fed, we came at last to Garm Chashma. Here for three days we enjoyed ourselves skating, hawking and 'taking the waters'. Next day, before sunrise, we started on our ponies towards a narrow gorge of reddish rock, through which a torrent of water thundered amongst enormous boulders. This was the route to Badakshan in Afghanistan whence came our polo ponies. The track crossed the river three times by cantilever bridges of local design, which seemed to hang together in defiance of all engineering principles. Once through the gorge, our way led through calmer scenes; terraced fields came down towards the river banks and little orchards of apricot and peach decorated the humble villages. At a turn in the road we looked behind us and saw the sun gleaming on Tirich Mir, dominating the valley in isolated majesty at 26,000 feet.

On our way back to Drosh we passed a caravan of *hajjis* from Turkestan; in spite of many weeks of hard journeying, they still looked fat and cheerful. Round Mongolian faces, vivid blue eyes and startlingly pink complexions, beamed out from under furry caps. Wrapped up in quilted cloaks, they made a formidable load for their small under-fed ponies, whose raw backs gave sickening evidence of merciless treatment from their masters. To pay their way from Central Asia to Mecca they carried money, silks, carpets and attractive pieces of Russian porcelain, which they peddled as they went. I bought a 'Gardner' teapot for my mother.

Some weeks later, we heard that the snow at the ski-hut was in good condition and we decided to spend ten days there. The ski-club of Chitral had been founded some years before and comprised a hut which could house ten people in great warmth and reasonable comfort, a miscellaneous collection of skis, and two Chitralis 'George' and 'Albert' who, taught by successive sapper officers, were fair performers. The runs started at 14,000 feet and varied from some suitable for the novice, to hair-raising descents, daunting to all but the experts. The heat of the sun and the consequent danger of avalanches necessitated very early rising. The climb on skis could start as early as 4 a.m.

After ten days of this paradise, the change from the snow-covered slopes to the terraces of Drosh was sudden and surprising. The first signs of spring had begun to appear. Narcissi and daffodils were shooting up and the wild primulas and hyacinths had reappeared in the valleys. The time for polo had arrived.

In Chitral, as in Gilgit, where it was first played, polo is the national game. Every man who could beg, borrow or steal a pony took part. The polo ground held the place of the village green. Here the great men of the district mingled with the peasants, hospitality was extended to visitors and entertainment offered to the officers of the garrison.

The *Jalsa*, the annual polo tournament, was played throughout the summer between a dozen or more village teams, with one from the British Garrison and one from 'the Royal Family'. Our garrison team captained by Lieutenant-Colonel Jackie Smyth with two gunners, the Assistant Political Agent and myself, all on Badakshani ponies, reached the final in which we defeated His Highness's team on the very bumpy palace ground. This happy event was followed by a 'banquet' (mostly out of tins) after which there was 'polo by moonlight', in which a visitor, Brigadier Harold Alexander, commanding the Nowshera Brigade enjoyed himself greatly. 'Alex' was forty-six : to me he seemed very boyish and debonair. Physically fit, good-looking and seemingly carefree, he entered into the fun with genuine enthusiasm. Jackie knew him well and had admired his conduct of frontier operations. All of us were pleased that he had taken the trouble to come so far to visit our small garrison. I was to see much of him later in sterner surroundings.

Six years of 'fun and games' were drawing to an end and already I suspected that dire events lay ahead. Many friends and a great assortment of sporting activities had come my way and I had learnt something about the command of Indian troops at a junior level. But I was far from being a professional soldier.

Yet in retrospect, I believe that in an important way, those two years in Chitral prepared me for the more critical duties that lay ahead. Two years entirely on horseback, with no radio sets, with primitive engineering equipment (our rock blasting was done by hand without compressors) and for fire support the historic mule-borne 'screw guns' of the Mountain Gunners immortalised by Kipling, how could this experience be relevant to facing a German *blitzkrieg*? The answer must be that I was given the opportunity to grow up. No sapper officer inspected me in two years; I was my own master, working out the year's training programme for the detachment including a permanent engineer project which by tradition was carried out annually. Mine was a reinforced cantilevered cliff gallery to improve the bridle track from Drosh to the Lowarai Pass and, for the first and last time, I used my Cambridge engineering notes. All stores had to be ordered five months ahead, as they had to be carried sixty miles over the 10,000 foot saddle by coolies, before winter closed in.

Again I was lucky with my friends, particularly 'Coco', the dark-skinned Artillery Captain, a dyed-in-the-wool mountain gunner. Five years later in Cairo I was horrified to hear that his corpse had been unloaded from an SOE caique returning to Alexandria from Nazi-occupied Crete.

All of us in Chitral were lucky with our garrison commander, Jackie Smyth, vc. He was a great games player and sportsman; if you did not take a fortnight's leave every alternate month in winter, he would ask the reason why. I got to know him well, as my luxurious garden, embellished by generations of sappers and provided with a swimming pool and peach orchard, contained the only tennis court, and he was a keen player. With ski-ing and shooting markhor, I was able to meet his winter specification for the sane officer. In addition I read a great deal, with a flow of books sent from London. I have them still: Fuller, Liddell Hart, Churchill, Walter Page, Blunden, Lawrence, Guedalla, Siegfried Sassoon ... not to mention many novels, which seem today to stand above their modern counterparts. The air mail *Times* used to arrive three weeks out of date; nevertheless it kept me well-informed of the darkening international scene.

I have often wondered since those days why we were ever located in this young man's paradise. Perhaps as in *Kim* we were playing Kipling's 'great game'? Certainly the Russians were our only possible enemy, but to us they seemed very far away. Our predecessors, helped by sappers of the survey of India and directed by the resolute young Viceroy Lord Curzon, who had visited Chitral in 1894, had contrived to establish an artificial tongue of Afghanistan, the 'Wakhan', to ensure there was no common frontier between British India and Russia. On our skating jaunt I had reconnoitred one of the entries into Chitral from Afghanistan, a track in a river gorge no wider than a small room, with sheer rock faces rising vertically on either side to 1,000 feet. It was clear that substantial enemy forces would find it difficult to invade Chitral: it was only Russian agents that needed to be watched and countered by our Assistant Political Agent. Forty years later, however, Soviet neo-imperialists realised their ambitions, occupying first Badakshan, and then the rest of Afghanistan.

I had two short breaks from Chitral: one to Gulmarg in Kashmir and the other to Simla for a course preparatory to taking the Staff College exam. Dick Keenlyside was also there with his charming wife, and we had a very jolly time. There appeared once again 'Chink' Dorman-Smith, the infantry captain at Chatham in 1928 who was now Auchinleck's Director of Military Training. The great Auchinleck, whose reputation ran very high in India, addressed us at the start: it was a good soldierly exhortation with nothing subtle about it, but the power of the man's personality certainly came across. 'Chink' had not greatly changed. Novel ideas at two a penny tumbled from his lips. I felt that he was determined to convince us that if there was anyone who could plumb the future and produce the right answers, it was he. How many of his ideas were really practicable, I wondered?

In 1938 I had already overstayed my five years' tour of duty by two years and had come to the conclusion that if I did not break the spell of India then, I never would. I applied to go, but this was inconvenient to our masters in Delhi. However I was due again for some leave, so the agreed solution was to leave Chitral, return after short leave in UK to serve in Kohat on frontier operations. There I found myself acting brigade major in the room of an officer who had just committed suicide.

Finally in 1938 I cut adrift from 'dreamland' for good and handed my Mahrattas over to my successor; I was to have the privilege of meeting fifteen of them thirty years later, when revisiting Kirkee as a member of the British Army Board. Many of them, old men by then, had fought alongside us in the Middle East and Italy and had done well; my second and last farewell was a very sad moment.

Early in March my ponies were assembled, followed by my bearer and the donkeys, and off we set along the familiar track up to the Ziarat Levy Post at 9,000 feet. Next morning I walked along the coolies' track through six feet of snow to the top of the pass and ski-ed down ten miles to Dir.

I was thirty; my apprenticeship was finished, and the Second World War was one year away. For all of us it was the end of an era.

CHAPTER THREE

Phoney War

After India, England in 1938 seemed dull and doom-laden. The spacious life with adventure never far to seek, the Indian soldier with his innate courtesy and simple loyalties, the friends of seven years' standing – all these had been left behind. My mother and my recently married sister were cheerful but anxious, living in flats in London with air raid precautions as an active topic.

I was not expecting scenes of gaiety and glamour. In 1937, beside the log fire in my bungalow at Drosh, I had read with dismay the repeated warnings of Winston Churchill, dubbed by many as a warmonger, and had studied with scepticism the account of Halifax's visit to Goering's shooting lodge and to Hitler in Berlin. Could Hitler's manifestly aggressive intentions really be assuaged by parley in such a charade?

The general attitude in England under the Nazi threat was one of watchfulness, resignation and seeming impotence. It appeared to me that there were many experts who must be privy to secret information yet had resolutely buried their heads in the sand. Essential military preparations to equip the RAF, to improve air defence and to produce tanks and other equipment for the Army were constantly postponed, either on grounds of finance or for fear of provocation.

In January 1938, Chamberlain attempted fruitlessly to appease Hitler by proposing concessions over African Colonial Development. The removal of the German Colonies after World War I had been worked up by the German leader as a 'genuine' grievance against Britain and France, although compared to his ambition to master the whole of Europe, it must have rated very low in his priorities.

There followed a succession of headlong steps towards the abyss : the assumption by Hitler of command of all the German armed forces : the browbeating of the Austrian Chancellor and the imposition of the Nazi Seyss-Inquart as his Minister of the Interior : the resignation of Anthony Eden frustrated by the Government's attempted appeasement of

Mussolini : the long-foreseen annexation of Austria : the French guarantee to Czechoslovakia, and the final drawn-out shame of Munich.

This was the scenario against which at Chatham we went about our 'humble duties'. We were not of course, well-orientated to the approaching crisis. In the minds of many of the senior officers there, memories of World War I, including a great respect for the size and efficiency of the French Army, were uppermost. Some of us were conducted on a battlefield tour in the area of Vimy Ridge : no-one suggested that within a year we should be 'at it again', not far from there. My job at Chatham was Assistant Adjutant in the Training Battalion RE, where the commanding officer was my friend Kit Woolner, now a lieutenant-colonel. The battalion received new recruits for their basic training and also newly commissioned officers. I had been through the process myself ten years before, and the nostalgia associated with Chatham, the 'home' of the Royal Engineers with its beautiful early Georgian Mess, was still a welcoming emotion.

But recruiting, country-wide, was poor; units were under strength and money was scarce. The doubling of the Territorial Army by Mr Hore Belisha, the Secretary of State for War, was a courageous political step, but it could not quickly transform the serious situation on the ground, and was to take many months to mature.

As Assistant to the Adjutant I deputised for him 'across the board', and had two subjects delegated to me completely : courts-martial and mobilisation plans, both providing ample scope for the detailed accurate work expected of all sapper officers. For these I dealt direct with Colonel Woolner, and learnt a lot from him as he set the highest standards. But the mobilisation plans, which involved the removal of the unit on D-day to a different location, and the posting of all its officers to active appointments of higher priority, soon convinced me that an element of fantasy had crept into our affairs. New units which, on paper were to be set up with the men, vehicles and stores to make them effective, exceeded by a wide margin the resources known to exist. The whole process became more and more frustrating and depressing.

We had plenty to do in the normal peacetime routine, improving where possible the standard of training of our recruits now greater in number, but still of indifferent quality, and consolidating our paper plans for mobilisation. Recreation continued as of yore : I went skiing in Davos with another sapper who had been at St Ronans. In the hotel there was a large friendly German skier whose teutonic greeting to me at breakfast, with a twinkle in his eye was :

'Good morning, you bloody imperialist.'

He had learnt one of the Nazi battlecries !

Later in 1939 I went on the Cowes-Dinard Ocean Race with Bill Fryer as our skilful and most entertaining skipper. Our French hosts at the Dinard Yacht Club also seemed blissfully unconcerned for the future.

Meanwhile to those who read the newspapers it was evident that the total subjugation of Czechoslovakia was proceeding rapidly. Week by week, said Churchill in the House of Commons, the forces of conquest and intimidation were being consolidated. Presently another stroke would come. After criticising the Government's inertia, he went on : 'If mortal catastrophe should overtake the British Nation and the British Empire, historians a thousand years hence will still be baffled by the mystery of our affairs; they will never understand how it was that a victorious nation, with everything in hand, suffered themselves to be brought low, and to cast away all that they had gained by measureless sacrifice and absolute victory – gone with the wind.'

We also were baffled; but it was clear that an immediate confrontation with the immense, well-publicised power of the Nazi war-machine would spell disaster. Appeasement, as an alternative, was now discredited. At the time of Munich some preparations for mobilisation were put in hand; most of them seemed half-measures carried out in a half-hearted way, and cheerfully reversed after Chamberlain stepped from his aeroplane declaring, 'Peace for our time.'

Despite the Government's attempts at political 'presentation', the betrayal of Czechoslovakia could not be concealed, but it was not until many years later that I learnt from a BBC programme how truly appalling that betrayal had been : the Czech delegates had been kept under SS guard in a locked room while Chamberlain was discussing the future of their country with Hitler. In the circumstances, Chamberlain's subsequent guarantee to Poland, another 'far off country' beyond the reach of any British military support, seemed illogical, but its significance gradually dawned on us; Britain had irrevocably thrown down the glove to Hitler.

Individual appointments on mobilisation were graded as 'secret' partly because they were subject to frequent change; as guardian of the secrets I found that my destiny was to be Adjutant of 1 Corps Troops Engineers, a territorial formation allocated to the BEF and consisting of three field companies and a field park company with officers and men from Manchester and Liverpool.

By September 1939 the Army was certainly in better shape; and when war was declared, it was with a sense of relief that I handed over to an elderly reserve officer in Chatham, and prepared to cross the Channel. My sister, by then a pathologist, was mobilised into the blood-transfusion service and my mother accompanied her to Kent; my brother-in-law was commissioned into the Royal Engineers. I was thankful to have no dependants.

We expected a German attack on France which, on the evidence available, could hardly be resisted effectively; but the die was cast and there was no point in worrying. The 'move to battle', as we deemed it to be, was a calm, peaceful and agreeable experience; by sea to Cherbourg followed by a drive in perfect autumn weather through the picturesque fields of Normandy onward to the less attractive neighbourhood of Northern France. Churchill, as First Lord of the Admiralty, took pride in having transported an Expeditionary Force to France twice in twenty-five years in complete safety.

Throughout that cheerful sunny journey we were quite unaware of the strategy which we were destined to implement. As we now know, it was the subject of acute controversy in the highest circles. The German High Command themselves, still retaining respect for the French Army that had totally defeated them only twenty-one years before, were apprehensive of the idea of a Western offensive at the beginning of the winter, despite their recent successes in Poland. Chamberlain, who had always hoped for some détente with the Germans, had recently had to turn down an approach from Hitler. But he, brushing aside military advice and confident of the inertia and irresolution of the French, was determined to attack France and Britain before their rearmament should redress their inferiority. This offensive was to be through the Low Countries, thus outflanking the Maginot Line.

That immense system of fortification, constructed along the Franco-German frontier, was intended to prevent any German breakthrough into France. It had been visited on several occasions by Churchill and in 1936 he had commented on the 'gravity and competence' of the

French officers he met. By 1939 these same 'grave' officers had sunk into a dangerous mood of defensive apathy, subsequently called the 'Maginot mentality'. The British CIGS, Field Marshal Sir Cyril Deverell, aware of the German Army's immense offensive potential, had expressed serious doubts as early as 1937 about the ability of the line to resist renewed attacks. There was in any case the undefended gap of 150 miles along the Belgian frontier.

However none of these controversies was in my mind as we drove towards the area of Lille. Our final destination was Fresnoy-en-Gohelle close to the Belgian frontier. Late at night and in pouring rain our headquarters' convoy drove into the village square. With my commanding officer, Lieutenant Colonel Gerald Pym, I advanced on the 'Château', a substantial, ugly but well-built red brick house at the end of a drive guarded by a lodge. We pressed a bell, the door opened and a large elderly lady emerged : Madame Colombel, the owner.

'*Bonsoir, Messieurs, entrez, s'il vous plait, et soyez bien venus.*' I paraded my Swiss-learnt French, and it soon became evident that we had landed in clover. Madame's husband was the Mayor of Fresnoy and, as a lawyer, had been mobilised into the French Army's Legal Service in Paris; in his absence she ruled the village. In her youth she had had an English governess, and was an enthusiastic Anglophile with two particular desires which in perfect *franglais* she confided to us: '*le bridge*' and '*le bacon*'. We were happy to supply both ! She, for her part, placed everything at our disposal. I slept in the second best bedroom in elaborately embroidered linen sheets; the Colonel was of course even better served, and the two field engineers who had been with me at Chatham, were also billeted in luxury. The housework was done by Françoise, the pretty *bonne à tout faire* in the Lodge, assisted enthusiastically by our batmen, who found her 'very easy to get on with'.

On arrival, there was no sign of enemy activity either in the air or on land. To our surprise we found that our task was to build a large number of concrete pillboxes, on a defence line already reconnoitred which claimed to be a northern extenion of the controversial Maginot Line. By now it seemed even to us that its importance in the eyes of the French was exaggerated. Our surprise increased when we learnt that the necessary stores – cement, reinforcing bars and timber for shuttering – although figuring in the War Office mobilisation plans – were not due to arrive until the spring of 1940 at the earliest. We were ordered to get our stores by local purchase. There followed an extraordinary scramble in which the Engineers of all the British divisions and ourselves competed in buying hundreds of tons of cement and steel and the entire output of various timber mills from the delighted French. There was no financial control, nor could there be; urgency was the order of the day, and every morning I loaded the Field Engineers with vast quantities of francs and sent them hot-foot to any supplier that could be located. After a suitable pause for the French to count their gains, the stores arrived, accompanied almost invariably by a case of champagne for the 'Genie Britannique'.

We lived well and we worked hard. Our sappers, though territorial, were mostly highly skilled artificers, and their officers in many cases were experienced civil engineers familiar with the control of large projects. So amidst the notorious mud of Northern France the pillboxes rose steadily, and the French became richer and richer.

In October, the 'Alice in Wonderland' atmosphere was abruptly changed : warning was received of a possible German attack. However the pill-box building continued undisturbed and soon our routine returned to normal. We did not know that, but for appalling weather, Hitler would have had his way and marched into Belgium then.

Our Mess in the Château, with its garden embellished by shells of World War I, was a haven of comfort and cheer. Our colonel, Gerald Pym, wearing the ribbon of the Military Cross from 1917, had a delightfully light touch, and an eye and ear ever open to relish the comic aspects of our situation, which on reflection could only be defined as desperate. Professionally he was highly competent; he was killed after great endeavours in the Dunkirk operation.

However that disaster was not discernible as yet, although few of us were confident that by rushing forward into Belgium, when permitted by our ally to do so, we could achieve miracles against a better equipped and better trained German army.

I retain a memory of great hospitality and generosity from Madame Colombel, whom I was able later to track down in Paris in 1945. Soon after our arrival she told us how relieved she was when the French army moved out of Fresnoy, and the British moved in ! I believe that the excellent relationship between us remained unimpaired to the end. When our headquarters finally moved into Belgium in May 1940, by which time I was elsewhere, we all subscribed for a silver cigarette box with an embossed RE crest on the lid to register our appreciation of her generosity. She was a chain smoker, and we had always kept her well supplied with NAAFI cigarettes.

In 1945 when I was able to call on her in Paris, she was living in a smart *appartement* in the Quai D'Orsay devoid of any heating. The bouquet and the cigarettes which I presented to her were much appreciated.

In November, deeply involved as I was in the day-to-day management of a construction force of nearly a thousand men and frustrated by the onset of winter, I was surprised to learn that I was to attend a short 'War Course' at the Staff College, Camberley, in January. Moreover to educate us in the mysteries of the BEF, we were to be led on an instructional tour from the base at St Nazaire to GHQ at Arras by Major Neville Mitchell, 15/19 Hussars.* We had attached to us in our Engineer Formation a French *Agent de Liaison*, an intelligent smart young man who had intended to become a lawyer. His English was severely limited but we had many discussions together in which the dominant topic was 'would the French fight?' His answer given with some reservations was 'No'. He accompanied us on the tour of the BEF on which we encountered many French Army units; they seemed a dispirited lot and I saw no reason to dissent from his view. With little encouragement from the twenty-five British officers in our party, he assumed it was necessary on all possible occasions to guide us to a brothel; but I was never able to admire his judgement and was, I fear, a sorry disappointment to him.

Another interlude which relieved the monotony of pillbox building was an attachment to a medium regiment Royal Artillery to learn of their special tastes in the preparation of gun emplacements. It seemed unlikely that in Belgium, when the time came, an opportunity for building elaborate emplacements would be provided by our ruthless enemy; however the visit was most enjoyable for me because the commanding officer 'Mossy' Marshall had commanded the battery in Nasirabad in whose Mess I had lived, and Dick Keenlyside was one of the captains. His satirical comments on our situation were most entertaining.

---

* Major-General N. Mitchell, who when commanding the 6th Armoured Division in BAOR, died as the result of an accident in 1954. I was ordered to command the Division temporarily for six months.

As Christmas 1939 approached we decided to invite Madame Colombel to join us for dinner in the principal reception room in the château, a large hall in baronial style with an appropriate fireplace. What could be more fitting than to sit down to dinner in front of a roaring log fire? Logs were duly collected, and just before Madame's arrival my batman applied a match. For a few seconds nothing happened – then smoke in great quantities billowed into the room. We had forgotten that in France fireplaces are seldom built to be used, and that the chimney was firmly closed with a steel door. However the party recovered, Madame enjoyed herself, and we retired late. I was awakened in the early hours, and came slowly to the conclusion that I was experiencing the romantic device of gravel being thrown at my window. A voice below cried persistently, '*Françoise, Françoise, es tu là?*' I padded down to the massive front door and found a poilu standing there in uniform. He told me he had three days' leave from the Maginot Line and '*Françoise est mon amie*'. Naturally I admitted him, and he crept silently to the attics. This scene had a happy sequel in 1944 when I revisited Fresnoy; Françoise and her husband, the poilu, entertained me in the Lodge. A packet of NAAFI tea, which had been carefully concealed from the Germans and husbanded for an exceptional occasion was with some ceremony brought into use. I was almost overcome by the warm generosity of my hosts. Françoise told me then that after Dunkirk, the Château had become an officers' mess for Goering's Luftwaffe. The basement had been converted into a *Bierkeller* in which Françoise was required late at night to serve beer to the young pilots bombing England. In September 1940 it was not unusual for a senior Luftwaffe officer to descend to the *Bierkeller*, loaded pistol in hand, to order a reluctant pilot at 3 a.m. to undertake yet a third sortie over England. I was not surprised that Françoise, so gentle and sympathetic, had felt sorry for the young pilots!

The course at Camberley was conducted at high pressure; although in reality we were still captains we were given the local rank of major. I remember particularly the verve and instructional skill of a Lieutenant-Colonel Horrocks.* On the rostrum he used to stand with legs crossed and deliver a torrent of witty incisive instruction which riveted his audience. However I did not believe him when he said, 'In a year or two you will all be brigadiers.' I discovered once again my ignorance of infantry tactics, despite the grounding I had received at Chatham and Simla from Captain Dorman-Smith, and my masquerade as a brigade major in Kohat in 1938. The more general aspects of the military arts, however, presented no problem; and in retrospect I must have performed adequately as, much later, I found I was to be an instructor.

Throughout that period of four months of sheltered study, which was dominated more by our elderly Commandant's recollections of World War I than by the revolutionary concepts of Liddell Hart which I had read in the long winters of the Hindu Kush, the newspapers' headlines told of a succession of disasters: Hitler's unforeseen invasion of Norway, and heavy losses of shipping relieved only by the dramatic triumph over the *Graf Spee*.

Britain, under Chamberlain, not yet united in resolve, seemed all too slowly to be gathering her strength, and only one clarion call was to be heard: that of Churchill from the Admiralty.

We, at Camberley, expected and indeed hoped to return to the BEF, and were aware that there too the background had changed. The low morale of the French people and their Army, which on our pre-Staff College tour we had privately observed, was now the subject of public debate. Our four hundred pillboxes with their tank traps, trenches, barbed wire and signal cables had been completed. The strength of the BEF had been substantially increased, and Allied strategy had at last been decided. The option of remaining in the heavily fortified defensive line, yielding the initiative to the Germans and abandoning Belgium to its fate, had been discarded and, despite grave misgivings, it had been decided that a German onslaught should be countered by a forward move to a selected defensive line in Belgium. The Belgians, nevertheless, still clinging to their traditional policy of neutrality and fearful of provoking the Germans, declined to collaborate openly in planning for an Allied advance, although some secret contacts were utilised.

On 1st May 1940 we all dispersed from the Staff College to our various appointments, and I found I was to join the headquarters of 4th Division of the BEF commanded by Major-General Dudley Johnson, VC. It was located in the same region of France that I had left in December.

After the alarms of the previous winter and the intelligence that had fortuitously come to hand, despite the rudimentary intelligence agencies of that time, there was a general acceptance by the British, if not the French, that a massive German thrust into France from some quarter would soon take place. In the 4th Division the only doubt, which in my mind was never resolved, was whether we should proceed on 'Projet D' or 'Projet E'. This was typical of the ultimate confusion of Allied planning, and was to bear some very sour fruit in the operations that lay ahead.

My recollection of the next thirty days in which my contribution to the battle was almost negligible, has remained vivid, and has recently been fortified by re-reading *My First War* a delightful book by Captain Sir Basil Bartlett, Bt.,* the Field Security officer of our division. It was published in 1941, and gives a humorous and dramatic account of this period, with many profound observations well worth recalling.

Basil and I were in the same Mess with two other officers who were to become my life-long friends: John Stevens the Intelligence Officer, an amateur captain from a TA unit of the City of London; and a regular officer, Henry van Straubenzee of the 4th/7th Dragoon Guards, who occupied the position of Deputy Assistant Adjutant General, dealing with personnel.

Basil was a playwright, and indeed one of his plays was running in London at that time although I was unaware of it. My impressions of him were of an insouciant, intelligent and charming amateur; his secret activities seemed to be entirely linked with the French, whose language he spoke superbly. In carrying out his itinerant duties, thwarting enemy attempts at espionage, sabotage and propaganda, he exercised a superb talent for acquiring notable bottles of wine at knock-down prices. Hardly an evening passed without a splendid contribution from Basil, negotiated '*en passant*' in some *épicerie* while pursuing the track of one of His Majesty's enemies!

It was indeed fortunate for me that John Stevens and Henry Straubenzee were there, since my opposite number by definition was the GSO II operations, a major ten or more years older than me. At that time, in the minds of many die-hards in the Army Staff, there was an unfortunate tradition that the General Staff (with whom I was to spend the rest of my career until I became Quarter-Master

---

* Chatto & Windus, 1941.

General) were the 'twice-born', to use an old Indian term. As such, they operated on a platform above those like me who dealt with such mundane matters as rations, supply, repair, etc. It was axiomatic that these less exciting functions could not be planned or implemented without frequent guidance from the 'twice-born' Brahmins who, despite the uncertainties of this particular operation, were expected to be able to forecast at least forty-eight hours ahead the future trends of the battle. My colleague, if that is the right word, made no attempt to carry out this essential function. However Captain John Stevens, who turned up later as one of my majors in Cairo in SOE in 1941, was already showing those qualities of forethought, intellect and courage, which eventually carried him post-war to the chairmanship of Morgan Grenfell, a meteoric career in the City and in international finance, and a knighthood. From him I was frequently able to gain valuable guidance as to the likely outcome of our chaotic operations. Staff officers with responsibility for logistics almost invariably have to order the positioning of ammunition and supplies well before the next operational move takes place. John's forecasts of how long we were likely to remain in our present position, and where might be our next one, were seldom wrong. Henry, a charming major of immense ability, who was eventually to be cut off from the highest positions in the Army by arthritis, was well on top of his responsibilities, and was always ready to help me, the Deputy Assistant Quartermaster General fresh from the Staff College, unaware for some days even of the Divisional Commander's name, and manifestly 'wet behind the ears'! Without them I would indeed have been lost.

I was to get to know General Dudley Johnson as the critical scene unfolded. He was aged fifty-six, which was old for the chaotic events that were to follow, but he was quite imperturbable and much admired by his staff, and by many of the soldiers who knew him well. In the First World War, as an infantryman he had been awarded two MC's and two DSO's as well as the VC. The GSO I was Colonel Basil Dening, MC, a sapper, and the Commander Royal Signals Lieutenant-Colonel H. E. Rance, who later as Major-General Sir Hubert Rance became Governor of Burma.

On 10th May the balloon went up. Basil Bartlett in his book faithfully recorded the scene :

'So there's to be a real war after all.' I was woken up at six this morning by Allo [one of his warrant officers]. He was standing saluting at the end of my bed wearing a tin hat and with a smile on his face.

'I told you so, Sir,' he said. 'Germany has invaded Belgium, Holland and Luxembourg.'

I haven't any comment to make. I feel rather sick. War is something that happens to other people. In my heart I'd had a faint, mean hope that perhaps it wouldn't happen to me. That hope is now shattered. I must take hold of myself and see what courage I can muster.

The news didn't reach Division until breakfast-time.

All the morning the local inhabitants stood about in huddles and chattered. There doesn't seem to be much enthusiasm. I remember around Christmastime the cheerful way in which the Belgians declared that an invasion would be the finest New Year's present the Germans could give them. And the French felt much the same. Now it's different. I believe the majority of the French feel as I do. They hoped that the Germans would attack in the East or blow up inside or somehow lose their vindictiveness.

There's been great aerial activity all day.

At lunch in the Mess I looked at my fellow-members with new eyes. For months they've been bored. They've grumbled a lot. They've dragged themselves wearily to their dull offices and dutifully attended dull exercises. Today they seem to have taken on a new lease of life. They're calm. But they're extremely cheerful.

There's a great sharpening of knives going on all through the Division. Even my Field Security Police who aren't technically a combatant body are full of fight.

By contrast the French are sullen and scared.

We've learned with relief that the Belgians and the Dutch are both fighting and have asked us to come in and help them. There's been a doubt in many people's minds as to whether the Dutch might not pack up without a struggle.

I went up to the frontier and watched one of our divisions going through. The Belgians were welcoming them enthusiastically. They were travelling at a good speed, but were too closely spaced, I thought. They'd suffer heavily if the Germans took it into their heads to bomb them.

We had dinner to the accompaniment of guns firing and a few bombs dropping. In time I suppose I shall get used to them. At present they seem like noises off in a war play.

That afternoon John Stevens and I were summoned by Colonel Basil Dening, the GSO I (operations). He had in front of him a map of Belgium on which were drawn certain circles, the 'goose eggs'* of the

---

* Rough circles drawn on a map to indicate areas to be occupied by units.

Americans that became all too familiar when I joined General Mark Clark's Army in 1943.

With the clarity and courtesy for which he, a senior member of the General Staff, was renowned, he said :

'We move into Belgium at dawn tomorrow. The General wants you, Richardson, and you, Stevens, to cross the frontier at 0500 hours tomorrow and move to this locality and organise the bivouac arrangements of the three brigade groups and divisional troops in these particular areas that I have marked. Units of the division will advance on these routes and the GSO II (ops) will give you the order of march and expected time of arrival of the first units.

'Are there any questions?'

Resolved to 'sell our lives dearly', John and I withdrew from the presence and prepared ourselves for an early start on the morrow.

Colonel Dening was to die in a destroyer leaving Dunkirk four weeks later.

CHAPTER FOUR

Dunkirk

Early next morning John and I set off in our truck, expecting all hell
to be let loose, particularly from the Luftwaffe. Nothing happened! We
drove peacefully in the bright sunshine towards our destination. However, as we progressed, the signs of Belgian military activity increased.
Medium and heavily artillery, mostly drawn by equally heavy horses,
appeared to be occupying most of the narrow lanes. If this was to be
our division's bivouac area, already there were cuckoos in our nest.

We enquired in French, in which John also was fluent, what these
units might be and where was their headquarters. We persevered
through battery commander to brigade, and in every case were told
that the Belgian units intended to stay, and that nothing was known
about the arrival of the British 4th Division.

The situation looked highly unpropitious, and time was passing
rapidly. In growing desperation, we demanded to see a senior commander and eventually were shown into the presence of the Belgian
corps commander. He was very, very old. Politely we said our piece,
which he greeted with surprise.

'*Une division britannique arrivera içi ce soir? Impossible!*' he said.

We persisted with our request for him to move his corps, and eventually he said he would consult his staff. After half an hour we sat down
with a dozen or more Belgian staff officers at a long table in a farmhouse.
We repeated our request. 'No,' they said, 'there must be some mistake.'

After twenty minutes of futile discussion, we were getting nowhere.
Suddenly a small group at the end of the table abandoned their comments in French, and started to talk Flemish. John listened, pricked up
his ears, and to my amazement intervened in Flemish, one of the six
languages which I afterwards discovered he spoke. This *tour de force*
seemed to act like a catalyst, and after a further ten minutes of Flemish
debate, the corps commander agreed that he would indeed move his
units to permit the entry of the 4th Division.

61

But now it was too late. Two hours after our respectful farewell to the Belgian corps commander, John and I reported to Colonel Dening, who had just arrived on the scene. Together we watched with dismay while the incoming columns of British lorries became hopelessly blocked in the narrow cobbled lanes by outgoing horse-drawn vehicles and guns of the Belgian corps. This state of chaos was to continue in a mounting crescendo until our final evacuation from Dunkirk.

That evening, the divisional staff were gathered together in our temporary headquarters. Our commander was as usual quiet and unruffled. My immediate superior was an elderly colonel, Evelyn Smith, responsible for personnel matters and logistic support. As we shared a staff car, I was to get to know him very well in the next fourteen days. Amongst the brigade commanders was Brigadier Kenneth Anderson, the future commander of the British First Army in North Africa, whom Montgomery after his triumph at Alamein, was to categorise accurately and mischievously as 'a good plain cook'. I found him dour, fretful and humourless. The other two, 'Bubbles' Barker and 'Ginger' Hawksworth, were more congenial. In the adjacent 3rd Division, my old friend Kit Woolner now a Brigadier commanded a brigade under Montgomery. I well remember being warned that 3rd Division were very sharp; if you didn't watch out, you would find they had grabbed the centre of the stage, were occupying the best billets, and had acquired the lion's share of any resources available. This was a telling reflection of the dynamic personality of the instructor from the Quetta Staff College who now commanded 3rd Division, and under whom I was to enjoy such a rewarding year's service in North Africa in two years' time.

My responsibility in 4th Division was to assist my colonel in his task of ensuring that units, throughout a period of precipitately mobile operations, should not lack ammunition, petrol or rations. We were fortunate in having a first-class commander of the Royal Army Service Corps who was to be a tower of strength when others had been killed or had become useless through exhaustion. He had fought in the First War and was no longer young. I used to meet him every evening. After his long day of twenty hours or more, he had covered a great deal of ground issuing instructions to his transport columns and ensuring by personal supervision that his orders were faithfully carried out. I noticed, when we met, that a bottle of whisky was always within easy reach, but he was never less than a hundred per cent effective. If he could thus sustain himself, I thought, while others all around were crumbling from exhaustion, then 'more power to his elbow'! He had an uncanny knack of anticipating events; as a result the division was never short of ammunition or petrol and, if rations were scarce, they could always be supplemented by produce from the farms which the owners seemed quite willing to provide.

Very soon we moved forward to the area of Brussels, making contact with the Belgian Army on our north-western flank. We did not expect to be able to stay there long : the operation was to be a series of controlled withdrawals. In those circumstances, the divisional engineers had a vital part to play in demolishing bridges, laying minefields and strengthening whatever obstacles could be found to stem the advance of the German panzers. The commander of our Royal Engineers was Colonel Coxwell-Rogers who in Aldershot in 1929 had commanded the First Field Squadron, RE, an élite body of sappers devoted to, if not obsessed with, the horse. Under his guidance, I had attended a well-run course on 'Horse Management' which to my surprise had proved extremely useful during my two horseborne years in the Hindu Kush. I must confess that in 1929 I had wondered whether this boot-slapping *beau-sabreur*, who excelled in the show-jumping and hunting fields and seemed to personify the amateurism of the British Army, ever concentrated his mind on the less beguiling techniques of military engineering. Now in the Dunkirk retreat, I saw with admiration this tireless, devoted and forceful commander achieving outstanding successes by his professionalism and personal leadership. Later as a major-general he was Chief Engineer to the Allied Armies in Italy.

Very soon we were to be engaged in a series of short defensive actions terminating in hasty withdrawals, in which the major problem was control. Radio sets were few, and after my Indian training, which had been primitive in terms of military technology, I was far from adept at working them; this weakness seemed to apply elsewhere. My uncooperative colleague, the G II (operations), had a reputation for competence in this black art, but I doubt whether any portion of the division was in sustained radio contact with headquarters during our repeated nightly withdrawals. On one such night, when as I learned later our division had been transferred to a different corps after orders for the night had been given, I discovered that our destination had been completely changed. Lacking any radio communication, the best I could do was to write the new destination on a large blackboard taken from a school, prop it on the side of the road, illuminate it feebly with a torch, and attempt to draw the attention of drivers to it as they somnolently moved past at 3 a.m. : a highly unsuccessful example of modern staff duties !

Basil Bartlett's journal again brilliantly captures the surrealist scene :

There were no more British traffic police to be seen. And the mix-up was indescribable. Half Belgium appeared to be on the move. I've never seen such a queer collection of vehicles. The Belgian Army and the Belgian police seemed to be evacuating themselves as purposefully as the civilian population. The roads into France are temporarily closed to refugees, so their destination is obscure. When we stopped to ask the way or to find out how things were going, everyone – including Belgian soldiers – said :

'We're getting out as quickly as possible. The Germans are coming.'

This attitude rather took us aback.

We found our Divisional area chock-full of troops of all sizes and shapes. There appears to have been a muddle. Two Belgian Divisions are already billeted in the area allotted to us. And they refused to move. The King of the Belgians has persistently declined to have Staff talks with the French and British.* As a result there is no co-operation whatever between his Army and ours. I suppose it will all straighten itself out in time.

To our horror, we found the whole of Headquarters lumped together in an enormous school on top of a hill overlooking Brussels. It was the only building available. The two Belgian Divisions had very sensibly decided it was too vulnerable for them.

The school is quite beautiful. It is modern. The classrooms are on three floors. They are light and cheerful, and all have huge plate-glass windows. The school is equipped to teach everything from laundry to botany. If it is at all representative of Belgian education, I don't really see how a German occupation will be beneficial.

Our office is the Second Form classroom. It has only recently been abandoned. There are flowers still on the teacher's desk.

On the walls are gay railway-posters.

Our exposed position makes us a certain target for every kind of German missile. But the view of Brussels is magnificent.

As my Field Security Police came in I sat them down, one by one, at

* This was Basil Bartlett's impression at the time; but in fact King Leopold had had talks with the British on 12th May.

Morale-boosting at Munich time. Mr Hore-Belisha who had doubled the Territorial Army on paper visiting the Royal School of Military Engineering, Chatham. Lt Col 'Kit' Woolner, the author's Commanding Officer, in cheerful mood on right.

France in 1939 with Territorial Sappers of the BEF. Building concrete pillboxes to extend the Maginot Line.

As we advanced to Brussels May 1940, Belgian horse-drawn artillery was a frequen obstacle on the cobbled roac

'The Germans are coming': Belgian refugees moving West, their possessions stacked on carts and perambulators.

Dunkirk: a last look at the t in flames.

desks in the classroom and made them write letters home.

Then I went down to breakfast in a local café.

The news is shocking. Queen Wilhelmina is in England. And the Dutch are folding up. It makes me shiver to think of all those Dutch ports in German hands.

On my way up the hill after breakfast I nearly had my ear clipped off by the wing of a German reconnaissance 'plane which was tearing along very low and at a great speed, trying to get away from two Hurricanes. We shot off rifles and pistols at it : but without success. Later we heard that the Hurricanes had brought it down.

The area is thick with enemy agents. We have posted special guards all round Headquarters. Reports come in hourly saying that the signallers are having their telephone-wires cut as soon as they're laid.

At midday the two airmen from the 'plane that was shot down were brought in by a guard from an anti-tank regiment. I took them over to Corps for interrogation. They were very impressive. They were both Warrant Officers who'd had six years' ground service. They were good-looking and well mannered and know their job thoroughly. They weren't the under-sized half-starved lunatics we'd been led to expect.

All the prisoners so far taken are violently Nazi in outlook. They say that Hitler is a man of destiny and that everything he does is intuitive and right. What do 100,000 casualties matter as long as he achieves his purpose?

I am billeted on an exceedingly old woman who has sons and grand-sons and great-grandsons in the Belgian Army. She invited me to tea and gave me Chivers' strawberry jam. The pot dated, I think, from the last War; but it was a moving gesture.

My own recollection, more mundane, is of repeated night moves in the staff car with Evelyn. I had heard that an important facet in training for war was to take sleep whenever operationally possible regardless of conventional hours. This was not organised or encouraged in our division, although Montgomery in his 3rd Division had strongly emphasised it before the advance into Belgium; Kit Woolner told me forty years later that the system worked. With them there were no surprises, as the operations had been meticulously rehearsed before they moved forward. With us the result was that after ten days of continuous operations in which I, like many others, had had perhaps twenty hours' sleep, some of our senior officers, with lion hearts and unsurpassed keen-ness to remain continuously 'on duty', had begun to show obvious signs of wear.

While still on their feet they were beginning to talk nonsense. My colonel by this time was reaching that stage, and instead of dozing en route in our staff car from 1 a.m. to 4 a.m., which was perfectly possible, he would prattle away all night. At every unscheduled stop, due to the intervention of retreating Belgian units, he would become obsessed about spies: 'Charles, do you see that dark-haired man over there dressed as a Belgian soldier?' he would say to me at 3 a.m. 'I'm sure he is up to something odd; look at the way he keeps glancing up that street.' And I would have to volunteer to interrogate him. Had these suspicions ever been borne out, I have to this day no idea as to the next step we should have taken.

Throughout those days and nights I felt frustrated and impotent. There was no possibility of forward planning; even John Stevens seemed to have lost his talent for anticipating the next move in our increasingly chaotic situation. When I visited the headquarters of the three brigades they seemed to be reasonably content and adequately supplied with ammunition and petrol though food was getting short, despite using whatever was to hand locally. How much longer, I asked myself, could these impromptu withdrawals continue, and was the French Army capable of withstanding the strong German thrust which was directed at them. And what of the Belgians on our left?

On 15th May, the Panzers of German Army Group A broke through the French Ninth Army in the area of Sedan, thus splitting the Allied line in two. The French defence at that point disintegrated, and German Army Group A advanced westwards at astonishing speed in a wide outflanking movement south of the BEF directed on Amiens and the Channel Ports. Withdrawal of the BEF became inevitable, and on the evening of that day we received orders to move back from our positions near Brussels to the line of the River Scheldt.

Unaware of the full horror of this situation, I went about my prosaic business as best I could. But the increasing flood of refugees moving westwards with their possessions, stacked on farm carts and perambulators, was clear evidence that our situation, and indeed theirs was far from good. The Luftwaffe too was very active by day, and our movement was frequently interrupted by their Stuka attacks, and by long-range shelling of road junctions.

As to the French resistance, Basil describes the scene with a memorable vignette of our gallant divisional commander.

The situation map in the Intelligence Office is getting most alarming. I sat and watched it, fascinated, as the movement of the German push was chalked in. The break-through at Sedan seems to have been completely successful. And now there's another one higher up, the German Armoured Divisions must be travelling at a tremendous pace. I wonder what the French are going to do. They anticipated that the attack would come exactly when and where it has come. So I imagine that they have guns placed one behind the other all the way from Sedan to Paris. I hope they have.

The General was not impressed by the break-through. He put on four pairs of spectacles and stared at it calmly for a minute or two. Then he rubbed it out. 'It hasn't been confirmed,' he said.

On 27th May the disastrous situation was exposed all too clearly when we learned that the King of the Belgians had sued for an armistice, and our left flank was in the air. Only then did we junior officers start to talk about evacuation. I was not alarmed by this development; in my mind the Royal Navy supported by the Royal Air Force was still supreme in the English Channel. But gloom certainly prevailed, relieved by one incident which gave me great encouragement.

On one of our usual nightly excursions Evelyn Smith and I, being driven with minimum lights through the rain, got lost near Kemmel. In the distance I saw one of the dim marker lamps which were used to indicate a headquarters. Evelyn was persisting in trying to read a map, but I insisted on stopping the car to investigate the marker lamp. I knocked on the door: it was opened by Jackie Smyth! He had been brought to England to command a brigade. As usual, he was in great form despite the fact that his brigade had been training in England with pickhelves. Unfortunately our situation did not permit a 'Chota peg' nor reminiscences of Chitral.

To patch up the situation brought about by the Belgian collapse, great improvisations involving Montgomery's 3rd Division were successfully carried out. Eventually we reached La Panne in our final refuge, the Dunkirk bridgehead.

What emotions were appropriate to a situation such as this? I think mine were a strange mixture of professional despair, compounded with a juvenile feeling that 'somehow all would be well'. This naïve hope was strengthened by two unlikely but significant details, the first of which was the appearance on the roadside near La Panne of Lieutenant-General Sir Alan Brooke, our Corps Commander. He appeared to be full

of confidence and cheer and, as a counter to the chaos through which
we had passed, he was immaculately dressed with a gleaming Sam
Browne belt and a pair of symmetrically laced 'lion-tamer' boots,
identical with those of my gunner father in World War I. If he was not
worrying, why should I?

Gradually the scene unfolded : we were to embark for England. By
what means? This vital aspect appeared somewhat vague. Meanwhile
there seemed little that I could do other than visit the headquarters of
our three brigades and find out if they had any problems. Then I moved
further afield to find who our neighbours were, and was surprised to
discover an echelon of GHQ.

There I found an amiable sapper colonel in the 'Q' department, with
whom I had a cup of tea and a gossip. As I was leaving he said :

'How are you off for rations?'

'Not too good,' I said. 'Farms with geese and chickens seem to be a
thing of the past.'

'All right,' he said. 'There is a Belgian train at the station full of bully
beef. You had better take it.'

I drove rapidly back to our headquarters, summoned twelve 3-ton
trucks and drove to the station. The Belgian railway official evinced
surprise, verging on opposition, but *force majeure* overcame his doubts.
We drove away with our prize which was much appreciated by our
units. This was the only practical achievement that I could claim
throughout the Dunkirk operations.

Not long afterwards General Johnson held his last 'Order Group'
detailing the procedure for embarkation. I found I was to be a 'Beach-
master' and I was told to arrange the embarkation of any units that
arrived on my patch of beach in any vessel that might appear. Meanwhile the battalions were to fight a series of withdrawal actions as the
Dunkirk perimeter was closed in. The General as usual was calm
and unruffled, and the GSO I, Colonel Basil Dening, noted down the
verbal orders. These included precise instructions about the lining up
of vehicles and equipment preparatory to their destruction. There was
a deadening finality about this. Then came the second significant detail
which inexplicably raised my spirits. Basil Dening, in the space of an
hour, produced an impeccably typed and duplicated operation order,
complete with appropriate diagrams which he had personally enlarged
from the small-scale map provided. My suspicion that we were in for a

shambles, my anxiety at the evident lack of shipping, my inner questioning of the possibility of survival in a small beachhead under concentrated attack from land and air, all these doubts were diminished. Perhaps, after all it was business as usual!

My optimism was short-lived. I forget how many days and nights we spent waiting in the sand, at first with no shipping in sight and then gradually an increasing number of all shapes and sizes, but all standing far off. German shelling with methodical precision came nearer and nearer while the Luftwaffe bombed out to sea and occasionally on our beach; however they seemed unaccountably uninterested in totally destroying us as we stayed there impotently. My beach was near a hotel in which I was told a Joint Army/Navy headquarters was sited. I had no radio, so one night I ventured there in the hope of gleaning some cheerful news. Not so; a very exhausted and harassed naval captain was on the telephone to Admiral Bertram Ramsay's HQ in Dover reporting our desperate situation and pleading for more shipping to be sent most urgently. I concluded that a prisoner-of-war camp or a shallow grave seemed to be the likely outcome for most of us.

Eventually I was able to embark a large number of soldiers who arrived mostly in 'penny packets', and finally the order was given to embark whenever we could by whatever means were available. I collected up my posse of twenty soldiers and we waded out towards a naval sloop, where the sailors hauled us ignominiously on board. A young and energetic naval officer said: 'Down to the boiler room and strip off, while we dry your clothes.'

We then sat in a line like sparrows stark naked on the warm asbestos covering of what I took to be a boiler. Bereft of my own plumage, I observed that the British private soldier and his officer were strangely identical.

Shortly afterwards clad in damp battledress I went up on deck, and observed the scene for some time until peremptorily ordered below. The Luftwaffe and the RAF were very busy. Here and there warships were on fire or sinking. At first glance, the small boats seemed comparatively immune, perhaps because they did not easily catch my eye or indeed those of the German pilots. Our sloop was lucky; others were not so fortunate. Basil Dening was killed at sea by a Luftwaffe bomb.

Surprisingly soon, Dover harbour appeared with the white cliffs gleaming in the sunshine. At the railway station we were organised with

great efficiency and despatch. Cups of tea and buns were brought to
the carriage windows by those legendary characters, the 'excellent
women' who attend on British military disasters, and off we went to
Aldershot to bed down on a blanket in a bell tent : I slept for thirty-six
hours.

After two days we were ordered to rejoin our units; our divisional
headquarters was at Crewkerne. On arrival I found that about a
hundred miles of coastline was our parish; initially to defend it we had
about fifteen French 75mm guns with about 10 rounds of ammunition
per gun, and twelve boxes of small arms ammunition.

How soon could Hitler invade England? There were many who
thought 'quite soon'. As part of the BEF that had returned I had no
illusions that we were a deterrent : it would be months before our transport and heavy weapons could be fully replaced. The Royal Air Force
and the Royal Navy, still powerful, would have to give the Army a
breathing space.

The sense of relief at being back in England, ready in due course to
fight another day, soon gave way to shame. How had it come about that
a resolute army such as ours had been called upon to undertake such a
futile manoeuvre alongside allies of dubious worth against an enemy
with greatly superior equipment? How were we to recover from this
appalling disaster?

As for the French, my sympathy for them, generated by my love of
their language, was now extinguished. Had we lost the war? I thought
we probably had.

Soon we were given a week's leave and I went to stay in a small
cottage near the Cheddar Gorge belonging to an honorary 'aunt'. My
mother had taken her first grandson there for safety as my sister was
living dangerously under the Luftwaffe's attacks in Kent, engaged in the
Blood Transfusion Service. It was very peaceful and quiet with a
wonderful view across the sunlit fields of Somerset. The old ladies were
not despondent; the grandson, only six months old, so well-behaved and
pretty, was to them a pointer to a better future. I kept my counsel, but
a sober military appreciation seemed to lead to only one conclusion:
defeat. This mood persisted until on the radio I heard the voice of
Winston Churchill :

'. . . I expect that the battle of Britain is about to begin . . .

'Upon this battle depends the survival of Christian civilisation. Upon it depends our own British life and the long continuity of our institutions and our Empire. The whole fury and might of the enemy must very soon be turned on us. Hitler knows that he will have to break us in this island or lose the war. If we can stand up to him, all Europe may be free, and the life of the world may move forward into broad, sunlit uplands; but if we fail, then the whole world, including the United States, and all that we have known and cared for, will sink into the abyss of a new dark age made more sinister, and perhaps more protracted, by the lights of a perverted science. Let us therefore brace ourselves to our duty and so bear ourselves that if the British Empire and its Commonwealth last for a thousand years men will still say, "This was their finest hour".'

Perhaps by some miracle we could survive. I returned to Crewkerne, and after some weeks of uninspired activity, I found on my table an order from the War Office saying I had been selected to be an instructor at the Middle East Staff College at Haifa, Palestine.

I could scarcely believe it : England was about to be invaded and I was being shunted off to an unknown blind alley. In sombre mood, I 'braced myself to my duty' and packed my bags.

CHAPTER FIVE

Middle East

'They', those anonymous insubstantial figures in Whitehall, whom I was to join twenty years later, gave me seventy-two hours' leave to equip myself for service in tropical climates and to say farewell to my next of kin. The N of K, my mother and sister, were as usual undaunted; my brother-in-law, as a temporary sapper officer, was away in Scotland.

I found myself in the hands of a strangely reticent organisation called Movement Control, largely officered by Royal Engineers. Their behaviour to me seemed to be unusually eccentric. I reported in the south of England and was ordered to move to the Midlands. After a further journey of 100 miles, I was told to go to Liverpool. A few hours later, I found myself on the quarterdeck of a battleship: HMS *Valiant*. Security had been safeguarded: the mystery was solved!

This seemed to be a promising situation. The Navy's welcome, as always, was encouraging. With another eight young officers I was led below to the Admiral's 'Dining Room' a large void space well aft in which a number of camp beds were laid out with blankets. From there we were led to the wardroom and, as the sun was over the yard arm, pink gin was offered. Our delightful host was the Commander, Peter Reid, and the captain was Captain H. B. Rawling. Later they both became admirals.

There was a palpable atmosphere of quiet, disciplined activity, similar to that I was to sense before the Alamein battle: no hectic bustle, no hysterical emotion but the almost perceptible heartbeat of hundreds of men, each discharging his particular duty with sober devotion.

On 30th August 1940 as darkness descended we put to sea. Once again I heard Churchill's voice pre-recorded for an address to the ship's company by tannoy. HMS *Valiant*, with the aircraft carrier HMS *Ark Royal* and several cruisers and destroyers, was bound for Gibraltar to join Force H, another powerful group of warships; thence we were to go to Malta and Alexandria. Churchill indicated that on the success of this major operation, the first since the declaration of war by the Italians on 10th June, major issues depended. In fact, this operation, 'Hats', had originally been conceived as a convoy to pass merchant ships with troops, tanks and equipment urgently through the Mediterranean to Middle East Command, thus avoiding the long delay by the Cape route. However the First Sea Lord, Admiral Pound, had persuaded Churchill that this concept was too hazardous. Hence, in strategic terms our passage through the Mediterranean was now to be a challenge to the Italian Navy and Air Force.

Unaware that I was an infinitesimal part of the bait for Mussolini, I decided that if one had to leave beleaguered England in the hour of her greatest peril, this was not a bad way to do it. To the soldier, a British warship prepared for battle carries with it an impressive atmosphere of assurance. Having been 'rescued' by the Royal Navy at Dunkirk, I was perhaps readily susceptible. Unlike the soldier accustomed to wallowing in mud and blood, and never too certain that natural obstacles, quite apart from the Queen's enemies, may bring his plans to nought, a sailor in a capital ship of the Royal Navy, self-contained, well-ordered, logistically independent, master of sea and weather, and with all her mechanical and lethal machinery fine-tuned for the challenge of battle, has good reason to be supremely confident, notwithstanding that disaster may suddenly strike with awesome rapidity. Certainly as we ploughed through the Bay of Biscay, this was the predominant impression given to our little group of khaki drones.

From time to time, abandoning our limited social pursuits or our attempts to keep fit in the face of naval hospitality, we were summoned by tannoy to 'repel aircraft'. For me this involved climbing from the wardroom to another deck, running along a catwalk with 4.5″ LA/HA guns below, and descending into a 15-inch gun turret presided over by a petty officer. We seemed to do this rather too frequently, but for us it was the only evidence that a war was in progress. Life otherwise was like a holiday cruise; but not for Captain Rawling, who never descended from the bridge.

After passing the Rock, an atmosphere of greater tension became evident. Our naval friends in the wardroom were rightly observing the security principle of 'need to know', but perhaps by this time they had gained some confidence in our discretion; at all events I learnt that there would be a formidable threat of submarine attack as we passed through the Sicilian Channel. Naïvely I felt that in some cranny of this vast warlike edifice, there was a place for Major Richardson to 'do his stuff'. Politely but firmly this was declined! Nevertheless I slept that night only fitfully, got up early and at dawn went up to the quarter-deck.

The sight was unbelievable. Spread over an arc of about two hundred degrees and at a distance of two to eight miles there appeared a vast array of battle-grey warships as far as the eye could see; the Mediterranean Fleet had joined us! Shortly afterwards *Valiant* steamed into Malta. In any age at any hour the Grand Harbour provides a dramatic setting which no impresario of stage or screen could ever match; on this occasion the circumstances fitted perfectly the emotional scenario. The people of Malta, cut-off from what at that time was their mother country and besieged by an avaricious and ruthless enemy, watched from the natural battlements above the harbour the entry of this majestic symbol of British naval power, with her Royal Marine Band playing 'Rule Britannia', on the quarter-deck, while the cheers of the ship's company mingled with those of a multitude of Maltese.

We disembarked several Bofors AA guns and ammunition, with officers and men to man them and many tons of warlike stores. A few hours later, heartened by this display of Maltese loyalty and spirit, we resumed our journey to Alexandria. Sleep again was fitful, perhaps through excitement or through the oscillation of my camp bed. The propellers of HMS *Valiant*, designed in World War I, did not seem to be balanced with perfect precision, with the result that the admiral's dining room rose and fell to an irregular rhythm throughout the night. Although no admiral was aboard on this occasion, I assumed that the traditional dinner parties, with lovely ladies flashing their diamonds and their bright coquettish smiles, would invariably take place on arrival in harbour.

The next day at about pink gin time, 'repel aircraft' sounded once again. Expecting the familiar practice, which we must have undertaken twenty times since leaving Liverpool, I leisurely finished my drink. Passing along the catwalk as usual, I was surprised by a loud bang and felt a wave of hot gases entering my khaki shorts: one of the 4.5 guns in its AA role had fired. I was the last to reach the gun turret, our funk hole, and the petty officer remarking that I was late, pressed me to enter.

'What's going on?' I enquired.

'The Italians are bombing us, sir,' he replied. 'You had better get inside.'

I asked for and was reluctantly granted a few minutes' grace to view the scene, which was most remarkable. Six Italian light bombers were flying very slowly at about 2,000 feet in a dead straight line, dropping their bombs on the assembled warships, all of which, or so it seemed, were throwing at them everything they had. Not a scratch of paint was damaged on either side! Fire control in those days was extremely primitive, and heat-seeking missiles were still to be invented. As the Italian pilots withdrew northwards, I felt that they had certainly deserved a medal.

In early September 1940 I arrived at my destination, the Middle East Staff College in Haifa, which was in a Jewish hotel, Telsch House, close to Mount Carmel. It had been established a few months before I arrived, and the first course of students was still in residence. The Commandant was Brigadier 'Chink' Dorman-Smith, my tactics teacher at Chatham in 1928, and my mentor in Simla in 1937. Our paths seemed to be linked ever more closely.

The senior instructor, who virtually ran the place, was Lieutenant-Colonel Freddie de Guingand. Almost at once I fell under his spell. Highly intelligent, humorous and articulate, he performed his professional duty as a teacher with unsurpassed zeal, but without a trace of pomposity. As a lecturer he was fluent and witty; he drew the best not only from the students, but from us his colleagues as well. He brought to Telsch House a whiff of the clubland of St James's, where he would have been welcome as a bon viveur and gambler, and hardly recognised as a soldier. A bachelor, he had been Military Assistant to Mr Hore Belisha the Secretary of State for War, and after the latter's eclipse had been despatched for his own good to remote foreign service, or so we understood. It was through this singular chance that he was to become at a moment of dire crisis General Montgomery's trusted adviser and Chief of Staff, and thereafter to render unsurpassed service to his country.

To work as one of his team was an exhilarating experience; seldom was there a dull moment. Nor were opportunities for relaxation ignored, whether it be shooting *chikor* at dawn only a mile or two from Mount Carmel, or an evening at the local night club, the Piccadilly, where good food, drinkable Palestine wine, and the innocent attentions of attractive Jewish 'hostesses' were readily available.

The Middle East Command in September 1940, controlled by General Wavell from Cairo, covered a vast area: Kenya, Eritrea, Abyssinia, Somaliland, Sudan, Egypt, Palestine and Iraq. Though not facing such a dire threat as the United Kingdom which was beating off Goering's Luftwaffe, Wavell with minimum resources had to cope with Mussolini's incursions, launched from bases in the Italian Colonies in East Africa and Tripolitania.

Already in June, a very small British force had surprised Italian forces on the frontier between Egypt and Cyrenaica, inflicting significant casualties and capturing many prisoners. There were other alarms in Somaliland, Kenya and the Sudan. By the end of 1940 the main Italian threats would be reduced to two: against Egypt, and in the Balkans as a result of Mussolini's invasion of Greece in October of that year.

From Freddie, I learnt that I was the only instructor who had as yet faced the German Army in war. Those who, until then, had been skirmishing with marked success against the Italians, seemed to look to me for 'all the answers'. At an early stage after discussion with Freddie, I took steps to disabuse them. At Dunkirk, we had learnt how not to do it; like them, I was still searching for the right answers.

I found that my principal subject was to be logistics. Ruling out the experiences of Dunkirk as irrelevant, I illustrated my theme in my first lecture by reference to Chitral with its mixed line of communication, five hundred miles long, comprising a rail link, followed by road, then porters and finishing with mules and donkeys. This theme was not as fantastic as it then appeared. In Italy in 1943 mules were to be a godsend; in any tactical discussion with my French colleague he would invariably take refuge behind the statement: *'C'est une question des mulets.'* Moreover Major-General Gerald Templer, then commanding 56 Division, had to convert a gunner regiment temporarily into human porters to carry ammunition to the tops of the snow-clad peaks facing him at Monte Cassino. My Chitral diagram was captioned with a Russian bear since that had been the only purpose of our presence there; ironically the Bear, dormant in our day, was to spring into violent action forty years later.

'Chink' Dorman-Smith, well known to General Wavell and a close friend and protégé of General Auchinleck who was still in India, was obviously restive in his appointment and, perhaps legitimately, left the running of the course almost entirely to Freddie and his Assistant Commandant, a Colonel Tiarks (King's Dragoon Guards) who exercised a vague paternal supervision. 'Chink', fired as always with ambition, was intent on demonstrating his tactical expertise and qualities of leadership, both of which he overestimated, in the more rewarding environment of the battlefield rather than in the backwater of Telsch House. For this purpose, he would absent himself for long periods, move to the Western Desert and there seek 'lessons from the battlefield'. On his return, the more critical members of the staff and of the students, found the harvest somewhat meagre. Late in 1940 Chink played his hand even more boldly; he succeeded in translating himself to an 'operations' appointment in GHQ and took part in General Richard O'Connor's brilliantly successful operations, led by 7th Armoured Division under Major-General John Harding. We always suspected that 'Chink' hoped for an unexpected casualty amongst the generals, permitting him instnatly to stand forward with the cry, 'Here, sir, am I, ready to take over.' After the arrival of Auchinleck, who succeeded Wavell in June 1941, such an apotheosis could indeed have been possible.

To most of us he became a figure of fun. Though gifted with a sharp intelligence and a creative, unconventional mind, his rhetoric, amply larded with his native blarney, seemed seldom based on any sustained study of the problem. He was certainly not a good tutor for young majors who were about to face the full force of the German Afrika Korps in mobile battle in the Desert.

Our students were a hand-picked lot, and included Captain Carver, a very bright young officer of twenty-five in the Royal Tank Regiment, who had already distinguished himself in 7th Armoured Division, and Captain 'George' Baker, a gunner aged 28. Both were to become field-marshals, but as students they were markedly different. Mike Carver, a Wykehamist with a brilliant mind, was intellectually dominant; he was seldom prepared to accept a point from his teachers without challenging its validity and digging deeply into it. George, whom I could remember arriving at Wellington College when I was on the point of leaving, had an equally discerning mind but adopted a more patient, diplomatic approach. Mike was a constant challenge to his teachers, while George often put them right by more subtle means. My friend Dick Keenlyside was appreciated for his keen sense of the ridiculous and for his lack of respect for the instructors!

Our small band of instructors included another sapper, Lieutenant-Colonel Eddie Myers, who later was to lead a brilliant SOE operation in occupied Greece. We were all tied very firmly to the preparation of lectures and correction of students' work, but there were two benefits ready to hand : first the war in Syria just 'up the road', well-furnished with corpses, most of them black, which the French seemed to disregard, despite the hot weather. This war between the Free and the Vichy French offered convenient illustrations of battlefield techniques, such as the firing of a divisional concentration of artillery, which one of the contestants would obligingly provide at our request. Our second benefit was a wide variety of sporting activities, swimming, sailing and even duck shooting at the Lake of Tiberias. Our tactical exercises without troops were conducted sometimes in neat orange groves where Israeli children evinced friendly surprise, or at Tel Aviv, crossing the river Auja from North to South in the reverse direction to Allenby's operation, or in the Plain of Esdraelon, as suitable for tanks in 1941 as it had been for Joshua's war chariots in Old Testament times. We were surrounded by the ruined monuments of ancient wars such as the Crusaders' Krak des Chevaliers and, nearer at hand, the remains of the Templars' castle at Athlit built in 1218 AD. In the short intervals between courses most of us tried to get right away, in my case to Jerash, to Luxor, to Baalbek and Northern Syria after the French war was over, and in the spring of 1941 to El Agheila in Libya, seeking like my master for 'battlefield lessons'.

This latter jaunt was both hilarious and informative. The Assistant Commandant, Colonel Tiarks, felt the very proper desire to visit his regiment, the King's Dragoon Guards, who occupied the honourable role of the foremost unit in Libya at the conclusion of General Richard O'Connor's victorious campaign, in which over 100,000 Italian prisoners had been taken and Benghazi had been captured. 'Would I accompany him?' he asked.

'Delighted,' I answered.

The age gap of about fifteen years would not be awkward, as 'Sharks', as he was known, was a charming person. Military ambition had long been renounced, leaving a benign aura, seasoned with a quiet sense of humour.

'How do we get there?' I asked. 'There' was 1,200 miles away.

'We'll take the staff car,' he airily replied.

And so we set off. The staff car, a vintage Humber of uncertain age, gave out two hundred miles from Haifa. Sharks showed no sign of concern.

'We can hitchhike quite easily,' he said. This we did for over two thousand miles; and to me the extraordinary feature of our hike was the number of personal friends in all walks of military life who greeted Sharks along the route. All were eager to provide transport, rations and a place to doss down at night. At Mersa Matruh I slept in a caravan belonging to the late Italian General Maletti, who had been killed at Sidi Barrani, while the Colonel slept in an underground dug-out, of which there were plenty. Initially in our car we had laid in a good quantity of whisky, with which friendship and hospitality were partially repaid. Every night stop, be it with a well-known regiment previously encountered by Sharks in India or with a Polish battalion eager like the others to receive us, was invariably entertaining.

I wrote home: 'Colonel Tiarks is a vague, easy-going sort of person. Rather a trial when I was trying to "organise" the expedition, but the perfect companion once we started. He has great confidence in something turning up, and it always did!'

As, somewhat insecurely, our journey continued through Sidi Barrani, Derna, Tobruk – place names which had figured in newspapers on the British breakfast table but were as yet unknown to me, I pondered on the scene that might greet us beyond Benghazi when we reached 'the Regiment' at Agheila. There seemed to be a marked thinning out of fighting units: many of them had recently been withdrawn for the abortive operations in Greece. At Cyrene, in the beautiful green-clad *jebel*, I reported to the local headquarters, and found an old school friend, Lieutenant-Colonel 'Bob' Priest, in the appointment of GSO I (Intelligence). He was a robust gunner officer, but was definitely alarmed. He may have been provided with intercepts from Ultra, of which I knew nothing at that time. His message to us was on these lines:

'Between her and Tobruk we have only 150 captured Italian tanks being repaired in our workshops; if something starts up again, particularly with German backing, we shall be on the run to Matruh very quickly.'

With this sombre reflection, we moved on in our borrowed transport to Benghazi and thence down the coast road to Agheila, a patch of sand, with the Italian fort guarding the coast road just visible some miles to the west.

By this time enemy air attacks became uncomfortably frequent. I could not help thinking that our lone British staff car on the dead straight stretches of the only road in Libya must be a very conspicuous target! On arrival, Sharks and his unknown companion were courteously greeted by the commanding officer. I sensed an unusual atmosphere. It was as if we had arrived at a country house for the weekend, unaware that the son and heir had just blown his brains out!

Darkness, the instant darkness of the Desert, was approaching, and our bedding rolls were taken to the slit trenches provided by our hosts. After a welcome drink, the story came out: a troop of their armoured cars had been sent that morning to reconnoitre the neighbourhood of the fort. No sound of firing had been heard, but the troop had never returned. I learnt much later that the troop had been ambushed by a German detachment recently arrived; this was the advance party of the German Afrika Korps under a General Rommel, who in February had arrived in North Africa to support his Italian allies. Very soon he was to revolutionise the whole progress of Desert operations and, by his successes, exert a dominating influence on the forces opposing him.

The Americans, whose language I learnt when later serving with them in Italy, have an illuminating phrase: 'A visiting fireman'. This defines a visitor who arrives with some official pretext, but is definitely unwelcome. The next day I reckoned we were in that category.

The armoured car regiment, whose nearest tank or infantry support was very many miles away, were justifiably apprehensive; doubtless they felt they should not be lumbered with two guests who were virtually non-combatants. So after two uncomfortable nights we said farewell. I was not loth to do so as enemy air attacks had been persistent; to me our safari from Haifa seemed hardly to call for a supreme sacrifice.

Slowly we wended our way back. In Cairo I lunched with 'Coco' Cumberlege from Chitral; he had been with an Indian division in the operations in Eritrea; and I met a number of our previous students now installed in their first staff jobs.

It was at about this time that General 'Dick' O'Connor, the victorious commander of Western Desert Force, was captured by the Germans together with Lieutenant-General Sir Philip Neame, vc, a distinguished

(Above) On passage to Haifa by battleship, September 1940.

(Right) At the middle East Staff College, Haifa, we were surrounded by ruined monuments of ancient wars: the Templar's Castle at Athlit.

(Left) Staff College Exercise: 'Armour in the advance', on the Plain of Esdraelon, author pontificating. *(Right)* The Senior Instructor: Major 'Freddie' de Guingand, later to become General Montgomery's invaluable Chief of Staff.

Instructors at work, but Colonel Tiarks, Deputy Commandant, relaxes with pipe.

sapper who was with him in the same car. They both escaped two years later, and General O'Connor re-emerged to command a corps in NW Europe. Dick O'Connor was a very friendly, small and modest general loved by all : he was to win the admiration both of Chink Dorman-Smith and of Montgomery – a difficult 'right and left' !

Thereafter disasters came thick and fast to the British forces in the Western Desert and later in Greece, where for political reasons they had been diverted on a hopeless task.

After nine months at the Staff College, I fully expected to become involved in these operations as a regimental sapper, but found to my surprise that I was posted to Cairo to join a secret organisation as GSO I (operations) with promotion to the rank of lieutenant-colonel. This was SOE, Special Operations Executive, engaged, I understood in supporting resistance and sabotage in enemy-occupied countries. I knew nothing about it, so I could but raise my eyebrows at this strange turn of events, say goodbye to Freddie and my friends, and prepare for the journey to Cairo.

CHAPTER SIX

Cloak and Dagger

Soon after arriving in Cairo in the summer of 1941, I was fortunate in finding that Dick Keenlyside, my friend from India and France, who had survived my tutelage at the Staff College, was in a job at GHQ, and was looking for a flat. Eventually he and I and another friend rented two floors of a house belonging to the Shell Company, in Gezira the best residential area in Cairo. This developed into a particularly happy nest. Below in the basement resided Idris el Senussi the exiled ruler of Libya, who was under British protection as a refugee from the Italians. Although we made no social contact with the basement, perhaps because the future King Idris was a strict Muslim recluse, two advantages accrued from his presence. When our *suffragi*, an ineffective Egyptian butler, ran out of soda water, he invariably acquired emergency supplies from the basement: a further more substantial advantage lay in the person of King Idris' bodyguard Mahomet, an Arab in untidy uniform who lounged at our gate, but was always willing to help, particularly if rewarded. Dick had to report at 9 a.m. at 'Red Pillars' as GHQ was known, and I had to appear at 'Grey Pillars', the undercover address (or so it was hoped) of SOE. Dick's elderly car was our only transport, and despite Cairo's balmy climate it seldom started without great exertion by Mahomet, who was grateful for a few piastres.

In Grey Pillars I met for the first time my immediate boss, Colonel Terence Airey, who later became a lieutenant-general; from him I learned something of SOE and G(Raiding Forces), known as G(R). Both SOE and G(R), and indeed the first concept of Commando units, had grown principally from the ideas and proposals of three sappers working in 1938 in London. They were Lieutenant-Colonel J. C. F. Holland, Major L. D. Grand and later Major Millis Jefferies. A branch of the Foreign Office under a Canadian, Sir Campbell Stuart, was working independently of the War Office on somewhat similar lines.

Lieutenant-Colonel 'Joe' Holland, medically unfit for active command, engaged himself in research on irregular warfare; he had seen something of the exploits of Lawrence of Arabia in the First War, winning a DFC, and had gone through the 'Troubles' in Ireland in 1919–20. Lawrence Grand had a striking personality, a fertile imagination, a ready wit and sometimes an abrasive tongue, but he led a happy and energetic team. Millis Jefferies, whom Churchill later was to adopt as his private adviser on explosive devices, had a most inventive mind as well as a determined personality. From those tentative early days, much had developed, and I was now to be involved in SOE operations.

I took to Terence Airey immediately. He was a very intelligent and charming infantry soldier; we shared a common bond of frustration caused by the extraordinary circumstances around us. In temperament he was highly-strung, and when angered by the many mishaps in Grey Pillars, he would visibly froth at the mouth! Fortunately he had a lively sense of humour, and after a long exasperating day, ending perhaps at 10 p.m., we would often seek solace at Le Petit Coin de France, where excellent French food and passable claret were still available.

At these sessions, Terence would sometimes regale me with stories of his experiences in the Egyptian Army to which he had been attached, acquiring fluent Arabic in the process. Also, as a staff officer in Khartoum, he remembered all too well the remarkable and eccentric Orde Wingate, who was to become a legend in his lifetime. Terence objected to Wingate's habit in camp of walking around stark naked with his pubic hair inadequately concealed by an alarm clock as a form of sporran. The nakedness was to demonstrate symbolically his savage ruthlessness, and the alarm clock the inexorable onset of time!

I learned from Terence that we were both unwilling participants in the consummation of a shot-gun marriage: SOE, established on Churchill's initiative soon after Dunkirk, was controlled by Dr Dalton the Minister of Economic Warfare from Baker Street. Churchill had told him 'Set Europe ablaze'. The Cairo branch had been set up in 1940 on a civilian basis to operate in the Balkans. Meanwhile there had grown up a parallel military organisation controlled by the Commanders-in-Chief Middle East: G(R). Both organisations operated under a cloak of secrecy: this effectively concealed the operations of the one from the other, but did not invariably conceal either from the enemy. In such a dangerous and sensitive endeavour, two cooks in the kitchen, blindfolded from each other, was one too many and could only lead to disaster. After many unintentional crossing of wires, creating incidents which imperilled the respective agents, General Wavell complained to Dr Dalton, and it was wisely decided that the two organisations should be married under SOE direction, and that a military staff should be inserted into SOE to control operations.

It was a situation familiar in the matrimonial world, which General Wavell summed up neatly: 'SOE think they have taken over G(R), and G(R) think they have taken over SOE, so I suppose everyone is happy.'

I was to be the central controller of operations, while Terence Airey was to provide military advice on the policy level and act as Chief of Staff to the civilian director, who was responsible direct to Baker Street.

To a regular soldier trained to foresee the hazards of military operations and to cope with them by the use of clearly defined machinery proven in war, SOE was a peculiar organisation. Its executives were drawn from many sources, politicians, business men, bankers, financiers, academics, secret service operators, etc. Most of them were intelligent and dedicated amateurs. There were compensations: they were supported by a group of charming and talented young ladies. One of these was Lutie Sweet-Escott. Before I joined Dick Keenlyside's 'nest', she had accepted me into her female 'chummery'; Lutie, quite a veteran of SOE, had left Belgrade and Athens in a hurry after burning the legation's archives, and some months later was to face the same task in Cairo when Rommel attacked.

In a letter home at that time I wrote: 'I am surrounded by mountebanks: the place is a madhouse, but there are no dull moments.' After the war I found confirmation in Bickham Sweet-Escott's comment: 'Nobody who did not experience it can possibly imagine the atmosphere of jealousy, suspicion and intrigue which embittered the relations between the various secret and semi-secret departments in Cairo during that summer of 1941, or for that matter for the next two years.'*

It would be a mistake to attribute this abrasive situation solely to clashes of personality. There was an underlying and fundamental difficulty: those authorities such as MI6 which were engaged on intelligence gathering needed to conduct their business quietly with the minimum of aggression, while those such as SOE, engaged in sabotage, must

---

* *Baker Street Irregular* by Bickham Sweet-Escott. Methuen & Co. Ltd.

invariably attract attention, and indeed needed publicity after the act
to encourage their supporters.

Our parish was the Balkans, occupied by the enemy, together with
'the Middle East' extending eastwards to Syria and Iran, and westward
to Libya. Turkey, though cleverly sitting on the fence, was also in our
orbit. Our directive, I assumed, was to support by resistance activities,
sabotage and black propaganda, etc., any groups in those countries
which were prepared to oppose Germany.

Although by this time SOE had made contacts in many of the Balkan
countries, little of any strategic significance had been achieved. Its
mission in Romania had come out in February 1941, and touch had
been kept by a wireless set left behind with a sympathiser. An SOE agent,
De Chastelain, a business man in Romania before the war, whom later
I was to meet in Istanbul, had parachuted in to assess the possibilities
of subversive action and had been taken prisoner. He emerged safely
when Romania surrendered.

In Yugoslavia, SOE had had several emissaries including Julian
Amery and D. T. Hudson, and there was great optimism in Cairo that
the contact with Mihailovic would bear fruit. Soon I was to watch bags
of gleaming sovereigns being packed into parachute containers which,
not infrequently, landed unexpectedly at some mountain shepherd's
door! The successful operations in support of Tito were still to come.

The story in Albania was much the same. The groundwork had been
laid, but the SOE mission had had to withdraw hurriedly when the
Belgrade legation, which controlled SOE in Albania, had had to be
evacuated.

In Greece, little had been done by way of preparation before
invasion took place. Thereafter, some sabotage had been successfully
achieved by Peter Fleming and N. G. L. Hammond, and contacts
maintained with Colonel Bakirzis and a naval officer Koutsoyian-
nopoulos; they were known as Prometheus I and II. It was after I left
SOE, that the first and only SOE success to have strategic significance
at that time was achieved by Colonel Eddie Myers, RE. In the autumn
of 1942, SOE was asked by the C-in-C Middle East to block the railway
line which ran through central Greece towards the Peloponnesian ports,
and Eddie was hurriedly recruited for the task. With C. M. Woodhouse
and others he succesfully demolished the Gorgopotamos viaduct on
the night of 25th November 1942. This was a month later than had

been hoped, and did not affect Rommel's supplies at Alamein, but was certainly effective in succeeding months.

Eddie had not only achieved a remarkable military feat; he had also united a miscellaneous collection of Greek Resistance groups under his personal direction. Unfortunately many of them, as in Yugoslavia, were communists, the unification was only temporary, and complications were to ensue.

From the airfield in the Greek mountains which they had built under his direction he brought a representative group to Cairo where the King of the Hellenes, still supported by Britain, resided. The Foreign Office representative in Cairo was far from enthusiastic at his arrival; but Eddie was sent to London to report to Churchill and was received in audience by King George VI. On returning to Cairo, to his amazement he was ordered never to return to his followers in Greece.

Thus ended a great act of valour, sustained for over a year; Eddie received the DSO, but no public acknowledgement until years later. His operations had caused a political 'entanglement', embarrassing to the Government.

Although on joining SOE I lacked experience in secret service work, and indeed in operational intelligence, it soon seemed to me that the introduction of a co-ordinated control of operations and of communications was long overdue. One of the first anomalies that caught the military eye was the system by which SOE activities in any particular country, e.g. enemy-occupied Yugoslavia, were personally and exclusively controlled (if that is the right word) by the man in charge of the Yugoslav 'desk'. This system, derived perhaps from Foreign Office procedures, and suitable maybe for the passive collection of intelligence, in the case of SOE operations placed the agent's activity exclusively in the hands of one controller, who often opposed disclosure to those other parts of the organisation capable of rendering support in an emergency. I gathered that it was not unusual for such a controller, squirrel-like, to cache his juiciest nuts, lest others might find them and claim the credit!

The system was doubtless intended to minimise security risks, but the operational hazards inherent in it were brought home to me soon after I arrived. We had infiltrated into Yugoslavia by submarine an agent who was charged with making contact with the Resistance groups under the leadership of General Mihailovic. Despite the comprehensive training provided for this agent, covering the use of personal weapons, secret radio, codes, survival procedures, and a political briefing, nothing was heard from him as week after week went by. Then, one morning I heard with relief that contact had been made, and a message had been received. Later, I discovered that this message had reached us only because the controller of the desk had remembered at 3 a.m. to string an aerial between the poles of the clothes line on the roof of his Cairo flat! It did not seem profitable to enquire whether this process had been faithfully carried out at all the other times laid down in the agent's radio schedule. What happened when the controller was indisposed, or absent on other duty, or even forgetful? Would the unfortunate agent, desperately tapping out his morse at the top of a snow-clad mountain, receive no acknowledgement?

I disclosed this extraordinary state of affairs to Terence Airey, and he agreed that we must immediately organise a proper signals reception and transmission unit with a twenty-four-hour service and emergency back-up.

At that moment there arrived a war-time Major of Royal Signals flown out from England to join SOE. He had a wide technical background from his civilian career, and combined great determination with tact. As a result of his forceful but diplomatic handling of Egyptian officials, a suitable site on the outskirts of Cairo was soon selected and, several months later, a massive station for receiving and transmitting wireless traffic was erected. Clothes lines, as a military adjunct, were discarded!

I found some of the senior civilians in our organisation difficult to admire. They seemed to be resting their reputations solely on the volume of political intelligence which they had previously acquired in some other walk of life. Thus they would pontificate at length on the secret peccadilloes and the vivid private lives of the particular Balkan 'Quisling' who figured at that moment on their 'desk'; such information, though useful perhaps at times, did not contribute directly to the safe instalment of a SOE agent and to the provision of the effective support needed to achieve the military objective.

I was personally very well served by my small military staff. There were three majors: one a regular, John Commings, and two war-time officers, one of who was my old friend from Dunkirk days, John Stevens, and the other Kenneth Greenlees, who after the war became senior partner of stockbrokers Laing & Cruickshank. Later they both carried out hazardous and successful clandestine operations. John went twice to Greece and twice to Italy and France, winning a DSO and OBE. Kenneth joined Mihailovic in Yugoslavia and received an OBE, followed post-war by lukewarm recognition for operating with 'the wrong man'!

As to our agents, their dedication, courage and self-sacrifice were unsurpassed. In the main, they seemed to be quiet modest men, often with some special qualification of language or experience. When briefing them in anticipation of a submarine journey followed by a lonely passage to a hostile shore by folboat,* or sometimes a parachute descent into wild and rugged country hopefully to meet a friendly 'reception committee' with whom radio communication had been established, I was amazed and humbled by their quiet courage and calm devotion to their chosen near-suicidal role. I remember well a young captain, wearing the badge of the Royal Army Service Corps, who spoke modern Greek with fluency. He had volunteered to join 'our man in Athens', and take with him the equipment needed by a Greek resistance leader to liquidate a traitor who held high political office. He was warned of the hazards in landing from a submarine on the Greek islands, occupied intermittently by the Germans, but nothing deterred him. Many months later, we heard that he ran into a German post immediately after landing and was killed, we hoped instantly.

John Haselden was another man of superb courage. He was a cotton-broker in Alexandria, not in his first youth, but remarkably fit. He had bright blue eyes and aquiline features and spoke Arabic fluently. On very many occasions he was infiltrated in Arab clothes behind Rommel's Afrika Korps, which at that time was posing an increasing threat to the Delta. Although he was received by the Senussi, and invariably acquired useful intelligence, he was never able to galvanise them into direct sabotage action, for which there was ample opportunity in the lightly guarded airstrips and vehicle parks of the Afrika Korps.

SOE's inheritance from the old G(R) organisation was valuable and highly effective. First there was the Long Range Desert Group, the LRDG. They were a small band of selected officers and men who perfected the techniques of living, navigating and moving in the inner desert, which extended for nearly a thousand miles south of Libya and

* A small collapsible canoe which could be carried in a submarine.

Tripolitania. They had evolved from a peace-time band of enthusiasts in Egypt, under Brigadier Bagnold of the Royal Engineers, who had organised expeditions to distant oases, making a scientific study of sand formations and methods of crossing them. Lieutenant-Colonel Guy Prendergast, a New Zealander, took over from Brigadier Bagnold and led them with great distinction.

The unit, although under the control of GHQ, was available to assist our operations; they were masters of the desert, and using astral navigation they could be relied upon to make a rendezvous specified in precise terms hundreds of miles from Cairo within an error of a minute or two. Repeatedly they inserted John Haselden, or collected him for his return journey. They played a vital part in the abortive raid on Rommel's headquarters, in which Lieutenant-Colonel Keyes was killed* and assisted Lt-Colonel David Stirling in his initial SAS operations, particularly the spectacularly successful raid on Benghazi aerodrome. David Stirling, who came to see me before this raid, impressed me greatly. As a young man he had been a keen mountain climber and at the outbreak of war, had joined the Scots Guards and then one of the first Commando units. He had come to the Middle East with Robert Laycock's 'Layforce' which later, with no operational role in sight, was threatened with disbandment. Stirling, however, decided to experiment with parachuting; he had a bad crash and ended up in hospital with paralysis.

From there, he put forward proposals for parachute attacks on enemy airfields and was encouraged by General Neil Ritchie, DCGS, at GHQ. Becoming aware of the operational potential of the Long Range Desert Group, he then decided to move with them by land to Benghazi Airport, using his special jeeps which he had liberally armed with Browning machine guns. These he showed to me with pride. I was greatly struck by his offensive spirit at a time when Rommel's influence was beginning to create in some quarters a cautious defensive mentality, and by the sober confidence with which he assured me that the operation was practicable.

The raid was a great success, and others followed; within a few weeks, twenty men of his Special Air Service 'Brigade' – the word 'brigade' being, he said, for purposes of deception – had destroyed over a hundred German aircraft. From this initiative the SAS was successfully

---

* Lieutenant-Colonel Keyes was awarded a posthumous VC.

developed. They achieved many triumphs in all the subsequent theatres of operations.

In 1962 after attending a combined exercise with the United States Special Forces in South Carolina, I was able, as Director General of Military Training, to contribute to their further evolution in their counter-insurgency role in peacetime.

A new military asset which unexpectedly appeared at this time was a band of about twelve young 'kamikaze' Jews. Their origin was never revealed to me, but I was much impressed by their vigour and ruthless determination. I was involved with their training in sabotage and demolition skills and the use of weapons and radio. They were all 'mad' keen to have a go at the Germans, in revenge for the sufferings inflicted on their families; they all spoke German fluently.

Long after I had left SOE, a plan was evolved for them : dressed in enemy uniform, they would drive into Tobruk, held by the Germans since June 1942 and destroy the coast defences and other targets. The Jewish band and John Haselden were to be conducted through the Desert by the Long Range Desert Group; Haselden, dressed as an Arab, would take up a position overlooking Tobruk, observe the procedures of the German garrison and advise the Jews by radio on the method of attack. SOE would provide the lorries with appropriate unit signs and give them intelligence of passwords, etc.

Unfortunately this hazardous but simple SOE plan started to attract enthusiastic support in GHQ. A Royal Marine Commando was allocated followed by a cruiser and some destroyers and light bombers. The operation code-named Tulip was then taken over from SOE. Haselden and the Jews passed under the control of the Commanders-in-Chief Middle East. Thus was evolved the disastrous Raid on Tobruk in September 1942. Later I heard that Haselden and the Jews had achieved their particular objectives, but at a very high cost in lives. Haselden was killed.

After I had joined General Montgomery, he used to cite this to us as a classic case of how not to conduct a military operation. 'An operation commanded by a committee,' said he. 'Useless, quite useless!'

For operations by sea to Greece and Yugoslavia, to Derna for the Rommel raid and to Crete after the island fell to the Germans in May 1941, we depended on the submarines of the Royal Navy. For such missions I used to visit, cap in hand, the venerable Sammy Raw, Captain

(S) in the Submarine HQ ship, HMS *Medway*, in Alexandria. The captain who later became a vice-admiral, treated me, a bumped-up lieutenant-colonel of thirty-three, with quiet courtesy, never sought to magnify difficulties despite the manifest hazards to his submarines involved in our missions, and met my requests with immediate and helpful decisions. Our principal supporter was Lieutenant-Commander Tony Miers with his submarine *Torbay*, in which he performed prodigious feats, while putting our agents and weapons into Crete and bringing back as many as a hundred passengers gathered up from soldiers not yet rounded up by the Germans, patiently waiting for a submarine to be beached to rescue them. In subsequent exploits in *Torbay* Tony Miers was to be awarded two DSO's and a VC.

Despite this magnificent support from the Navy, we decided that SOE required its own 'fleet' for clandestine operations nearer to base. An old sea-dog, 'Skipper Poole', with First War medals and the stripes of a Captain RNR joined us, and was directed to acquire suitable craft in Alexandria. He also started to recruit skippers for the caiques he was buying from the Egyptians. Soon a very dashing young yachtsman, who had been crewing yachts for American millionaires in Florida, arrived in Grey Pillars with a handsome sunburnt face and a large gold earring in one ear. His name was Cumberlege and I understood he was related to my friend Coco, to whom I had said goodbye in Chitral three years before.

The 'pretty playboy' appearance of 'Sailor' Cumberlege was misleading; it concealed a courageous, skilled and determined seaman who successfully carried out numerous trips to Crete in his SOE caique. He planned his trips to ensure that he was well to the southward of Crete by first light when the Messerschmitts started to investigate; if he was well clear of the island there was little to distinguish him from other similar Egyptian craft which were not worth attacking. On the last trip scheduled for Crete, by which time several hundred British and Commonwealth soldiers had been rescued by various agencies, he found his cousin Coco who had served there with an Indian division, awaiting transport on the beach. But on this trip Skipper Cumberlege's luck failed. When dawn came, a Messerschmitt flew over and directed a burst of machine-gun fire at the caique. Skipper and crew survived, but my friend Coco was killed.

In contrast to our relations with the Royal Navy, our RAF support

presented problems. Certainly they were hard-pressed and heavily
involved in bombing Rommel's communications and his ports in Libya,
while the British Army continued its ineffective operations. In the early
days of SOE operations, the aircraft provided were always short of
range, and this severely inhibited our missions. Then our prospects
suddenly improved : three Liberator bombers with a range greatly
exceeding anything we had known before, were sent from England for
the specific purpose of supporting SOE operations. To us this seemed
to be a vast improvement. Inevitably and properly the aircraft were
placed under the command of C-in-C Middle East Air Force. We
started to form a close working relationship with the Liberator crews,
studied their particular requirements as transporters of our secret agents
and stores, and began planning a series of operations into the future. Full
of confidence we started a more ambitious programme of training agents
for their anticipated missions. A few days before one such mission was
due to depart, I learnt by telephone from RAF headquarters that 'our'
Liberators, as we certainly deemed them to be, had been lost in a
bombing raid on Benghazi.

In the angry heat of youth I went immediately to see Air Vice-
Marshal Wigglesworth, the dour Senior Air Staff Officer to Air Marshal
Tedder the Commander-in-Chief RAF. We had never met before, and
he was not accustomed to receiving young unknown lieutenant-colonels
in his office ; however, white-faced and boiling with rage I was admitted.
The conversation as I recall after forty-four years went as follows :

AVM :   Sit down, why have you come to see me ?

Lt-Col R : I want to know why you sent our SOE Liberators on a
            bombing raid, with the result that they have all been lost.

AVM :   What do you mean 'our' Liberators ?

Lt-Col R : Were they not sent out from the UK specifically for SOE
            operations ?

AVM :   That was one of their tasks, but they were under command
            of the C-in-C who can use them as he wishes.

Lt-Col R : Don't you realise that this has set back our secret opera-
            tions for months ?

AVM :   That may be, but I am not going to sit here listening to
            your complaints. You'd better go.

I went : but the next day Terence Airey, whom I had not been able to consult, told me the sequel. The AVM rang him, and the following dialogue took place. The printed page cannot do justice to the virulence of the AVM's protest :

AVM :   'Is that Colonel Airey ?'
Terence : 'Yes, Sir.'
AVM :   'Have you got a chap called Richardson ?'
Terence : (doubtless frothing at the mouth) 'Yes.'
AVM :   'You must sack him : he's truculent.'

Terence's response is not recorded, but I wasn't sacked and I heard no more. He had backed me up, not for the first time ! My reputation for truculence seemed to be growing : to be truculent to an air vice-marshal in 1941 was better than to a lieutenant-colonel in 1934 !

From this incident it could be deduced that I was pledged heart and soul to the success of SOE's business. Nevertheless I could never visualise myself in some desperate cloak-and-dagger operation 'selling my life dearly'. I did however carry out one secret mission, in which Turkish bedbugs proved to be my most dangerous enemies !

The government of Turkey – the 'Land of Delight' as I cryptically wrote to my mother – was engaged in a clever game of playing off the Allies against the Germans, thus maintaining her neutrality, and enjoying the material advantages of being courted by both sides. They had agreed to allow a British contractor to build airfields so that RAF squadrons could be flown in at short notice for defence against a possible German attack. Similar activities by the Germans were also taking place. Amongst the labour force of the British contractor there were many sappers in civilian clothes.

There came a time when the British Government became highly apprehensive that the Turks would succumb to German pressure, and would declare war on the Allies. This would enable a combined Turkish and German force to advance through the Taurus mountains into Northern Syria ; thence through Palestine to Cairo and the Egyptian Delta, from which came the heart blood of the British Army facing Rommel.

SOE was requested to report what covert steps we could take in anticipation of such a disaster. Rail and road communications between

Turkey and Syria went through the Taurus mountains, much of the routes through tunnels. If these could be blown up instantly when the Turks succumbed, the southward advance could be significantly delayed. This proposition did not seem impossible, since we had the Sappers, thinly disguised already in Turkey, though some distance from the Taurus area; and explosives were being sent in overtly for rock blasting. A secret plan was drawn up by the Military Attaché in Ankara, and likely Anglophile Turks were discreetly recruited. However one vital adjunct was missing: radio communications to alert our supporters and set the plan rapidly in motion. For this purpose I was ordered to take three 'suitcase' radio sets to Turkey and distribute them to Turkish agents in different provincial towns.

Urgency was the order of the day, and the SOE 'Despatch Department' which I could scarcely forget had sent some of my friends to instant death, took charge of me.

'You need a civilian suit,' they said.

'Correct,' I replied, 'but where do I get one?'

'Ibrahim Mohammed in Rue Tewfik (or some such name). He is the best tailor in Cairo.'

I had visions of acquiring a perfectly tailored lounge suit, and all for free on His Majesty's Service, and I rushed thither in a taxi. The outcome was disappointing. Ibrahim had one roll of suiting left, a somewhat woolly Lovat green. At a range of a hundred yards it shouted 'Spy'. Moreover Ibrahim, in the hurly-burly of the Cairene 'War', fought over cups of coffee at Groppi's the pastry-cook, had lost his head cutter. The result, when I put it on was appalling. I appeared dressed for a minor part in some third-rate amateur theatricals! A brown trilby hat completed the illusion. 'Despatch' then rushed me to a photographer, and instantly from the British Embassy appeared my passport: 'Mr Charles Richardson, Civil Servant'. Next I was briefed by the Head of the Turkey 'desk' and given the names and locations of the Turkish sympathisers to whom I was to hand my 'precious burdens'. I found it difficult to keep a straight face when instructed on the recognition codes. A folded *Times* newspaper in the Alec Guinness manner was ruled out, as my contacts were in the category of 'jungle wallahs'; nor was a crimson carnation appropriate as Turkey was in the depths of winter:

'You will say to him,' said the Head Despatcher: ' "Has your uncle

Achmet recovered from his fall?" and he will reply: "Thanks to the doctor's skill, he is much better." You will then hand over the set and the schedule and wavelengths, and show him how to erect his aerial and work the set.'

'I assume he will speak English?' I enquired.

'Yes, but not very well,' was the ominous reply.

Thus prepared, I took delivery of three identical brand new suitcases, each weighing forty pounds and flew to Ankara where I was met by the Military Attaché. He welcomed me warmly, introduced me to the Ambassador, Sir Hughe Knatchbull-Hugessen who, according to some, was unwittingly harbouring Cicero the German spy as his valet. The Attaché then took me for dinner to the best restaurant in Ankara. On the far side of the room I noticed a group of close-cropped aggressive young men. 'Do you see that lot over there?' said my host. 'They are Germans, and doing exactly the same as you.' I could not make up my mind whether this was a good or a bad portent.

Next morning I left by rail for Afyonkarahissar. Sitting in my railway carriage in Lovat green with three identical suitcases on the luggage rack, each admittedly locked with an individual key in my trouser pocket, I pondered how I should react if some aggressive official were to ask me to open them. However the tedious journey continued undisturbed, and I reached my destination in the late afternoon. Snow was thick on the ground when I arrived.

The town was important to our Taurus plan as it was a communication centre on the route to the tunnels. Recognition with our agent was duly effected, and I was relieved that my 'precious burden' was now reduced to two cases. The hotel in which I had to spend the night was appalling: the sanitary arrangements were indescribable, and all night in a cold damp bed I fought a losing battle against the bedbugs, who seemed to be rejoicing at the arrival of a hot-blooded young Englishman.

The destinations of the remaining two sets were in more civilised areas. When they had been delivered, the Military Attaché said that I must not leave Turkey without visiting Istanbul. There I was shown the Embassy's impressive store of weapons and explosives; it was explained to me that Istanbul contained at least four secret British organisations, and not one of the four would tell the others what it was really up to! We had a very jolly twenty-four hours and an excellent fish dinner.

On my return to Cairo, the bizarre aspect of the venture was once again underlined: my green 'spy suit', which I had hoped to preserve at least as a memento of the trip, was called in by the authorities. SOE, though secret, was a Government Department, ever vigilant in the tax-payers' interest! So the suit was returned to store in case someone else could use it. The brown trilby hat, however, I was permitted to retain.

A hat of a different sort figured in the last SOE 'operation' to be recorded here. The German Army was not only building up a powerful threat in Libya; other forces on the Russian Front were penetrating rapidly towards the Caucasus oilfields. What could SOE do to stop them?

We had no agents in the countries adjacent to the USSR but we did have experts in oilfield demolition. Some of these had attempted without success to impede the flow of Rumanian oil to Germany by blocking the Iron Gates on the Danube. After interminable argument and negotia-tion, the Soviet Government agreed to receive a British mission, which eventually was whittled down to one officer to advise them on demolition. This robust SOE officer was kitted out as a lieutenant-colonel and we accompanied him to Cairo Airport for his departure to the USSR. As this was an overt operation, a representative also arrived from the British Embassy to say farewell. Immediately he expressed dismay at the unimpressive appearance of the lieutenant-colonel, large though the officer was.

'He must have a red hat,' said the Embassy official, 'otherwise the Russians won't talk to him.'

'But he's not a full colonel,' said Terence Airey.

'Can't help that,' said the official. 'He will be useless without a red hat.'

With only fifteen minutes to spare, an emissary was sent hotfoot to the 'officers' shop' in Cairo, and in the nick of time arrived on the tarmac with a screech of brakes and a red hat.

Despite the red hat, our SOE officer could achieve little with the Russians. He arrived just in time to see train-load after train-load of refinery equipment moving eastwards by rail, with every part carefully marked with white paint, ready for re-assembly in the heart of Russia. Advice clearly was not required; and, after a glass or two of vodka, 'our man in the Caucasus' despondently returned to Cairo. It was not the first or the last time that the British Government had under-estimated the Russians.

By June 1942 I had spent nine months at the centre of SOE's bizarre activities; little of strategic value had been achieved despite the sacrifice of many valiant men. Nor had the ebb and flow in the Western Desert ended to our advantage. General Wavell's offensive in June 1941 had foundered, resulting in his replacement.

General Auchinleck's offensive in November 1941 after long and bitter fighting achieved success, and British forces advanced through Benghazi to face Rommel, established in a firm position at Agheila. To the jocular military punters in Cairo this was the second 'Benghazi handicap'! But the capability of the Afrika Korps had not been irreparably damaged and, owing to British losses in the Mediterranean, substantial reinforcements and supplies soon reached them.

The phase of exhaustion on both sides did not last long, and soon it became clear that Churchill's expectation of a further advance to Tripoli was impossibly optimistic. On 21st January Rommel again seized the initiative; our forces were compelled to withdraw, Benghazi and Derna were evacuated, and we then occupied a defensive position stretching from Gazala to Bir Hacheim. On 26th May Rommel attacked with the prime object of securing Tobruk. Weeks of fierce fighting ensued in which there were heavy losses on both sides but Rommel demonstrated his superior mastery of desert tactics. On 20th June the garrison of Tobruk surrendered, and 25,000 men, largely South African, were taken prisoner. Rommel's victorious advance continued, and Eighth Army seemed to be in a desperate position. All our gains in Libya and Cyrenaica were lost, together with enormous quantities of ammunition, vehicles and supplies, much of which Rommel utilised. Mussolini was making preparations for a triumphant entry into Alexandria and Cairo, and Hitler was claiming that the 'English Eighth Army has been practically destroyed'.

It was at this juncture that I was summoned to join the headquarters of Eighth Army as GSO I (Plans). By the time I had hurriedly packed my bags, Eighth Army had suffered further disasters, and my journey to join them was shortened by a hundred miles.

CHAPTER SEVEN

Alamein

It was Dunkirk all over again! In Cairo, where the population, including many of the British, expected Rommel to arrive at any moment, there was a pervasive smell of disaster in the air. The chimneys of Red and Grey Pillars were smoking merrily as top secret documents were hurriedly burnt; charred remains floated accusingly in the sultry air. Warships at Alexandria hurriedly took evasive action, and women and children including the charming girls of SOE were sent in batches to Palestine for 'safety'. I put away my smart tropical uniform, the hallmark of a 'Gaberdine swine' as the desert warriors so kindly named us, got into battledress, checked my revolver, and left for the Eighth Army on 25th June 1942, five days after the fall of Tobruk. General Auchinleck, the C-in-C Middle East, had dismissed his Eighth Army commander and taken command of the retreat himself.

Despite the cloak-and-dagger environment in which I had been immersed for nine months, I was not completely out of touch with those more conventionally employed. In 1941 I had visited the HQ of Western Desert Force to appraise them of John Haselden's and David Stirling's operations. Such enterprises, by what were known as 'the Funnies', were not always well received by those engaged in the primary battle; but to my surprise I had been greeted with great friendliness and courtesy by the Chief of Staff, General 'Sandy' Galloway. At GHQ I had from time to time met Freddie de Guingand in his capacity as a GSO I (Plans) under General Wavell then C-in-C Middle East, whom he admired but found astonishingly remote. He told me that in the corridors of GHQ, the C-in-C could frequently be seen totally ignoring a senior staff officer, of whose name, after several months, he appeared to be unaware. Together we had admired the success of General Dick O'Connor's masterly campaign, and later had shared forebodings over the diversion to Greece, with which Freddie was closely involved. On the arrival of

General Auchinleck to replace Wavell, I was not surprised to hear from Freddie that the inimitable 'Chink' had installed himself in GHQ as an extra Deputy Chief of the General Staff, and thereby appeared to have cunningly skipped an intervening rank.

The RAF flew me after dark to the main HQ of Eighth Army near Fuka. The pilot of the Lysander, a very young carefree character, took the map reference of our destination and produced a very small scale map and a stub of pencil; then with the blunt point covering an area of several square miles, said :

'So that's where you want to go.'

Sensing that he was not greatly interested in navigation, I asked anxiously, 'Can you find it, do you think ?'

'Oh, I expect so,' was the answer, and off we went.

We stooged around in pitch darkness for quite a time, and then fortunately saw below the pinpoint of a torch, and landed clumsily on rough sand. Chink was there to greet me !

'We're having a great time here, Charles,' he said. 'So glad you've come !'

His eyes glittered with amusement and a broad smile wreathed his prominent teeth. Only Chink could comment thus on a cataclysmic military disaster !

He sent me forward to General Auchinleck's temporary tactical head-quarters : a small group of caravans, cars and lorries on that coast road that we came to know so well for the next twelve months. I arrived at 2 a.m., and reported to Brigadier Jock Whiteley, the Brigadier General Staff.

Jock Whiteley was a sapper aged 45, who justifiably was a very popular figure in the Royal Engineers. He had won a Military Cross in the First World War, and later had had a distinguished career. He was lying flat out in his caravan with an exhausted look in his eyes and a very red face. This was not surprising as he had been on continuous duty in a crisis situation for several days. It may be to him that I owed my escape from SOE ; if so, I remember him with gratitude.

Unlike some of the others I encountered that night, he was coherent and, for my benefit, described the military situation : withdrawal followed by withdrawal 'in the Dunkirk manner', I thought to myself. He then ordered me to go back to a wayside railway station called Alamein, and turn south to a map reference in the Desert. There next morning I

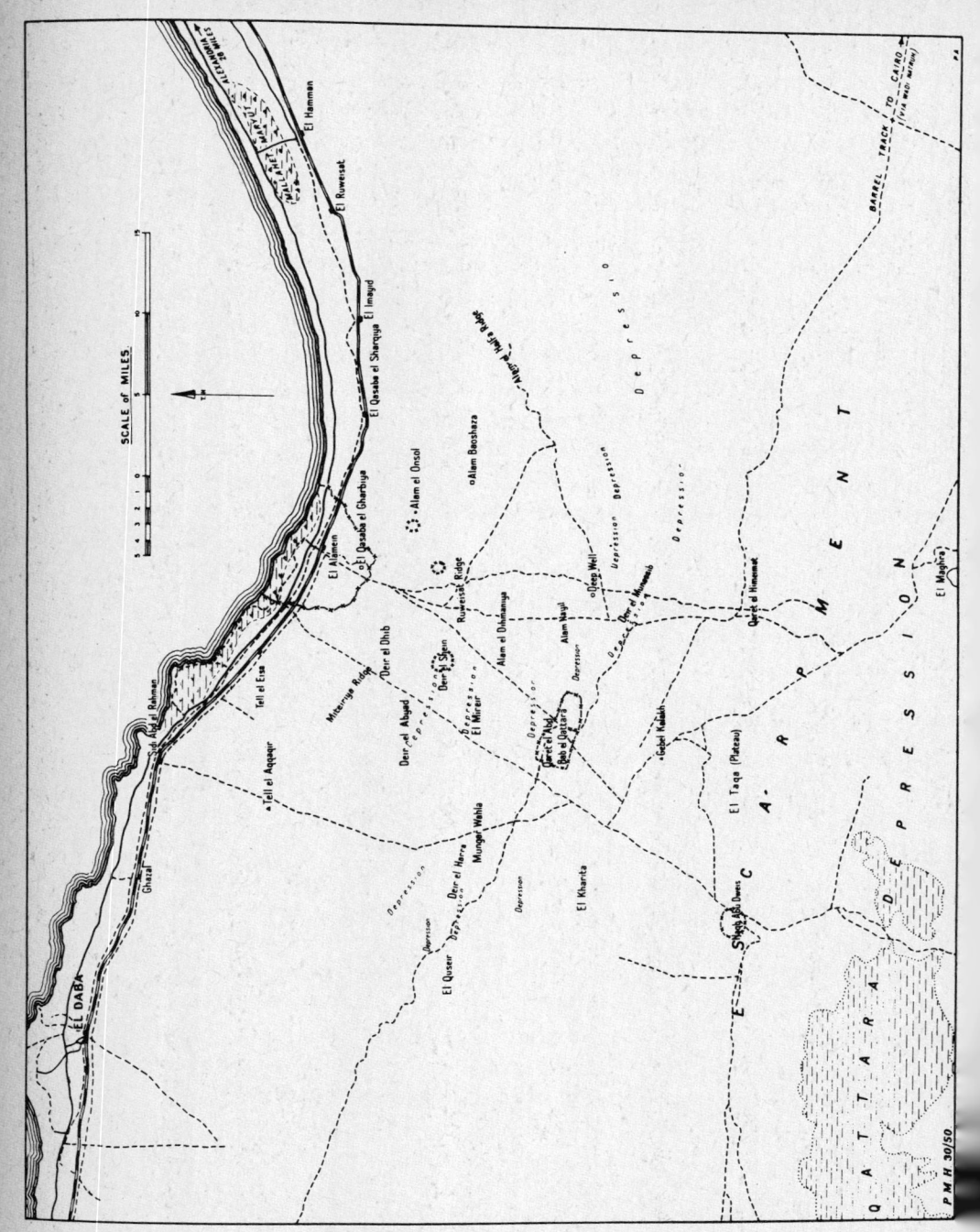

SCALE of MILES

QATTARA DEPRESSION

P M H 30/50

would meet Lieutenant-General Willoughby Norrie, Commander of 30 Corps, who had been sent back by General Auchinleck to reconnoitre 'The Alamein Position', and recommend a plan to hold it. I was aware that this was the last position capable of defending the Delta, Alexandria and Cairo, and that the Qattara depression, a vast area of salt marsh and soft sand, discouraged any outflanking movement at its southern extremity.

I was to get Norrie's plan and bring it back immediately to a junction of camel tracks near Ruweisat, which was to be Eighth Army's next Tactical Headquarters.

Dawn was breaking as I arrived at General Norrie's map reference. I had never met him before, but his Chief of Staff was a Canadian-born sapper, George Hatton, who had been a fellow instructor at Haifa. He generously offered me a hard-boiled egg and a cup of tea; but there was nothing festive in the atmosphere.

I explained my mission. 'Alamein position?' said Norrie. 'There isn't any position. We need sixteen divisions to hold this line.'

I knew we had six. Patiently I told the corps commander that I needed to take his plan, conforming to our existing order of battle, back to General Auchinleck as soon as possible. Our frugal and depressing breakfast was soon completed, and George Hatton nudged his commander to do his reconnaissance and get to work. An hour later, with the plan, I set off for the camel-track junction.

This particular spot in the sand, thanks to the comments of Churchill and Montgomery, has passed into history, and rightly so. Why General Auchinleck or Jock Whiteley chose it, and why we stayed there so long has never been explained. Certainly it was a track junction, not that that was particularly significant since one could normally drive anywhere by compass bearing. It was liberally supplied with camel dung and the attendant clouds of flies. It was unsuitably close to our forward troops; had our line given away seriously at any point, Army HQ would have had to retreat immediately. It was miles away from the headquarters of the Desert Air Force with whom we had to co-operate closely. I came to the conclusion that General Auchinleck decided not to withdraw from it, lest units should deduce that further withdrawals were 'in the air'.

We lived rough, sleeping in slit trenches with the covering of a 40 lb tent over us. Our half gallon of water per day was used for shaving, tea and washing; it was a strange sight at 5 a.m. to see miscellaneous naked figures, lance-corporals, colonels and brigadiers, standing in the sand sponging themselves all over! Our C-in-C lived rough as well; he had a caravan but slept beside it; we understood this was to share in a token fashion the discomforts of his soldiers.

I did not know him personally, but remembered him from Simla, and was aware of the great reputation he had brought from India. I tried to comprehend the ceaseless strain which he had endured through successive crises for many months. During the seven weeks I was with him, weeks of further anxiety ending in proud despondency when Churchill relieved him, his striking personality, which dominated almost without speech, his courage and his manifest integrity all impressed themselves upon me, and on many others far better able to judge.

In my own mind, I had no doubt that our situation marked a desperate crisis in the war. If we lost Egypt, the strategic implications were appalling. Was this general capable of lifting us out of dire disaster? I thought not.

My conclusion was partly influenced by Auchinleck's inability to make effective use of his staff. Unlike his successor, as yet unknown to me, he seemed to lack the art of successful delegation, nor did he seem to spend a great proportion of his time visiting his forward commanders, bending them to his will. When I observed him, day after day, sitting in the sand spending long hours staring through binoculars at the distant void horizon I asked myself:

'Has he anything left to offer?'

Looking back forty years later, I realise that I was privileged to be there in such a small select group, consisting of Hugh Mainwaring the GSO I (Operations), David Belchem (Staff Duties) and myself (Plans). Inexplicably, we had two 'Chiefs of Staff', although official recognition of the Chief of Staff system had not yet been conceded. Jock Whiteley as BGS was virtually in that position; Chink, of similar vintage, had outsmarted him in rank and, abandoning his Cairo desk, had super-imposed himself on Eighth Army headquarters in a most equivocal capacity. For us subordinate staff officers, this duplication produced chaos. The situation was a horrifying illustration of General Auchinleck's inability to select and gather round him efficient subordinates. All too often he enlisted friends from his distinguished Indian past, of which

Chink was one, and Corbett (CGS in GHQ Cairo) was another. To our cheeky group, General Corbett was known as 'Aunt Blanche'.

By this time, after observing Chink at Simla and Haifa I had formed a definite opinion of my mentor. His vigorous, restless and inventive mind was continually looking for clever, unconventional and daring solutions to the dire battlefield problems with which Rommel confronted us. Few if any of these solutions were attuned to the capabilities of Eighth Army, which had recently been disastrously defeated. Moreover, Chink was seldom content with pursuing only one solution. Ideas in plenty from the top of his head were liberally distributed, larded with Irish 'blarney', to any listeners available in our small group, more particularly, at the 'Evening Prayer' session which six of us attended every evening in General Auchinleck's caravan. The unfortunate Jock Whiteley, as the accredited subordinate of the C-in-C holding executive authority, seldom knew which particular hare of Chink's was running at the moment; and I felt sure he realised, as I did, that Chink's intellectual dominance of the Auk was such that it was not possible to arrange the removal of this dangerous supernumerary adviser.

The prayer meetings were very depressing; nothing constructive by way of seizing the initiative ever emerged. As the latest and youngest 'pseudo whizz-kid' to join the party, I was the last to be asked for my contribution, and I always felt that Chink was expecting his pupil to produce some brilliant *tour de force* out of thin air. I could offer nothing, and felt totally impotent.

From the intelligence reports which I heard, it was clear that the immediate destruction of Rommel's forces by any means, however hazardous, was essential not only to ensure the safety of the Delta and the naval base at Alexandria, but also to forestall a possible German attack into Northern Iran or through Syria to Iraq, expected in September. However, the advantages were not all on one side; Rommel's forces were in a weak condition, needing reinforcements and further supplies. His urgent pleas to Rome and Berlin for personnel and reinforcing units, and the arrival of many of them in North Africa were known to Auchinleck, though not to me, through Ultra signals. The C-in-C also knew that the Panzer Army's need for ammunition and petrol was also becoming urgent, due to heavy losses inflicted by the RAF and the Navy. By 18th July Rommel's supply situation was reported as critical. By comparison, our own logistic capability, which had been strained to the uttermost to reach Agheila, was now good and battle losses were being rapidly made up.

Much has been written since about our next period of 'stabilisation'. Certainly many small-scale attacks were mounted, often without adequate preparation, in order to convince Rommel that we were not an easy option. If one such attack was typical, they were the negation of that careful 'stage management of the battle', that was to be the hallmark of our next manager : Montgomery. A fellow instructor at Haifa, who by this time was commanding a battalion of his regiment, located far to the south of the Alamein position, received orders late one afternoon to put in an attack in the northern sector on the following night. He was given permission to reconnoitre the area, featureless as usual, but with only one other officer on the following day. This he did, while his battalion drove northward through the choking dust for many hours.

Reconnaissance by company and platoon commanders was prohibited 'to secure surprise'. At midnight the attack was launched; platoons got lost and not surprisingly the operation failed with very heavy casualties. My friend inevitably lost his command.

Certainly we remained on the Alamein position. If there was stability, it hinged on a knife edge. Perhaps the Auk at his evening prayers kept everything to himself; but to me throughout this period, there was no glimmer of light on the horizon. My depression deepened when I was ordered by Jock Whiteley to draw up a plan for the possible withdrawal of Eighth Army to Khartoum. Prepared with a school atlas bought in Alexandria, the plan looked far from convincing to me.

'Rather thin, Charles, isn't it?' said Jock. 'Lock it in your tin box, and don't talk about it to anyone.'

A barometer of our expectations was the device known as the 'water-closet', WC, short for 'worst possible case'. This was a signal that had to be sent every evening to Admiral Cunningham, C-in-C Med, giving Eighth Army's estimate in the worst possible case of the number of hours in which Rommel might reach Alexandria. The Navy, God bless them, had been much upset by the panic of 20th June. When I joined Eighth Army the 'water-closet', with which I was closely involved, was four hours. Andrew Cunningham was a fire-eater, and I sensed that General Auchinleck and Jock Whiteley were somewhat daunted by him, but after 'stabilisation', Jock took a deep breath, and said, 'Charles, let's make it 24 hours!'

Long after the war, in the historical process of allocating credit, some writers have attempted to glorify those weeks of piecemeal unco-ordinated attacks under the title 'The First Battle of Alamein'. Thus, the only Battle of Alamein that can be recognised by those of us who were there is accorded second place. I can state from my continuous presence as GSO I (Plans) throughout those weeks, that no battle entitled to the name 'First Alamein' ever took place. Unfortunately by now the phrase is firmly lodged in some of the history books.

When Freddie de Guingand appeared as our new BGS, things began to look up. In Cairo, General Auchinleck had recently promoted him to be Director of Military Intelligence Middle East and amongst the officers that he took over with the job was a Captain E. T. Williams,* who had been a troop commander in the King's Dragoon Guards, the regiment which I had visited a year before at El Agheila. 'Bill' Williams soon joined us, and thereafter was to play a most distinguished part in all our affairs.

In his book† published in 1947 Freddie described the scene on his arrival at Eighth Army:

> Late in the afternoon I arrived at Auchinleck's HQ. It was located in a rather unpleasant spot on the Ruweisat ridge. It was a sort of compromise between a Main Headquarters and a Montgomery Tactical Head-quarters. And I'm afraid, like many compromises, it was a most unsatis-factory arrangement, certainly as far as the staff were concerned. Every section or branch had to split their resources, and this spelt inefficiency, for the two echelons were many miles apart. It was also a bad piece of desert with much soft sand, and very inaccessible . . .
>
> . . . The various plans being worked out represented the state of mind of Eighth Army, or at least their High Command, at that moment. They were still looking over their shoulder. Other defensive positions far to the rear were being reconnoitred, and in some cases work was being done on them. A new site for the Headquarters had been selected on the Nile, sixty miles south of Cairo. I don't say that it is not prudent to be prepared for the worst, but on the other hand, if there is too much of this sort of thing it is most unlikely that the troops will fight their best in their existing positions . . .
>
> I very soon found I was becoming overwhelmed by having to examine a number of such plans and schemes, both defensive and offensive. There

* Sir Edgar Williams, Kt CB, CBE, DSO.
† *Operation Victory* by Major-General Sir Francis de Guingand, Wm. Collins, p. 130.

was a fundamental weakness in the staff set-up. The Commander-in-Chief had, as I have already related, taken up with him the 'D.C.G.S. in the field' ['Chink' Dorman-Smith], who acted as a sort of personal adviser to Auchinleck, but carried no responsibility in Eighth Army. His quick brain and fertile mind produced appreciations and plans at a quicker rate than anyone I have ever met; he was perhaps too clever to be wise. The usual procedure was for these papers to be marked by the C-in-C: 'B.G.S., please examine this idea'. At first I sat up all night conscientiously working on these projects, but I soon found they took up too much of my time and, I regret to say, wasted a lot of it as well. Some had merit and might have been of use when we became strong enough, but a lot were somewhat impracticable. I liked the D.C.G.S. a great deal, and he had no doubt helped to stabilise the front at Alamein, but I felt he would be better employed at his normal job in Cairo. We had a talk about it, and he agreed with me. The Commander-in-Chief allowed this move to take place when I had more or less got into the saddle, and then I found my work became a lot easier.

Our friend Freddie, a brilliant co-ordinator of staff work, accessible, diplomatic, humorous and with a remarkable intuition which he had further developed in intelligence work, soon brought a happier atmosphere and greater efficiency into our small group. 'Evening prayers' became much more business-like and slightly less depressing, but even so I was unconvinced that General Auchinleck could turn the tide, no matter what new resources might come our way.

We all expected Rommel to make one final push in the hope of reaching Cairo. Chink was still in ebullient form, and confided to me the tactical scheme which he had 'sold' to the C-in-C; his notes, in a clear round childish hand were on the back of an envelope. I can see them still! This was the theme: on warning of the attack, Eighth Army would withdraw seven miles from their present prepared positions. En route, divisions would regroup in two new 'Chinklike' varieties of battle group:

(a) Those required to man the 'Defended Observation Posts' in a static role. (These OPs were on the tops of the natural 'pimples' parallel to the coast road.)

(b) Those required to fight mobile battles against Rommel's seasoned battle groups (the recent victors of Gazala) in Chink's chosen 'killing ground', dominated by the OPs.

It would be difficult to conceive a tactical plan more unsuited to the units of the Eighth Army at that time. Depressed by defeat, dismayed by heavy casualties, and disillusioned by the collapse of all their hopes, they were in no mood to leave the comparative security of fixed positions, then marry up with units with whom they had never trained, and engage without pre-tested radio communications in mobile manoeuvres against an enemy who had proved himself master of this form of fighting.

One evening Freddie told us that Mr Churchill was visiting us next morning. I did not at first grasp its significance, but felt that the visit must at least be entertaining. Chink asked me to his tent for a drink :

'I'm for the Star Chamber tomorrow, Charles,' he said.

'What do you mean ?' I replied.

'I'm going to be sacked.'

I made a friendly reply, but in my heart thought 'thank God'.

Colonel Ian Jacob, military Assistant Secretary to the War Cabinet, who accompanied Churchill to Eighth Army, noted at that time: 'Everyone regards General Dorman-Smith as a menace of the first order, and responsible for many of the evil theories which have led to such mistakes in the handling of the Army. General Auchinleck thought Dorman-Smith had a brilliant brain, and also thought that he could keep him under control. In this he was quite mistaken.'

Chink then disappeared from our scene. Years later, I heard that he had been given command of a training brigade in Wales, which did not greatly appeal to him. The Military Secretary then tried to place him elsewhere, but with little success. So Chink retired to Ireland, changing his name to O'Gowan. In our lighter moments at Haifa, we had often asked him what he would do when the war ended, his reply was, 'I shall lead the League of Angry Men'. The identity of these men remained a mystery to us, but Chink's activities in Ireland may well have followed some such path.

After the war when I was serving in BAOR, I was asked by Sir Hartley Shawcross whether I would 'assist Mr Churchill' in a libel action brought against him by Chink. I was given to understand that Chink had taken exception to the manner in which Churchill had described his departure from Eighth Army's headquarters. By the time I reached London, the case had been settled out of court. Poor Chink ! So much talent wasted !

Churchill's visit was a remarkable tonic for us all. He arrived in his black siren suit carrying a black umbrella as a sunshade and wearing an extraordinary pith helmet. This particular type of *topi*, the Urdu word used in India, was made of a white satin-like material, not the normal khaki cotton; in India it was the distinctive mark of the Anglo-Indian railway guards : theirs were usually smudged with engine oil! A *topi* of that sort was regarded by all as highly unsuitable wear for a Sahib. How Tommy Thompson could have acquired such an inappropriate adjunct for his master has never been recorded. Nevertheless it added a finishing touch to what was, I think, an intentionally comic pastiche.

Soon after arrival, he stumped down to the crude enclosure around our mess table, which failed to exclude the flies but foiled their escape. He then surveyed the scene, and glancing at the camel dung, the flies, the slit trenches and our patent device, commented sibilantly : 'This austerity would satisfy Sir Stafford Cripps.'

Great events were of course afoot, and the Prime Minister was facing a decision which in the event changed the whole course of the war. We youngsters felt that the removal of Auchinleck was essential. The trio of Belchem, Richardson and Williams was certainly looking for a new dawn. Far more so was Freddie who, in answer to a question from General Auchinleck as to who should command Eighth Army when the C-in-C as planned should return to Cairo, had said Montgomery or Slim.

It was at this juncture that General Gott, Churchill's original choice to command Eighth Army, was killed in a plane crash. He was very popular and had a great reputation amongst the veterans of the Desert. Reflecting later on the changes brought in by General Montgomery, I became convinced that General Gott, inevitably exhausted mentally by the strain of successive defeats, would never have succeeded. Even after seven weeks, I realised we needed a fresh approach.

On 12th August 1942, the day after my 34th birthday and the day before Monty arrived, I wrote home, somewhat dejectedly :

I spent my birthday yesterday in a sandstorm recovering from Vincent's Angina, so the doctor called it – a three day sore throat to me. He gave me some captured German prontosil which was very effective. I am not very hardworked at the moment. My job is 'Plans', and I have a fairly roving commission. My boss is one of my old friends from Haifa [Freddie de Guingand]; we shared the same house when he was also teaching. I like him . . .

I have been very fortunate in this war and have fallen among very good friends. Dick Keenlyside is now teaching generals how to become good generals, and is a Lieutenant-Colonel himself!

You will have seen one of our Corps Commanders was killed a few days ago [this was Gott]. Such a charming man and very efficient too. We have had some very bad luck over our generals. I hope you will write a lot as your letters are more than ever valuable in this rather arid existence.

With the death of Gott, and on the strong recommendation of the CIGS, General Sir Alan Brooke, General Montgomery became our new Army commander. Freddie knew Monty quite well but we did not. He told us that he was due to meet him the next morning and that we were to be addressed by him in the afternoon. We asked what sort of man he was. Freddie painted a cautious picture of a commander who was sharp, very confident and very decisive. I think he felt uncertain in his own mind whether he would survive as Chief of Staff. Yet he remained in that key appointment until the end of the war, despite having been told by Monty soon after taking command that he intended to make a change.

The next day we all assembled, sitting in the sand under a blazing sun, waiting for the new commander. Freddie arrived leading a slight figure with a pale face and formal uniform, which was seldom worn in the Desert. The thought 'Doesn't look the part' flashed through my mind. Monty then started talking in that high-pitched dogmatic voice. We listened with growing amazement:

'A charter from the Prime Minister!' (holding up a piece of paper) . . .

'Hit Rommel for six out of Africa! . . .

'Here we will stand and fight; if we can't stay here alive, then let us stay here dead. . . .

'There will be no withdrawal, none whatever, none.' [I thought of my plan for Khartoum and was much relieved.]

'. . . The bad times are over. Fresh divisions from the UK are now arriving. Three to four hundred Sherman tanks are being unloaded at Suez now. . . .

'I understand there has been a great deal of belly-aching out here. By belly-aching I mean inventing poor reasons for not doing what one has been told to do. All this is to stop at once. I will tolerate no belly-aching. . . .

'This headquarters will move to a decent place where we can live in reasonable comfort . . . side by side with the headquarters of the Desert Air Force.'

The 'decent place' was Burgh el Arab by the sea. My little tent was by the beach and on many afternoons we could have a quick bathe 'in the buff', for purposes of hygiene as much as pleasure. When Churchill re-visited us after the Teheran Conference, I was privileged at dawn to watch the Prime Minister being led by the hand of the Army Com-mander for a naked dip. Monty's devoted attention to the aged Prime Minister reminded me of a nursemaid carefully leading her charge. I wrote home :

> Winston's visit was entertaining. The new regime is an improvement as far as we are concerned. The new boss is full of confidence and knows exactly what he wants . . . This was in marked contrast to the previous regime under which orders had often been regarded as a 'basis for discussion'.

At this time, Lieutenant-General Horrocks was called out from England to fill the gap in 13 Corps left by Lieutenant-General Gott. General Horrocks, like General Templer, who was to appear much later in the campaign, had been brought on by Monty; all through his career Monty had developed an eye for spotting likely 'flyers', and helping them forward. He told us :

'I've sent for Jorrocks – he's *very* good – enthusiasm, enthusiasm.'

This was emphasised as 'enthooosiasm'.

As the weeks went by, we found that this talent of Jorrocks, combined with great intelligence and remarkable flair on the battlefield, produced magnificent results all the way to Tunisia, where Monty 'lent' him to 1st Army to finish the war in Africa. Shortly after the final battle, while standing on a balcony in Bizerta, Jorrocks received what was feared to be a mortal wound from a Messerschmitt strafing the building. Later I visited him in a convent which had been converted to a US Army hospital, and I thought I would never see him again. But after several months, Monty brought him back to NW Europe. Jorrocks was not really fit, and Monty went on using him too long, as I was to discover at Nijmegen in 1944.

As GSO I (Plans) under the old Auk regime, I had been bombarded by a flood of Chink's ideas in an atmosphere of constant crisis, and found the role of planner frustrating and unrewarding. Under the new management, the first task I was given was clear and definite; to write an appreciation for Eighth Army's offensive, i.e. the battle of Alamein. This was not our *next* battle : Monty had confirmed to us that we had first to 'see off' Rommel's attack, expected in a matter of days at Alam Halfa.

The Battle of Alam Halfa extinguished for ever Rommel's hopes of a breakthrough to Alexandria and Cairo. For many weeks under the Auk, this had seemed a horrifying possibility : Alam Halfa erased that thought for all time.

But the victorious battle also had major effects on the men of the Eighth Army and on Monty's staff. Already we had been impressed with his clear thinking and his amazing confidence; but in many minds, certainly in mine, there lingered doubts : 'Is this just a technique, and will it fall apart when we face the crunch with Rommel, still the bogey-man?' As we responded vigorously to the new commands, some of us also watched and pondered.

The first aspect that struck me was the speed with which the Army Commander had made his plan, and the confidence with which he proclaimed in detail the unfolding of the future battle. I was not then on the Ultra list, so I was unaware that an appreciation by Rommel dated 15th August, decrypted at Bletchley, had reached Cairo on 17th August. Rommel, after estimating the relative strengths in artillery and tanks, and examining his critical logistic position, had concluded that he would be strong enough for a 'quick penetration of the front' at the end of August. Since the necessary regrouping of his forces for the attack must be done at the last moment a full moon was necessary: full moon would be on 26th August.

On 17th August Ultra further disclosed that, to avoid British suspicions, 'Panzer Army had prohibited reconnaissance near the Qattara depression.' Thus the strength, timing and tactics of the Panzer Army's thrust were made clear beyond all doubt. Exercises based on this certain knowledge of Rommel's battle plan were then carried out by 13 Corps under Lieutenant-General Horrocks. Monty had good reason to be confident.

The second aspect was Monty's decision to obtain 44th Division to hold the Alam Halfa ridge. He appreciated that this dominant feature, echeloned to the south twelve miles back from our forward minefields,

would have to be captured by Rommel if his initial outflanking movement was to be exploited into a deep encirclement and breakthrough.
No attempt had been made by our previous Army Commander to obtain
the resources necessary to strengthen this key feature. We understood
that 44th Division was not yet fit for battle: yet Monty by appealing
personally to General Alexander, the C-in-C Middle East, obtained it
in a matter of hours.

'Alex in Cairo,' he had said to us on arrival, 'very good, very good:
he'll give me everything I want.' He did!

The third remarkable aspect was Monty's verbal instruction for the
defence of the Alam Halfa Ridge. Infantry, tanks and guns were to be
dug in. The place was to be held as a 'fortress': were we going back to
World War I? What had happened to Chink's 'mobile battle groups'?
But we soon saw the logic of it. Lastly there was the intimate planning
with the Desert Air Force. Freddie and the SASO, Group Captain
George Beamish, thrashed this out in detail, based on 13 Corp's
requirements.

On 30th August, we waited for the onset of this critical battle so long
discussed, so long prepared and so meticulously rehearsed. That night,
Rommel's columns were reported advancing precisely as expected, and
at 2.40 a.m. the RAF's bombers, with their targets lit by parachute
flares, began their destruction. The Wing Commander (Operations) with
Hugh Mainwaring at his side in the joint Ops Room at Burgh el Arab, a
novel sight which I had not seen before, continued to exercise minute
by minute control.

The next day in my letter home, I said:

> The battle is going rather well for us at the moment, so much so that
> the Germans have had to call their advance a 'reconnaissance'; of course
> in actual fact it was a full scale attack by which they hoped to reach
> Cairo. The RAF have been bombing them day and night and this has
> been most effective. The new corps commander out here was a teacher
> at the Staff College when I was there. Lieutenant-Colonel to Lieutenant-
> General in two years, and now it looks as if he has won his first big battle,
> although it is too early for jubilation yet.

Later, I wrote: 'We really dealt with them very effectively, and they
won't be in a position to try again for some time . . .'

When on 7th September the battle was over and the victory won,

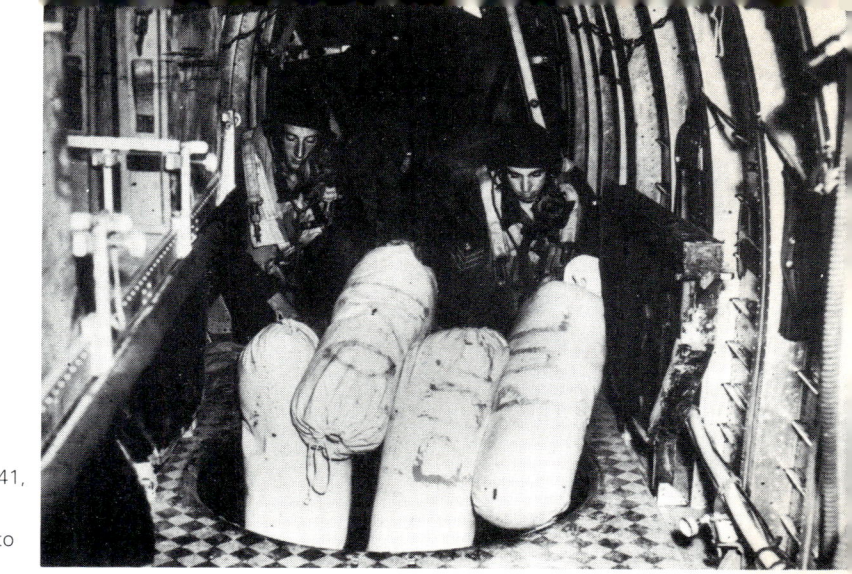

For SOE's operations in 1941, RAF bombers had barely sufficient range. RAF crew preparing to drop supplies to partisans.

Supply drop by parachute of arms, stores and sovereigns.

Partisans collecting a consignment from SOE

General E. E. Dorman-Smith, Auchinleck's duplicate chief of staff in conversation with General Sir Alan Brooke, CIGS.

Gen Auchinleck's farewell to Winston Churchill, Prime Minister, at Tactical HQ Eighth Army.

despite some disappointment that the Panzer Army had not been 'rounded up', there was great elation throughout Eighth Army.

To so many of us Monty had reiterated with that small emphatic gesture of his right hand : 'No more failures! No more failures!' Now with his 'uncanny' foresight, his clarity and poise, and his professional stage-management of the battle he had saved Egypt, and inflicted on Rommel his first defeat. We were ready for the offensive, and prepared to follow him.

Meanwhile, planning the forthcoming offensive, I was amazed to learn from Freddie that Monty already had very firm ideas where, when and how he would fight the battle; these ideas were passed on to me.

So I recognised that my appreciation, decked out, not with a school atlas as for the retreat to Khartoum, but with proper maps, and following zealously my Camberley masters of two years before, would inevitably be meretricious. It was shown to Monty who, since they were basically his own decisions, lost no time in approving them. I was off to a good start!

Not long after this I was told by Freddie to prepare a Deception Plan to complement the Army Commander's assignment. Deception planning had not been in the condensed Camberley syllabus of 1940; at Haifa because our exercises in 1940 took place so close to the 1918 scene, we had touched on Allenby's ruse by which a 'pocket book' with faked information was dropped from a saddlebag in the view of an enemy OP. In Eighth Army Freddie, together with Bill Williams armed with Ultra, had prepared an excellent spoof to mislead Rommel in his Alam Halfa attack by planting a false 'going' map of the desert. Although my SOE experience, particularly in the contacts I had made with the 'Black' propaganda branch, was not entirely irrelevant, I had never been asked to produce a concrete plan in this particular field: I was therefore much concerned that it should succeed; if it failed it would do far more damage than having no plan at all. Recognising by then the immense size of the operation, the magnitude of the preparations, and the inevitable activity of Monty's highly significant *Corps de Chasse*, the Armoured 10 Corps, all of which would be visible in part to Rommel's air reconnaissance, I was far from confident that any plan would be successful.

However, 'no bellyaching': so off I went to think. The object,

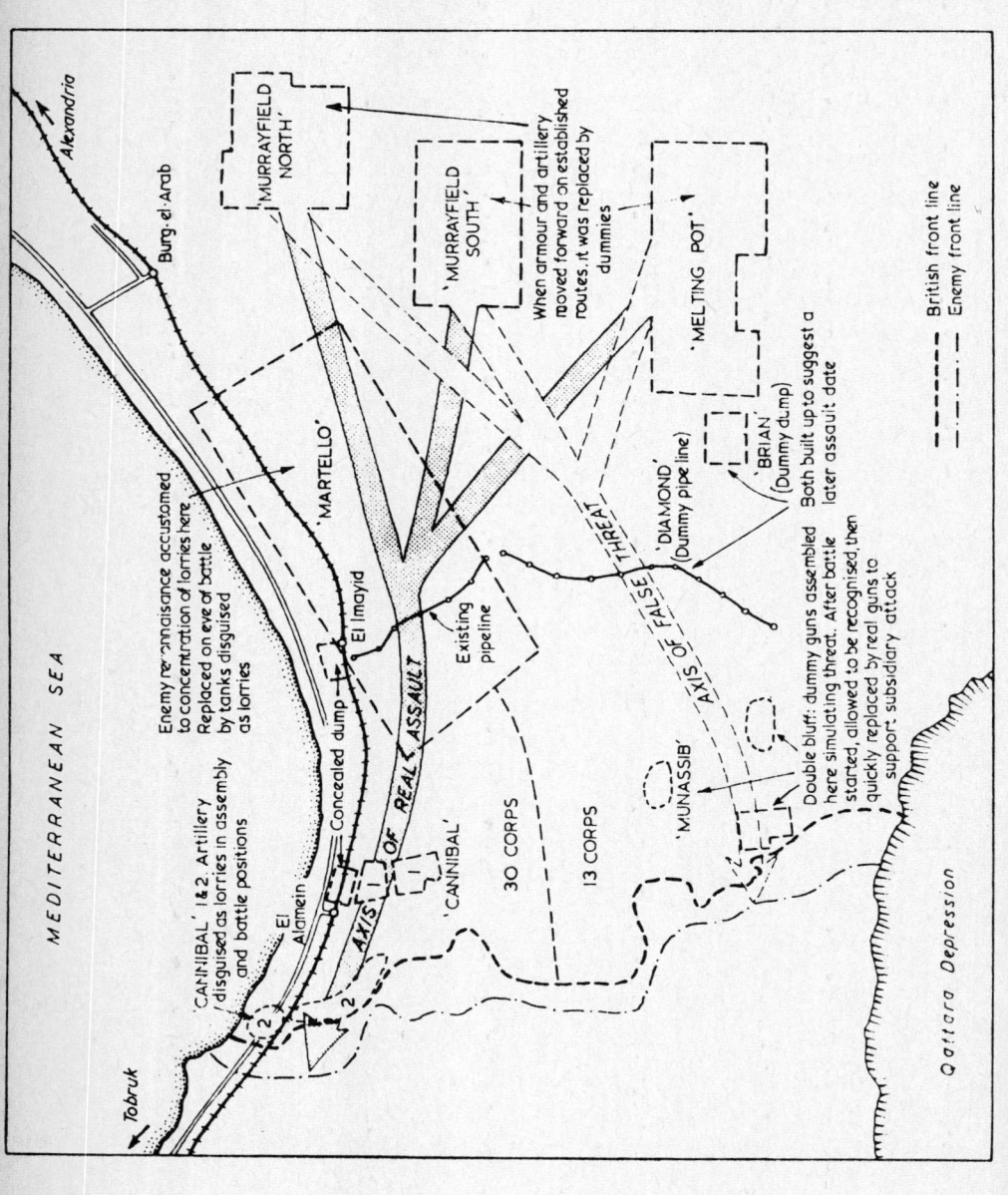

MEDITERRANEAN SEA

Tobruk

Alexandria

Burg-el-Arab

'CANNIBAL' 1 & 2 Artillery disguised as lorries in assembly and battle positions

El Alamein

'CANNIBAL'

Concealed dump

'MARTELLO'

El Imayid

Existing pipeline

Enemy reconnaisance accustomed to concentration of lorries here. Replaced on eve of battle by tanks disguised as lorries

'MURRAYFIELD NORTH'

'MURRAYFIELD SOUTH'

When armour and artillery moved forward on established routes, it was replaced by dummies

'MELTING POT'

'BRIAN' (Dummy dump)

'DIAMOND' (Dummy pipe line)

Both built up to suggest a later assault date

AXIS OF REAL ASSAULT

30 CORPS

13 CORPS

AXIS OF FALSE THREAT

'MUNASSIB'

Double bluff: dummy guns assembled here simulating threat. After battle started, allowed to be recognised, then quickly replaced by real guns to support subsidiary attack

Qattara Depression

- - - - - British front line
-·-·-·- Enemy front line

obviously, must be to deceive Rommel both as to the timing of the
offensive and the principal axis of attack, which I knew to be in the
north, close to the coast road. 'Horribly obvious,' I thought to myself.
As to timing, what interval could we sustain? Ten days at the outside,
I thought. Alamein was to be on 23rd October, that I knew. We must
persuade Rommel that it would start on 3rd November. As to the main
thrust, we must persuade him that this was to be on General Horrocks'
13 Corps front in the south. To fulfil both these requirements we needed
measures of passive concealment on a vast and comprehensive scale,
combined with some active pointers to emphasise the priority being
given to the southern front, and to indicate that the progress of our
preparations pointed to the first week of November at the earliest.

The active pointers to the south might include faked logistic activity,
dumps, etc., and a bogus water pipeline timed to reach an appropriate
terminal point by early November.* Freddie liked these broad ideas,
which were christened 'Operation Bertram', by the Army Commander.
Orders to implement them duly appeared briefly in Monty's operation
order for Alamein dated 14th September.

The techniques of camouflage and deception had been highly
developed in Middle East Command and used extensively in previous
operations with the enthusiastic approval of General Wavell and
General Auchinleck. The leader of this effort was Colonel Geoffrey
Barkas, the Director of Camouflage at GHQ. From the Camouflage
staff I was given a most devoted and effective sapper, Major Ayrton,
who became my assistant and worked miracles. The arrangements for
concealment and display were in the hands of Ayrton and Brian Cobb.

The armour of 10 Corps was to move forward to the assault by stages.
The staging areas were decided at an early date, and in the interim were
to be occupied by lorries. When the tanks came forward by night to take
their place they were to be covered with 'Sunshades' making them
appear as lorries to air reconnaissance. Simultaneously the lorries would
withdraw to rear positions.

Many other devices were to be used either to conceal or to deceive.
These included the positioning of bales of straw to resemble lorries, the
camouflage of 25-pounder guns to resemble 3-ton lorries, the stacking
of food supplies in the shape of lorries under intentionally ineffective

* See facing map.

camouflage nets; and the stacking of vast quantities of petrol tins in trenches to resemble fire positions.

As to the pipeline in the south, Major Ayrton assured me that this could easily be assembled from suitably 'doctored' 4-gallon non-returnable petrol tins which were everywhere available. A trench was to be dug normally in 5-mile lengths. At night the dummy pipes were to be moved forward to a further stretch and the trench filled in. For further verisimilitude, dummy overhead tanks, pumphouses, can-filling stations with dummy vehicles and men were to be added. As a final touch to the bogus activity in the south, a large dummy depot ostensibly for petrol and ammunition was to be created.

A few days before D-day, the armour of 10 Corps under very strict control was to move openly to the initial staging area which had been chosen to indicate a move to the south-west. The tanks were then to move further forward as planned while their previous positions were filled with over two hundred dummy vehicles and guns. The whole operation, which included similar activities in the other corps, was to be completed by 21st October.

All this seemed splendid; but I wondered whether perfect discipline during the coming weeks would be maintained throughout the Army areas; or would some stupidity ruin all our efforts? I confided my fears to Freddie. As usual he saw the point immediately and arranged that, preceded by a letter signed by General Montgomery, I would visit each corps commander personally, explain the implications of our plan to him and emphasise that detailed control of all activities would be needed if the plan was not to be rumbled by German Tac R. These interviews with the corps commanders, and with their divisional commanders to whom I was passed on, were incomparably easier than my visits to the brigade commanders in the Dunkirk operation to see how I could help them. Such was the aura of enthusiastic cooperation that Monty had already created. Throughout the many weeks of preparation we never lacked loyal, intelligent support to the plan, however frustrating and inconvenient it must have been to the units.

Meanwhile as a sapper I took a personal interest in the routes leading forward to the start lines for the attack. These routes were named by Brigadier Kisch, our remarkable Chief Engineer, Sun, Moon, Star, etc. Fred Kisch was a Jewish civil engineer who had served with distinction in the sappers in World War I. He had then supported the Zionist cause in Palestine. On the outbreak of war, he joined Western Desert Force where his effectiveness and popularity were quickly recognised. He remained as Chief Engineer Eighth Army until tragically he was killed in a minefield. His tracks were generously wide for a tank, and seemed to me to give the clearest possible indication to German Intelligence that the main attack would be in the north. I discussed the problem with him, but apart from getting the less significant work done early and delaying the most forward work of the bulldozers and scrapers until the latest possible date, there was nothing that could be done.

All was progressing well as D-day got nearer. Then one night there was an appalling dust storm; our straw 'lorries' were scattered in all directions. Ayrton worked like a black all through the night and the next day to get the 'scene' restored. German Tac R noticed nothing new. Every morning I received the intercepted Luftwaffe's report of the previous day. 'Nothing to report', was the phlegmatic message on about D-7. To my amazement this went on right up to D-day. We now know from Ultra evidence that the RAF's pre-battle offensive had so effectively established air superiority that no German aircraft succeeded in overflying Eighth Army's concentration area from 18th October up to and including 23rd October.

Various other activities by Colonel Dudley Clark's 'A' Force were also undertaken to support the plan, including wireless deception and other strategic measures under the control of GHQ Cairo.

On 17th October I wrote home :

> I have seldom been so busy. Things will be slacker for me soon. I slept extraordinarily well last night, and attribute it to the snake which my batman found in my bed this morning. It also was full of life and vigour. We have had a gale – it is still going on – and the poor creature came in for shelter.

Thanks to the unfailing support of the corps commanders, the discipline of every unit in the Army, the devoted work of Ayrton and Cobb, and of many other camouflage specialists, and the magnificent performance of the Desert Air Force's fighter pilots, the deception plan succeeded. Rommel was absent on sick leave when the battle started, and Eighth Army's Intelligence Staff informed the Army Commander that the enemy showed no sign of expecting the attack that night. This evidence came from Ultra and other sources : further confirmation came later when Ultra from the Luftwaffe disclosed that the Panzer Army had expected the main thrust to be *in the south* [my italics].*

On 23rd October as we waited for the battle which was to begin at 9.40 p.m., there was no further action we could take. Thirty-nine days of intense activity had passed since Monty had issued his plan to all his commanders and his Army staff on 14th September : to us assembled on that day the display of his technique of command, to be repeated before every future battle, had been a revelation. There had been no pomposity : indeed by contrived touches of informality he had identified himself with all those present down to the most junior. Clarity and simplicity had been the essence of the plan, backed by immense confidence derived from his own convictions and the many informal consultations he had already had with his corps commanders. At the end of this *tour de force* we had all been elated.

Many further discussions and coordinating conferences had ensued, when modifications were made. Now we, his staff, felt confident that all the loose ends had been tied up. We had read the Army Commander's 'Personal Message' :

1. When I assumed command of the Eighth Army I said that the mandate was to destroy ROMMEL and his Army, and that it would be done as soon as we were ready.

2. We are ready NOW.

   The battle which is now about to begin will be one of the decisive battles of history. It will be the turning point of the war. The eyes of the whole world will be on us, watching anxiously which way the battle will swing.

   We can give them their answer at once : 'It will swing our way.'

3. We have first-class equipment; good tanks; good anti-tank guns; plenty of artillery and plenty of ammunition; and we are backed up by the finest air striking force in the world.

   All that is necessary is that each one of us, every officer and man, should enter this battle with the determination to see it through – to fight and to kill – and finally, to win.

   If we all do this there can be only one result – together we will hit the enemy for 'six', right out of North Africa.

---

* *British Intelligence in the Second World War*, Vol II, p. 437, HMSO.

4. The sooner we win this battle, which will be the turning point of the war, the sooner we shall all get back home to our families.

5. Therefore, let every officer and man enter the battle with a stout heart, and the determination to do his duty so long as he has breath in his body.

AND LET NO MAN SURRENDER SO LONG AS HE IS UNWOUNDED
AND CAN FIGHT.

Let us pray that 'the Lord mighty in battle' will give us the victory.

This was stirring stuff, the like of which I had never read before. As this same technique was repeated before the next battle and the next, a cynic was heard to comment that God Almighty was now firmly under Montgomery's command!

Freddie then told me that for the duration of the battle he had decided to establish himself at a forward location close to Monty's Tac HQ, and he asked me to join him. My work, such as it was, was finished, so I was delighted at this move. But before going there, he said to our surprise at about 11 a.m.: 'We're doing no good here: let's go to Alexandria and have a good lunch.' This was typical of Freddie, and the reaction was instantaneous. Bill Williams, David Belchem and I bundled quickly into his car; Hugh Mainwaring, the GSO I (Ops), had to be left to mind the shop. The lunch with claret and champagne was excellent.

I wrote to my sister:

I am writing this in Alexandria where I have come for six hours relaxation as my work is finished. In a few days we shall see the results. It has all been very interesting, and I would not ask for a more congenial master than Freddie de Guingand who is the Chief of Staff. Having been 'schoolmasters' together, although he is eight years older than me, we can talk together absolutely freely and argue about plots for this and that. I am afraid I have neglected you both very much . . . but I have been working in 'predestinate grooves'* and it is difficult to think of anything else.

* There was once a man who said 'Damn'
It's borne upon me that I am
An engine that moves in predestinate grooves
I'm not even a bus, but a tram.
Maurice Hare, St John's College, Oxford, 1905

Finally I went forward at 7 p.m. to our new position, which was a superannuated Italian pill-box well forward near the Coast Road. We had a telephone to Tac HQ which was quite near, and to Main HQ still at Burgh el Arab. At 9.30 p.m. I went out to see the start of the artillery barrage, an astonishing sight. It was a clear starlit night; suddenly, all along the front there were continuous flashes, many of them behind us, and the roar of over a thousand guns, accompanied by the deeper roar of the bombers of the Desert Air Force flying overhead.

'If all this,' I thought, 'is going to the correct places [which the painstaking Intelligence work from our excellent air photos, supplemented by sound ranging and Y intercepts* should have ensured] a lot of Germans should no longer be alive.' But the battle wasn't going to be as easy as that; Monty had warned us all about the 'Dog Fight', which was to go on for several days.

By now, all the staff and the corps and divisional commanders had recognised Freddie's great qualities. His skill, reliability, tact and humour had won for him a dominant position as Monty's Chief of Staff and mouthpiece. I feel sure that Monty himself must have recognised by then how indispensable he was.

Freddie and I had adjacent bedding rolls in our pill-box, and I awoke about 2 a.m. on the second night of the battle to find he was fully dressed :

'What's going on ?' I asked.

Freddie replied guardedly, 'Things aren't so hot. I'm getting the Corps Commanders to come and see the Army Commander.'

Later, after the conclusion of that highly critical conference, which Freddie had so wisely prompted, I heard the whole story. At the conference, Monty's willpower had had to be forcefully brought to bear, otherwise we might well have lost the battle ! Freddie's intuitive decision to leave Main HQ, the normal and expected place of duty, and move forward in close proximity to the Army Commander had paid off handsomely. Monty, as usual, had retired early and was sleeping peacefully : only Freddie could have intervened.

Throughout the battle I was 'odd-job man'. Hugh Mainwaring, Bill Williams and David Belchem bore the brunt. There was little planning that could be done until the probable outcome of the battle could be

* The Y intercept service worked on enemy tactical transmissions in the battle area.

more clearly seen. Monty displayed his usual self-assurance and appeared relaxed; but as we got to know him better we realised that this was but the outward sign of a self-imposed regime, designed to ensure that the Army's morale did not deteriorate, and that he himself maintained the peace of mind necessary to manage the battle successfully.

Meanwhile the 'Dog Fight', far from proceeding according to plan, appeared to us to be running into great difficulties, and casualties in men and tanks were mounting. Before the battle I had been asked for my estimate of casualties. I had had to tell Freddie that I had no experience on which to base this. Freddie referred the question, prompted principally by the RAMC, to the Army Commander who immediately forecast with great accuracy a figure of 13,000.

We knew that Monty was watching the daily casualty reports of the 'Dog Fight' very carefully, not only because from his experiences in World War I, he deplored any futile loss of life, but also because he realised that the manpower of the United Kingdom forces was severely limited. As to the forces of Australia, New Zealand and South Africa, whose presence alongside the United Kingdom we regarded as perfectly normal, there were political as well as manpower complications that might at any time intrude. The manpower of the Indian Army was considerable, and the political factor did not, as yet, create any major repercussions.

Finally we came to operation Supercharge, which we all knew was the last remaining effort available to break the Afrika Korps. The Ultra decrypts, which Monty was receiving through Bill Williams, must have heartened them both; they knew that the enemy's already serious fuel position had not improved, his ammunition stocks had fallen to a very low level and his troop strengths had fallen still further 'on account of considerable losses'. Our own situation however looked to me far from bright: the battlefield, carefully 'stage-managed' as it had been by the Army Commander, was anything but 'tidy'.

The so-called 'Desert', far from being a vast flat area of sand did contain a few obvious tactical features such as Ruweisat Ridge, the eastern end of which I had reconnoitred when ordered in August to write my appreciation for the battle; but it also contained many minor features identifiable more by changes in the contours shown on the map than by easily recognisable landmarks. One such feature, 'Kidney

Ridge', which played a major part in the battle, was thought subsequently by some to have been a depression!

Add to this the frequent dust storms, the haze produced by the movement of tanks, the smoke of burning vehicles, the rudimentary tracks which served for roads and the general congestion of the battlefield, it was not surprising that many units were uncertain of their precise locations on the map.

The release of 10 Corps' Armour before 30 Corps had fully broken the crust of the defence, had virtually superimposed one corps on top of another, and 'real estate' was in short supply.

To help sort this out, I was delighted to be given an unusual odd job, not catalogued in normal staff procedures. General Freyberg was to be the commander of Supercharge; his GSO I, Lieutenant-Colonel Queree, and I were enrolled as a sort of 'Land Commission' to inspect the battlefield, find out which units were there, despatch to the rear those not required for Supercharge, and thus release positions for other units to come forward. We spent about a day doing this; armed with Monty's authority, we were not confronted with a single disagreement.

After Monty had given out his orders, clear and confident as usual, General Freyberg requested a postponement of the battle, and I heard to my surprise that Monty had agreed to it. The awful thought occurred to me: Were we at this crucial moment slipping back into the habits of the Auk regime, where this sort of thing had been all too common? I said nothing. I did not know, as Monty did, that Rommel with his supplies of petrol, ammunition and reinforcements further reduced by the successes of the Royal Navy and Royal Air Force in the Mediterranean, had reported on 28th October an 'extremely critical situation' and on 29th October had disclosed that his position was 'grave in the extreme', and issued an order of the day urging a 'supreme effort in a life and death struggle'.

For the final great attack, which we all recognised as crucial, Monty had regrouped. These procedures in the middle of a battle seemed to me to display the hall-mark of a masterly 'stage-manager'; they certainly demanded a high state of training from the formations concerned, and this by now they had achieved.

General Freyberg, in addition to his own division and armoured brigade, was given 8th Armoured Brigade and a brigade from each of 50 and 51 Divisions.

The attack was launched at 0100 hours on 2nd November 1942. After three days of fighting, as desperate and bloody as in the earlier phase of the break-in battle, Freyberg's improvised corps, with their commander leading as always from the front in his light tank, broke through Rommel's last position. The attack, the last shot in the locker, had 'done the trick'.

With Rommel defeated and short of supplies, with his Italian allies immobile for lack of transport, with the RAF dominating the Luftwaffe, surely the moment had arrived to round up Rommel's forces and destroy the Afrika Korps once and for all?

For some days, Freddie and I had been considering what form the pursuit might take if Rommel were to be completely defeated and had to beat a hasty retreat. Would there not be an opportunity for some daring, unconventional tactic? I was told to study this possibility and I produced a plan: Operation Grapeshot. This was to be a self-contained force under a major-general, consisting of 96 tanks and transporters (carrying also 5 tons of ammunition), two battalions of infantry, sixteen 25 pounder guns, forty-five armoured cars and three batteries of light AA guns plus the bare minimum of transport. Logistically the force was to be capable of reaching Tobruk, 360 miles away, and remaining there for seven days. I visualised them motoring fast along the coast road behind their armoured car screen, deploying their tanks and infantry into the desert to outflank Rommel's rearguards as soon as they met them, and thereafter repeating the process. We expected that Rommel would be bound for Fuka, fifty miles away.

Freddie liked my plan and obtained the Army Commander's permission to assemble the Grapeshot Force under General Charles Gairdner on 3rd November. But, little by little, troops were removed from the force for more immediate tasks until only a remnant was left. Soon it was cancelled.

For years afterwards, Freddie spoke in favour of this plan; but I wonder now whether in the stress of battle he had attempted to 'sell' it to his Commander with usual subtlety. Had he implanted a small seed of Grapeshot in the Army Commander's mind at a sufficiently early stage so that, undisturbed and unnoticed, it might grow into a Monty plan? This technique, in which Freddie excelled, was an essential feature in the handling of his master.

My concept would have required much modification, but I believe the principle of using a fresh, specially organised force was sound. The alternative adopted by Monty for the pursuit, the use primarily of General Freyberg's forces, with the addition of 4th Armoured Brigade, to by-pass Rommel's rearguard and move on Fuka, with intervening 'left hooks' by 1st and 7th Armoured Divisions did not succeed, although I and many others thought it would.

By 3rd November Rommel faced defeat. Throughout the period, Bill Williams had kept me up to date with the enemy's situation. Until the success of Supercharge was finally established, I had been far from confident that we were winning. Although aware that some high-level decrypted signals were arriving on the Ultra terminal which accompanied us, I was not on the readers' list. The decrypted signals during the night of 2/3rd November must have overjoyed Bill, Freddie and the Army Commander. Eventually, on the morning of 3rd November, Rommel's signal to Hitler, sent the previous evening, reached us :

> After ten days of extremely hard fighting against overwhelming British superiority on the ground and in the air, the strength of the Army is exhausted in spite of today's successful defence. It will therefore no longer be in a position to prevent a new attempt to break through with strong enemy armoured formations, which is expected to take place tonight or tomorrow. An orderly withdrawal of the six Italian and two German non-motorised divisions and brigades is impossible for lack of MT. A large part of these formations will probably fall into the hands of the enemy who is fully motorised. Even the mobile troops are so closely involved in the battle that only elements will be able to disengage from the enemy. ... The shortage of fuel will not allow of a withdrawal to any great distance. There is only one road available and the Army, as it passes along it, will almost certainly be attacked day and night by the enemy air force.
>
> In these circumstances we must therefore expect the gradual destruction of the Army in spite of the heroic resistance and exceptionally high morale of the troops.

As Bill gave me the gist of it, my heart missed a beat. The battle was won. I remember it still as the most dramatic moment in my life !

CHAPTER EIGHT

A Day's March Nearer Home

Euphoria was in the air. Thousands of our good men had been killed and tens of thousands of the enemy. But after all the failures of two years' fighting and the dashing of hopes after two runs of 'the Benghazi handicap', we were at last on our way to 'hit Rommel for six out of Africa'. We felt we could do it!

How had the battle been won? The men, broadly, were the same, though reinforced with new blood and given in many cases new commanders; their equipment, particularly their tanks, had been greatly improved; additional resources had been brought to bear. But above all, a new spirit had been created. Eighth Army had a new commander, confident, decisive and assured. He seemed to know his job; certainly he knew what he wanted of his staff. Moreover the fighting men, almost every one of them, had actually seen him and heard him speak.

At his headquarters, all of us had been amazed, and some even amused at his behaviour on arrival. After a very few days setting the scene for his first battle, Alam Halfa, he had resolved to see the soldiers and their officers. No pondering over a multitude of operational detail, no lengthy conferences with a coterie of advisers, just an intelligence briefing at 6 a.m. and an evening meeting with Freddie: then at 7 a.m. off would go 'the circus', as we cheekily called it: the Army Commander in an open Humber staff car, with one ADC and a supply of cigarettes and magazines.

As the pattern was repeated day after day we had asked Freddie, 'What on earth is he doing?'

'Visiting every unit, talking to officers and soldiers,' was the terse reply.

I think even Freddie thought his master might be overdoing it! But throughout the length of the sixty-mile desert front, the soldiers day by day had been assembled round his car. The message must have been the same as the one he had given to us in August; a message of

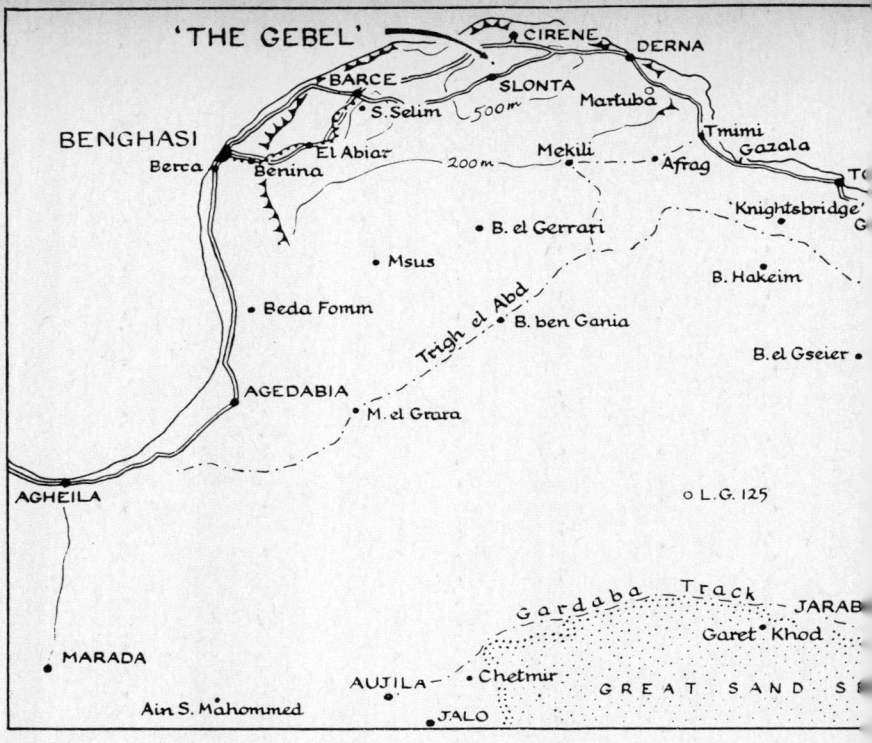

utter confidence and a clear indication of the way ahead. Then the cigarettes and magazines would have been dished out by the ADC. Through the intervening forty years I have never met anyone who, living through those days, has not admitted that he fell under the spell. To me it was an overwhelming contrast to the Auk, staring day by day at the distant blue and by night meeting with a disheartened and incoherent staff.

Some, in studying Monty's activity at that time, have sought to impute an egotistic 'cult of personality'. No; he sensed the bewilderment of the army that he had taken over, and wisely decided that to put that right was for him the highest priority.

Four talents marked him out as an exceptional leader: professionalism, self-confidence, an intuitive grasp of the psychology of leadership, and the ability to simplify the issues of battle.

His professionalism was based on twenty-five years of profound study of war, backed by tragic experiences from the First World War and the futile sacrifices of the Dunkirk operation. By 1942 he was without doubt a supreme master of the battlefield. From this professionalism and the personal successes he had gained as a divisional commander and as a

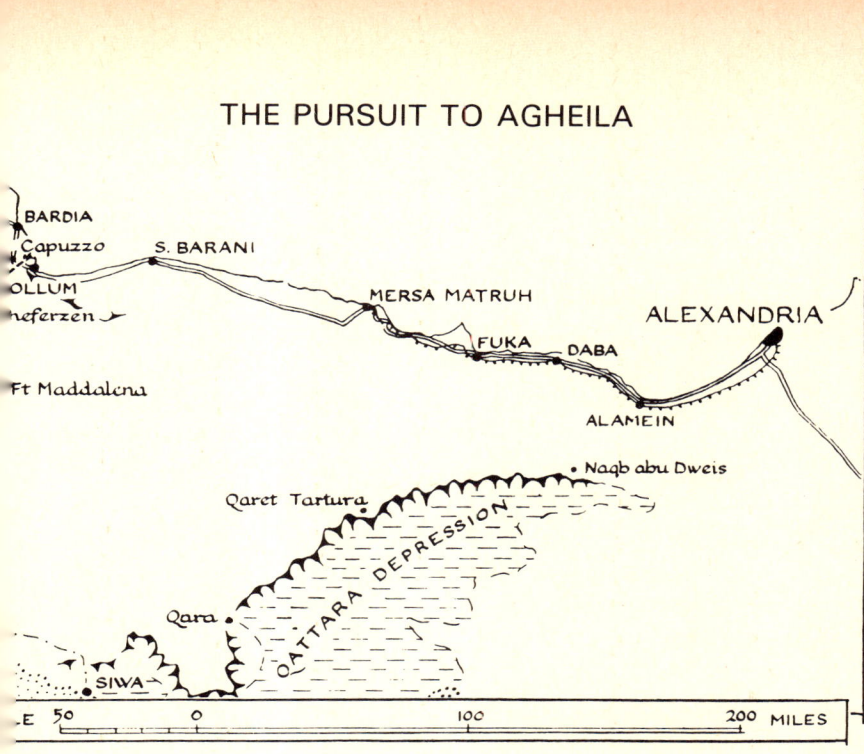

THE PURSUIT TO AGHEILA

BARDIA
Capuzzo   S. BARANI
OLLUM
heferzen

MERSA MATRUH

Ft Maddalena

FUKA   DABA

ALEXANDRIA

ALAMEIN

• Naqb abu Dweis

Qaret Tartura

QATTARA DEPRESSION

Qara

SIWA

E 50   0   100   200 MILES

trainer, he derived immense self-confidence. Though the outward manifestations of this, magnified for public consumption, were often criticised,
his confidence was genuine and profound.

Allied to this self-confidence was his innate understanding of the
psychological factors involved in the art of leadership. This extended
both to the leader and the led. The leader must at all times appear
confident of the outcome, and must so organise his staff and his personal
regime that the appalling pressures of modern battle can be mitigated
and controlled. Our leader's studied poise was not, as some thought,
evidence of relaxation, but of a highly organised system designed to
sustain his personal morale and hence that of his soldiery. As to the led,
he firmly believed that the British soldier, if clearly told by his officers
what was required and why, if launched into battle with the 'stage-
management' necessary to obviate chaos, and if inspired by the transmitted confidence of higher commanders, would never fail to face
successfully whatever sacrifice was demanded.

Lastly, his ability to simplify and to discard the inessentials was a
powerful technique both in his hands and in those of his subordinates,
who learnt it from him. War is organised chaos; any attempt to weigh

all the conflicting factors which beset a commander can only lead to mental breakdown. Monty had trained himself to discriminate and identify the critical factors, and formulate his plan on them, while delegating the remainder to a well-trained staff. Thus with an analytical mind shielded from the disruptive hazards of battle he was able to transmit his own resolution and serenity to those under his command.

Now, after Alamein, we were beginning to perceive what lay behind these manifest qualities of our new commander. From some of those who came out to join us, we heard of the profound impression he had made with his exercises when Commander of SE Army in England, and of the lead he had given in his confident pronouncements on professional doctrine.

From Freddie, who had been taught by him at the Staff College, we learnt of his record in World War I; how, after taking part as an infantryman in much of the fiercest fighting and being severely wounded, he had emerged as a temporary lieutenant-colonel with a DSO at the age of thirty-one. At Quetta he had been an outstanding exponent of battle tactics, and had put his views across with superb confidence.

We noticed that even after the initial 'circus' of August, he had continued with his custom of visiting formations in the forward area whenever possible; he seemed determined that the front-line soldier should always be assured that careful stage-management of the battle would be insisted on at every level of command; thus he would be given a fair chance of achieving the task set before him.

Freddie, after his daily discussions with the Army Commander, would often comment on Monty's ability to simplify the issues at stake; having decided the basic points of the plan of action, all else would be happily delegated to the Chief of Staff.

As to the bogeyman Rommel, the Army's attitude had completely changed. David Belchem, with whom I now worked in close cooperation, told me of General Auchinleck's extraordinary attempt to reduce the influence of Rommel by edict: the Eighth Army was ordered to avoid reference to the German commander and to desist from harping on him! This showed an amazing ignorance of the psychology of the British soldier.

Monty had no doubt that Rommel was a most able and determined commander. He had a photograph of his adversary installed in his

The Prime Minister in 'siren' suit with General Montgomery and General Sir Alan Brooke.

'Men behind Monty': Brigadier Sir Brian Robertson and Lt Col 'Bill' Williams.

Lt-Gen Horrocks enthusiastically explains a point to Monty.

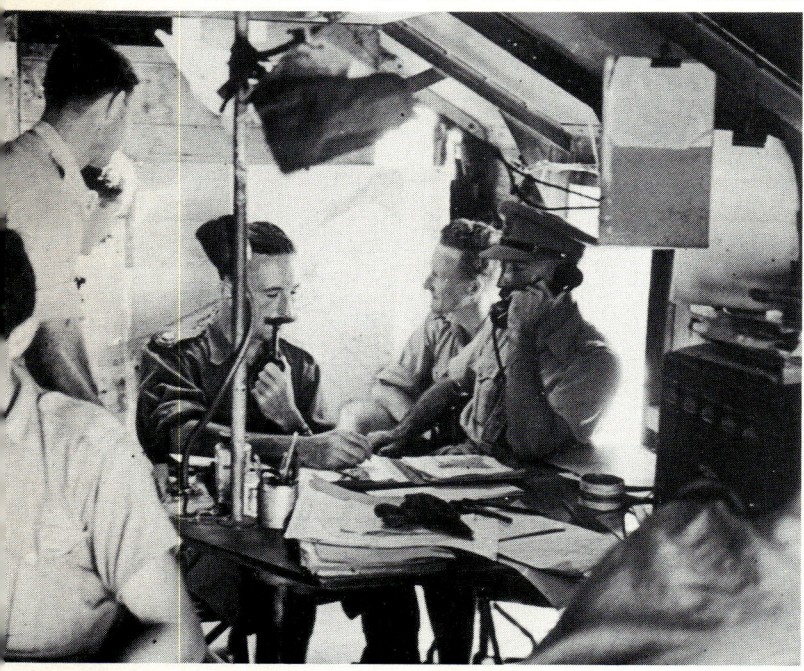

Inside the Operations Command vehicle of HQ Eighth Army: Lt Col Hugh Mainwaring, whom I was to succeed in November 1942

An artillery barrage by night feature of Monty's battles.

caravan, perhaps to emphasise that war is essentially a contest of will-power. We had no doubt after Alamein that we would 'hit him for six out of Africa', particularly now that we had heard of the Anglo-American landings in Algeria. Nevertheless Monty, though armed with Ultra information about the enemy's critical situation and Rommel's intentions, continued to treat his adversary with wary respect.

Rommel's Afrika Korps had not yet been totally destroyed, but he had certainly received what his opponent called a 'bloody nose'. Casualties of the Axis forces amounted to 39,000, and 450 tanks were left on the battlefield together with 1,000 guns and much other equipment. Rommel decided to abandon his immobile Italian allies and withdraw his German remnants at maximum speed; he would hold on to Mersa Matruh if possible for a few days and thus gain time to prepare hasty defences 270 miles away in the area of Sollum and of the nearby Halfaya defile on the Egyptian frontier.

Late on the night of 3rd November Monty had given to the commanders of New Zealand Division and 10 Corps his plan of pursuit. They were to bottle up Rommel's retreating forces between the Alamein battlefield and Fuka, about sixty miles to the west. The immobile Italians were to be rounded up in their thousands on the battlefield by 13 Corps. However the plan miscarried and Rommel's forces made good their escape.

On 6th November, we at Main Headquarters Eighth Army moved forward to Daba in anticipation of moving to the area of Mersa Matruh. Monty, in a tank of his tactical HQ, went forward to within about twenty miles of Matruh. Still filled with optimism, he thought Rommel would not stop short of the Halfaya Pass near Sollum, and was unaware of the Germans' temporary delaying position at Mersa Matruh.

At Main HQ an unconfirmed report was received that Mersa Matruh had fallen. At 0200 hours on 7th November, with Freddie's agreement, Hugh Mainwaring the GSO I (Ops) with the usual reconnaissance party consisting of Major Dick Carver, Monty's stepson, and a GSO III, went forward in two cars to site the new position of Army HQ beyond Mersa Matruh.

Freddie was held up by a torrential downpour but I was luckier, and met the Army Commander late that night. I had bad news for him: the entire recce party was missing. They had in fact been captured by a German rearguard. Monty told me immediately to take over from

Hugh, and replace Dick Carver with 'someone else'. I had feared that reporting his stepson as a casualty might result in a scene of some emotion, but on that dark rainy night my commander presented his usual demeanour of controlled professionalism. Hugh's reconnaissance party had successfully crossed one flooded wadi before running into a German rearguard. They were then hustled into a truck at pistol point, spent a night in a closely guarded trench at Rommel's HQ, then flown to Italy next morning. Hugh and Dick were to end up in the same POW Camp near Parma at the time of the Italian Armistice in 1943; their anti-fascist Commandant would let them out three hours before the Germans arrived to take the camp over. Later they succeeded in rejoining Eighth Army in Italy.

It was thus that Auchinleck's frustrated planner and the 'Alamein odd-job man' found himself at the very centre of the Army's operational activity. This was to last until the end of the campaign in Sicily in August 1943.

I shall not describe the sequence of battles in any detail; that has already been done, if not overdone. All I shall hope to do is to give some of the savour of those times which, despite the history books, we who remain look back on as days of unalloyed triumph.

How fortunate we were that our war was in the Desert. For most of the year we lived in a dry, bright sunny atmosphere with a sharp fall to near freezing at night. No ancient historic buildings, no lush landscapes attracted the eye, but the colours at dawn and dusk were ample compensation. There were virtually no refugees, nor homes to destroy nor children crying in the streets. It was a superbly sterile vacuum in which to stage military mass murder.

After the victory we had to move fast. It was essential to maintain at all times unbroken radio control with the headquarters of our two corps. Our friends in the Royal Corps of Signals were magnificent: Brigadier 'Slap' White, efficient, imperturbable and charming, and his young helper Major 'Andie' Anderson. The RAF frequently provided me with a Beechcraft aeroplane to fly forward, with a leap of a hundred miles or more, and land in a patch of desert near Major Bob Long, our genial Rhodesian Major who led our advance party. The Rhodesian Army, with insufficient white manpower, could not provide a unit but they supplied some splendid characters. Bob erred only once, near Tunis, when he positioned Army HQ only two miles behind the forward troops: at midnight when we had 'unpacked', we were ignominiously ordered five miles back by the Army Commander.

The functions of an Army headquarters are to keep track of the battle situation minute by minute, to ensure staff co-ordination of activity throughout the army area including all the support in men and material of the forward battle, to plan for future developments and lastly, but most important to co-ordinate with the RAF the minute by minute use of airpower in support of the forward units. The airpower of the Desert Air Force became at this time an overwhelming factor in our success.

Relations with the RAF had entered a new phase with Monty's arrival. 'Maori' or 'Mary' Coningham, a tall impressive New Zealander, was their C-in-C. Like many commanders he was a prima donna; but he took umbrage too easily. Co-operation in the Auchinleck days had not been close or cordial. Monty set out to change all that, and leant over backwards to generate confidence between the two Services and their chiefs. In this he was helped immensely by Freddie, who had the intellectual imagination to be able to appreciate the intricate problems of another service, and the temperament to ensure cordial co-operation.

I learnt the trade as we went along, and was greatly helped by Lieutenant-Colonel Jock McNeill, a friend of Haifa days, who had already firmly established himself as the GSO I (Air). Together we wove a dense tapestry of co-operation, which improved throughout the campaign, particularly with the arrival of Air Vice-Marshal Harry Broadhurst, first as Senior Air Staff Officer, then as Commander-in-Chief of the Desert Air Force.

Lieutenant-Colonel Bill Williams was an acute and engaging figure trusted by all. By origin a history don, and young to be exercising such immense responsibilities, he maintained his erudite humour at all times, and was sublimely competent in his intelligence role. Normally he composed the intelligence summary in the early hours of the morning, by which time all the various agencies, including Ultra, had delivered up their harvest. By the light of a pressure-lamp, a bent scholarly figure could be seen composing Rommel's daily story in the lean-to of a small truck, wrapped in a sub-fusc crochet jacket, once the property of a German general.

David Belchem, sharp as a knife, was clear, accurate and decisive in every emergency; he ran the 'Staff Duties' organisation which dealt with organisation, manpower and movements.

Every morning at seven o'clock, standing in the sand by my 'operations' vehicle, Freddie held his coordinating conference, going through
the pencilled notes of his agenda efficiently and informally. He would
call on me to describe the operational situation and on Bill Williams
for the intelligence picture. The head gunner, Brigadier Sidney Kirkman, might give us a point, likewise the Chief Engineer, Brigadier Fred
Kisch, and the other experts.

We lieutenant-colonels were young, intelligent and keen. We never
felt we were serving a hard task-master; Freddie so skilfully eliminated
much of the pressure. At our level, the way ahead was straightforward
and clear. Almost invariably we knew what was in 'Master's' mind.
I suspect that Bill Williams introduced this epithet : a cryptic hybrid,
with theistic as well as academic connotations! Seldom was any decision
changed. By this time I, a comparative newcomer to the Desert,
had acquired the technique of living – of keeping personally clean on
a minimum of water, of keeping fit and avoiding 'Desert Sores', of
moving quickly and accurately through the Desert sand and of reacting
immediately to any situation by day or night. How lucky were we to be
in such a party, as Master called it. He never needed to 'binge us up'!

Buoyed up by the Army's irresistible advance, responding gladly to
the clear direction from above, it was a time when every demand, many
of them 'beyond the call of duty' was gladly met. But there were many
moments when for an hour or two the pressure was off. Two of these
remain vividly in my memory.

We had reached Buq Buq : just a small cove in the Gulf of Sollum,
beyond Sidi Barrani. It was evening, and not a soul was there except
the small advance party of Army Headquarters. They had established
radio contact on arrival and reported all was well. We were to move
forward at 4 a.m. the next morning and already a score of soldiers,
young chestnut-coloured cannon-fodder, had raced to the glittering
white sand and plunged into the sea, which stretched in a green-blue
calm towards the sunset. We followed them. For a time the war seemed
very far away.

Many days later we arrived at the *Jebel*, the green hill-country of
Cyrenaica. After months of desert living, plagued by the fine brown
dust thrown up with every movement, it was a relief to see the scrubby
green trees on the slopes above our camp and to catch sight here and

there of patches of water. I well remembered this place with nostalgia from my journey with 'Sharks' in 1941. Now the victorious advance was going well and we with our RAF friends had settled into a happy routine which seemed to 'deliver the goods'. Every evening Jock McNeill and I met the SASO and Wing Commander (Ops), and jointly planned with them the next day's air strikes. A flexible reserve of fighter-bombers was always kept in hand, and by day the wing commander and I worked in a joint ops room with comprehensive army and air communications so that we could respond immediately to the changing battle scene.

The Desert Air Force by this time had achieved air superiority and dominated the Luftwaffe. The inconvenient attacks on Army Head-quarters by ground-attack Messerschmitts, which had frequently occurred in the early days of 1942, no longer took place. For the coordination of army units with our supporting air force we had excellent minute by minute information relayed by our 'tentacles' – small parties with forward units which were in direct communication with our Joint Ops rooms – and also by a special reporting organisation called 'J' developed by Hugh Mainwaring, my predecessor. This was a system which enabled reports from brigades or even regiments to reach Army HQ direct.

I described the scene to my mother :

In my job as GSO I (ops), I sit in a sort of control room with three telephones and four wireless sets around me, and lots of GSO IIs at my beck and call. The place is made up of lorries grouped together, and at the moment is far from waterproof. I am very glad of my down flea-bag at nights : the tent is rather draughty even when dug down three feet. My furniture consists of camp bed and a small shelf looted by my batman. You know I rather like my creature comforts : but I wouldn't have missed this for anything.

On one of these days when work was done, I was startled by the familiar cry of the chikor, last heard four years before on the steep hillsides of the Hindu Kush. My shot-gun and cartridges were in my 'ops lorry', locked up with Eighth Army's top secret files. With the sun about to set, three of us set forth immediately up the hillside. In half an hour we got six chikor; they proved a most welcome variant to the bully beef and biscuits, our staple diet, which occasionally had been supple-mented by enormous sand-covered parmesan cheeses and here and there a bottle of Chianti, left behind by Mussolini's heroes in their hasty flight. Unfortunately my gun, the files and the lorry were incinerated a few weeks later en route to a new location. The driver, unaware of a short-circuit in the lighting arrangements and the flames billowing from the rear of his lorry, interpreted the warning signs given him by passing drivers as normal gestures of goodwill. He came to a halt only when the entire vehicle, except for the driving cab, was burnt out.

We spent Christmas in the Benghazi area. Turkey and Christmas pudding were flown up from Cairo, and Lutie my friend in SOE sent me 'a very good stocking', 'containing 2 handkerchiefs, 2 bars of chocolate, 1 toothpaste, 1 tangerine, 2 jars of sweets, 1 cake of soap, 1 packet of safety pins, 1 packet of razor blades (very rare these days) and a bottle opener. Most welcome : she chose so well.'

Agheila, the previous limit of the British Army's advance which I had seen with the King's Dragoon Guards in 1941, lay ahead. Monty became cautious. 'There must be no repetition,' he said. 'Eighth Army must be properly "poised" with adequate logistic support built up behind them.'

In early December 1942 Freddie became ill and left for Cairo; while there in hospital, he recovered and got married. In his absence I enjoyed working under Bobby Erskine, who was BGS 13 Corps and came to Eighth Army HQ as Freddie's temporary replacement. His mind was not as acute as Freddie's, but he had a great capacity for friendship, which he extended to me in full measure then and afterwards.

Rommel was successfully manoeuvred out of Agheila and Buerat and all eyes were now focused on Tripoli. In the brilliant mobile operations that ensued, which resulted in Eighth Army entering Tripoli on 23rd January 1943, Major General 'John' Harding was very seriously wounded. He, like Monty, had finished World War I as a lieutenant colonel, aged only 22, and after service in India, had distinguished himself greatly in the earlier desert operations with General O'Connor and General Auchinleck. He had commanded 7th Armoured Division at the battle of Alamein, and in the pursuit after the battle had greatly impressed the Army Commander. After some months he was back in action as Chief of Staff to General Alexander in Italy.

When we arrived in Tripoli, Army Headquarters, in accordance with the Commander's policy, was not to be sited in the town; so we selected a place on the southern outskirts. Green crops in the adjacent fields bore testimony to the existence of water close at hand; nevertheless we settled happily in a broad dry riverbed. I had forgotten about rain. In the middle of the night, a torrent of brown water four feet deep arrived from the mountains fifty miles south of Tripoli and cut the headquarters in two. One officer was drowned in his slit trench, and at dawn the Army Commander found himself cut off; the GSO I (Ops) was not popular. It was carelessness again, just like the mules in Kirkee in 1931!

Rommel meanwhile, having preserved the remnants of his force from Alamein by a series of successful rearguard actions had his eyes on Tunisia, where the operations of the Americans were running into serious trouble. For us there was to be a period of 'make do and mend'. I was able to have a bath: the first for four months.

Our logistic tail, still based largely on Tobruk, had to be wound up to permit a further advance. Benghazi as a supply port had not come up to expectations; it had been blocked for far too long by sunken ships. That particular drama had occurred some weeks before, when Freddie had been out of action; the Army Commander had summoned Brigadier Brian Robertson, his chief of personnel and logistics, and myself to a meeting.

Brian was the son of the great Field Marshal 'Wully' Robertson who, without benefit of formal education, rose from trooper in the 16th/5th Lancers to become CIGS in World War I. Brian himself was a regular Sapper in that war, then served with great distinction in the Bengal Sappers and Miners on the NW Frontier of India. He retired and joined Dunlop in South Africa. In 1941 he had come up to North Africa through the campaigns in Eritrea and Abyssinia and, when I first met him, he still wore the shoulder flashes of the South African Forces. Despite an age gap of twelve years, we worked very happily together; I was greatly impressed not only by his effectiveness but also by his friendly courtesy. He knew the logistic business so well that he could be very firm on practicalities. On this occasion, he had to tell the Army Commander that Benghazi could not be opened for many weeks, and a new plan must be made.

'Why can't you open the port?' Monty had said quietly.

'Because the Italians sank a large number of ships in the harbour and unfortunately the recent storm has sunk many more. Ships are bobbing about the harbour like corks,' replied Brian.

'Well, tell the Admiral from me to get hold of his corks,' said Monty, with a glint in his eye.

'I will; but it will take time to catch them.'

Monty, having delivered himself of a splenetic 'rocket', even if only by remote control, then got down to business. In a matter of minutes, on Brian's recommendation, General Horrocks' 13 Corps was grounded, and its transport taken over to ferry forward petrol and ammunition for 30 Corps. To me it had been an eye-opener as to how a major strategic decision should be reached.

It was during the lull at Tripoli that I heard Monty first mentioning his 'Diary'. He told us it was 'Very hot stuff' and implied that he had commented on events and personalities with the utmost frankness. 'Everyone will know who is "useless" '; he said :

'It can't be read before I'm dead, or there'll be a frightful rumpus, frightful rumpus !'

He used to return to this theme quite frequently thereafter. I have no doubt that the Diary, now known to be much less explosive than he indicated, helped him to review analytically the tactical problems of the current battle. In referring to it so often, he may also have been trying to use it as a psychological weapon to inspire us to even greater efforts in the knowledge that our individual performances would eventually be recorded for posterity !

For a few weeks at Tripoli the business of war receded, and showmanship took its place. The first item was the Ceremonial Parade and march through the city. After our thousand-mile trek from Burgh el Arab, much 'spit and polish' was required. This was duly applied to men and vehicles with splendid results. The parade brought tears to the eyes of Mr Churchill, who watched with pride alongside Monty. The Prime Minister also came to the short open air Church Parade held at Army Headquarters. Monty's Senior Chaplain, Padre Hughes, who had been selected for the job by Monty himself, gave an inspired sermon and, at the end of the service, Mr Churchill addressed us. It was a wonderful impromptu speech :

'In days to come, when asked by those at home what part you played in this war, it will be with pride in your hearts that you can reply: I marched with the Eighth Army.' He finished: 'And, remember, you nightly pitch your moving tents a day's march nearer home.'

There was hardly a dry eye: mine was not one of them.

Then came Monty's four-day teach-in: 'How I win my battles', attended by officers from all the theatres of war. We assembled in a cinema and, as a backcloth, there was an enormous map showing the battles we had won, and the amazing distances we had covered. In front of this stood the small thin dynamic figure with the bright blue glittering eye holding forth in his repetitive high-pitched voice. He had a lot to tell, and many lessons to teach, but we youngsters wondered how the doctrines of our dogmatic Chief would be received. It is not every member of the 'Second Eleven' that relishes public instruction from the Captain of the 'First'! Later he registered disappointment at the response to his invitation: 'from the party from Tunisia . . . not one British general had come; no infantry brigade commanders; only one American general . . . an old man of 60'. This was Patton, whose comment has passed into the history books: 'I may be old, I may be stoopid but this don't mean nothing to me!'

I described the event to my mother as 'a party here for various generals from near and far – "Senior Jobs" as our AOC [this was Harry Broadhurst] calls them – for whom various lectures and demonstrations were arranged by "the victorious and efficient Eighth Army"! Our reputation now is such that we simply cannot afford to make any mistakes.'

We were all heavily involved in intensive rehearsals for the indoor and outdoor demonstrations we had been ordered to produce. I learnt a lot, particularly from Lieutenant-Colonel 'Pete' Pyman's presentation of an armoured regiment in action. He had commanded one himself with great successs.

Jock McNeill and I were ordered to put on a presentation on Army/Air cooperation. With our pal the Wing Commander (Operations), we staged, to a special scenario, what was really our normal daily activity, and we used our well-worn radio and operational vehicles. Our technique had been evolved pragmatically in a very cordial atmosphere: it became the model for others to follow until the end of the war in Europe.

In the less hectic atmosphere of our pause at Tripoli, I wondered whether the time had come for me to become a regimental sapper again, and I sought the advice of Brigadier Kisch, the Chief Engineer. He welcomed the idea, but surprised me by saying, 'Of course you will have to revert to major and command a squadron as a start.'

This was perfectly correct, but it had not occurred to me. We agreed to consider the problem when the North African operations were over.

We had paused in Tripoli for about four weeks, and expected to remain there longer while supplies were being ferried forward by General Horrocks's transport from Benghazi and Tobruk, when Freddie asked me to go with him to the Army Commander with a signal which had suddenly arrived from General Alexander, who had assumed responsibility for coordinating the actions of First and Eighth Armies. This signal told us that the II United States Corps had been strongly attacked and was in a critical situation : could Montgomery take some action to relieve the pressure?

I was surprised at Monty's reaction. With his well-considered policy of building up his resources and going on to the offensive only when *he was ready* as at Alamein, I would not have been surprised if he had answered that there was nothing he could do. Not a bit of it! His reaction was :

'Alex is in trouble : we must do everything we can to help him.'

It was Monty in his most generous mood and this was entirely genuine.

Immediately it was 'action stations', and 'full speed ahead'. Tactical and Main headquarters were to move at once into Tunisia. The New Zealand Division was ordered to move immediately to Tripoli, armoured and infantry formations were rushed forward to join 7th Armoured Division, and great efforts were made to prepare additional forward air strips. Our object now was to ensure that Rommel after his success at Kasserine should abandon his attacks against First Army and turn to face us. Monty sent an encouraging reply to 'Alex' in which with some glee he spoke of the prospect of Rommel 'running about like a wet hen between us'.

This 'wet hen' was a symbol which appeared frequently in Monty's vocabulary, both then and thereafter. His farmyard metaphor denoted a bedraggled but important bird (which in its role as a commander should really have been a 'cock' even at some sacrifice of onomatopoeia) rushing in panic from one side of the hen run to the other and achieving nothing at either destination. The 'wet hen' syndrome had certainly been present in General Gort's command of the BEF and, if Monty had studied General Ritchie's 'Crusader' operations in 1941, he would certainly have detected it there.

Monty's counter to the 'wet hen' was 'poise'; he aimed invariably to dispose his forces so that, whatever the enemy might do, his own forces would remain 'balanced' and need not react. This did not denote a defensive posture, nor exclude the planned re-grouping of his forces to prepare for a further attack; he had so skilfully done this in the Alamein battle, much to the alarm of onlookers in Cairo and Whitehall, who thought these moves denoted the imminent abandonment of the offensive.

Now, with his impish humour, he gloated on the prospect of Rommel, the defeated bogeyman, being forced by the combined squeeze of Eighth and First Armies to adopt that very 'wet hen' tactic, which he had so often forced upon the British.

Monty's generous reaction to 'Alex's' crisis was an interesting facet of the extraordinary relationship between them. Although GHQ in Cairo was nominally a superior headquarters, I was not aware that any strategic instructions ever emanated from them. It was Monty who planned the strategy, decided how far and fast he would go in each of the phases, and how each battle should be fought. To the extent that he was controlled at all, it was by the CIGS General Sir Alan Brooke who was kept minutely informed by the personal letters sent to Major-General F. W. Simpson, Director of Military Operations in the War Office, a trusted friend from the days when in England he had been Monty's Chief of Staff. 'Alex' was 'kept happy' by a series of personal signals drafted and despatched by Monty from his tactical headquarters. Every night I despatched my situation report to GHQ, but never received as far as I can recall any operational instructions. Monty in fact treated General Alexander, for whom he had very friendly feelings, as a subordinate, just as he had when teaching him at the Staff College. Now at Tripoli, which Monty had originally felt should be an objective to be taken from the west by the First Army, not the Eighth, the activities of General Anderson, 'the good plain Cook', became very relevant to our situation and Monty rightly demanded coordination from General Alexander at this juncture.

On the logistic side GHQ Cairo played a vital role, and General Alexander undoubtedly gave Monty 'everything he wanted'. With the inadequate ports which were invariably damaged by the enemy and the vast distances involved, over 1,000 miles from Alamein to Tunis, this was no easy task. Fortunately there were some very shrewd and farsighted generals at work in the Cairo base including Eustace Tickell, my 'tutor' at RMA Woolwich, who, arriving as a major-general in 1940 had startled his staff by saying 'order 1000 miles of ten-inch water pipe'.

One of his assistants was my old friend Bill Fryer, who had instructed me as a lieutenant in 1928 in the mysteries of electrical and mechanical engineering. In 1939, as a spare time job, he had brought up to date the Army Manual on Water Supply and, on arrival in Cairo in May 1940, found ample scope for practising his art. He planned and supervised the installations for the many new camps in Egypt, started the desert pipeline from Alexandria to Mersa Matruh and had thirty-six well boring rigs working throughout the Middle East. New sources of water were discovered principally with the assistance of a team of geophysicists from the Johannesburg Rand, working under the direction of Professor Shotton of Sheffield University. The Professor had discovered a source near Fuka by picking up small pieces of pottery in the desert :

'Roman pottery,' he declared; 'there must have been a village or a town here : so there must have been water.' The source, in a large clay basin 70 feet below the surface, was tapped at once with two rigs. Large quantities of water were found although there was no clue of vegetation or of habitation.

All this work required a vast amount of travel, for which purpose Bill used an aeroplane. He found a dusty Moth at a Cairo airfield which had been grounded for the duration of the war. He persuaded his general, Eustace Tickell, to buy it for him for £100, and to get the RAF to maintain it. He piloted it with RAF roundels 'usually above 3,000 feet to keep clear of pot-shots from rifle and machine-gun fire'.

After the Alamein battle it became urgent to build up supplies of petrol and oil at Benghazi for the advance to Tripoli. A bulk petrol station at Benghazi had been badly damaged, but the Sapper petrol team soon repaired it, and Bill Fryer sent up a floating pipe-line leading to a harbour buoy. A 20,000 ton petrol tanker manned by Merchant Navy men was waiting at Port Said without orders. Bill visited them to check their equipment, but did not disclose what dangers lay ahead for them; but he thought that his 'desert boots' might be a worrying sign for them !

Two days later the tanker entered Benghazi at dusk, pumped ashore 20,000 tons of petrol and was away by dawn.

Churchill had demanded reports of tonnages unloaded daily at

Benghazi; the tanker load of petrol caused a dramatic increase, which drew from Churchill an immediate signal : 'Well done – you are unloading history.' A nice pat on the back for the tanker heroes !

At Tripoli by February our supplies of ammunition and petrol had not yet been brought forward to the full extent needed for our eventual move to the Mareth position, where we expected Rommel to make his next stand. Nevertheless we were going to have to lure Rommel from the west and fight a defensive battle against him.

The battle at Medenine twenty miles east of Mareth, so quickly staged and so rapidly won, proceeded almost exactly as planned by our Army Commander and made a big impression on me and on many others.

I was not a reader of Ultra, althought I knew a good deal about it; we now know how successful the cryptographers had been. For ten days before Rommel's attack, the strategic intentions of the Axis Forces were known almost as soon as they were formulated. This Ultra information was supplemented by intercepts from Eighth Army's 'Y', and from air reconnaissance.

The battle had a resemblance to Alam Halfa. Our defensive position included a dominant feature, Tedjera Kher, on the southern flank giving magnificent observation. It was to be held by 201 Guards Brigade under command of 7th Armoured Division. The 51st Highland Division was to the north and the 5th New Zealand Brigade to the south of Tadjera Kher. Rommel, who had assembled three panzer and two infantry divisions, started the attack on 6th March, later than expected, thus providing a welcome period for further improvements to our positions. He did not follow precisely the sequence which Monty had forecast, but our position as usual was 'well-balanced', so that we could react favourably to enemy thrusts from any quarter. Moreover Monty had assembled 400 tanks and 600 anti-tank guns and a great mass of artillery. Rommel's Panzer thrusts were held everywhere by the well-trained determined veterans of Eighth Army, and Rommel withdrew that night with his tail between his legs, and left Africa for good. But the two protagonists were to confront each other again in Normandy.

While we had been at Tripoli and were considering the problems that would be involved in attacking the Mareth position, General Le Clerc had turned up on 1st February with his small force from Chad. Except for the blackened stinking corpses that I had observed in Syria where

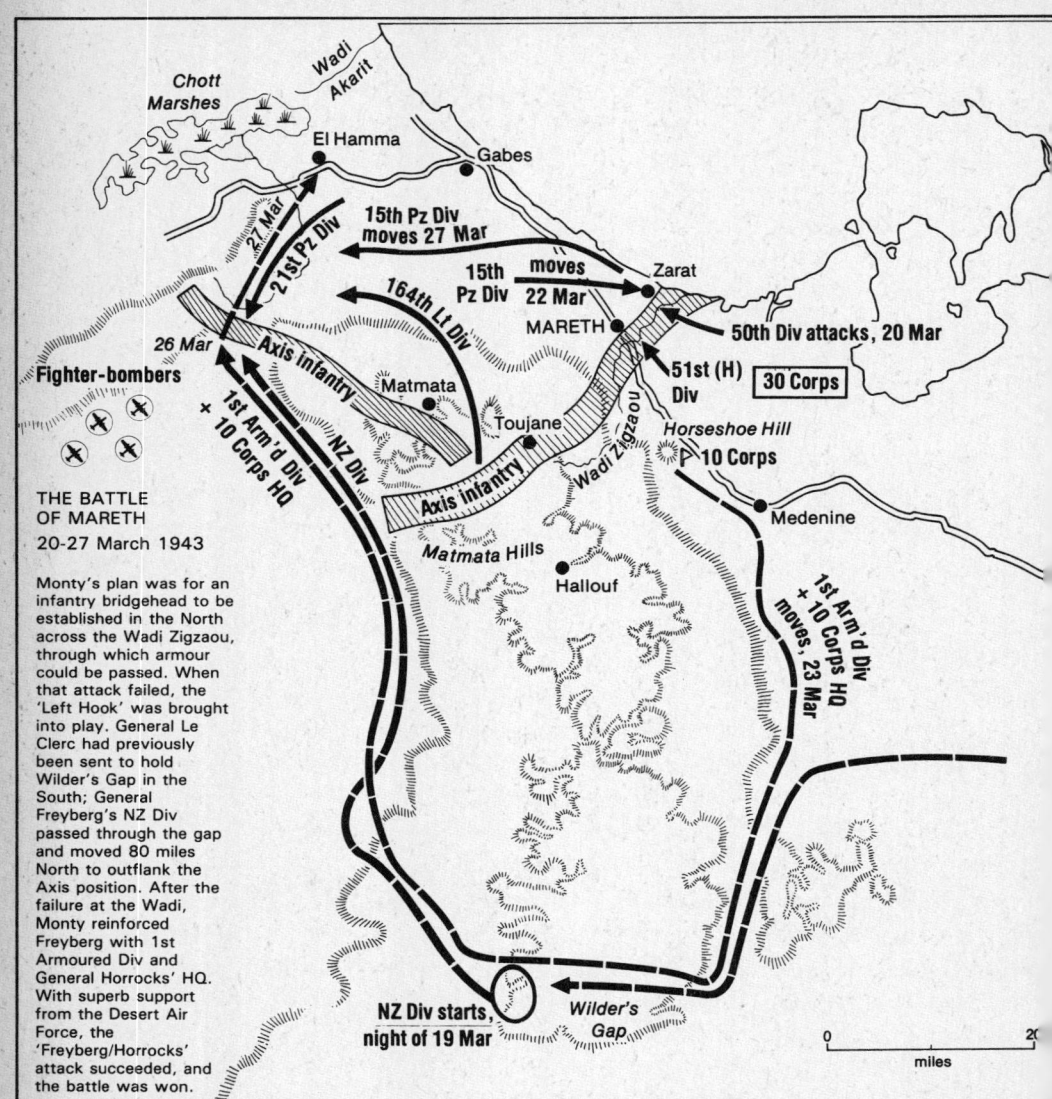

Chott Marshes

Wadi Akarit

El Hamma

Gabes

15th Pz Div moves 27 Mar

27 Mar

21st Pz Div

15th Pz Div

moves 22 Mar

Zarat

164th Lt Div

MARETH

50th Div attacks, 20 Mar

26 Mar

Axis infantry

Fighter-bombers

1st Arm'd Div + 10 Corps HQ

NZ Div

Matmata

51st (H) Div

30 Corps

Toujane

Axis infantry

Horseshoe Hill

10 Corps

Wadi Zigzaou

THE BATTLE OF MARETH
20-27 March 1943

Monty's plan was for an infantry bridgehead to be established in the North across the Wadi Zigzaou, through which armour could be passed. When that attack failed, the 'Left Hook' was brought into play. General Le Clerc had previously been sent to hold Wilder's Gap in the South; General Freyberg's NZ Div passed through the gap and moved 80 miles North to outflank the Axis position. After the failure at the Wadi, Monty reinforced Freyberg with 1st Armoured Div and General Horrocks' HQ. With superb support from the Desert Air Force, the 'Freyberg/Horrocks' attack succeeded, and the battle was won.

Matmata Hills

Hallouf

Medenine

1st Arm'd Div + 10 Corps HQ moves, 23 Mar

NZ Div starts, night of 19 Mar

Wilder's Gap

0   20
miles

Frenchmen had been fighting Frenchmen, I had seen nothing of our ally since leaving Dunkirk. Le Clerc's small band, answering a call of conscience, had quitted Chad and started northwards on the thousand-mile trek to get back into the war. It was a romantic and heart-warming event. Knowing my Frenchmen, I expected they might well want to exploit their situation *'pour l'honneur de la Patrie'*, with a bit 'on the side' for themselves.

I was wrong, but they certainly needed help. The force was a very mixed bag; colonial soldiers with white faces and others coffee-coloured; an armoured car or two; some artillery, machine guns and ancient lorries : even two aircraft. Le Clerc, having reported for duty to Monty, who immediately recognised his quality, was passed to Freddie and then to me to get down to detail. From the hip pocket of his heavily darned 'Huntsman' breeches* he produced a piece of paper about the size of four postage stamps, and very quietly made his first request : *'Deux camions, s'il vous plait.'* And so his modest demands continued, all of which fortunately we were able to meet. To me he seemed a very English *général!* He became 'one of us'; and Monty, who until then had firmly declined to depend on any French troops offered him, assigned him to what proved to be a highly critical role in the Mareth battle, which we were already beginning to plan.

For us, the battle of Mareth contained all those elements of intellectual interest and high drama that had attached to Alamein. But there was a strange contrast which even Freddie could not explain. We could never find out before the battle where Monty had 'put his money' : on the thrust along the coastal axis or on the 'left hook'. And it was with the 'left hook' that Le Clerc was concerned. Several weeks before the battle, Freddie had been studying with Bill the possibilities of turning Rommel's Mareth defences by an outflanking movement deep in the southern desert. Hearing that the 'going' was terrible, he ordered the Long Range Desert Group to carry out special reconnaissances in that vast area, which of course was not occupied by Rommel's forces. They eventually reported that a left hook, though very difficult in terms of movement, was possible, but that at one place, Wilder's Gap, there was a defile which guarded the only feasible passage through the sand obstacle. It was to Wilder's Gap that Le Clerc was sent with his small force.

* Huntsman was a renowned breeches-maker in London.

I have often wondered whether initially Le Clerc may have regarded his assignment as a token operation *'pour nous amuser'*. Having driven a thousand miles through the desert from Chad to join Eighth Army, then to find himself sent sixty miles back into the Desert, to sit in the sand with not an enemy in sight, might well have appeared as anticlimax! But this was not to be the case. His small force was discovered by the Luftwaffe and they set out to destroy him. We had a receiving set on his command net, but could not transmit to him as he was out of range. We listened, appalled, to Le Clerc's phlegmatic comments as the attack continued : alarming casualties in men and equipment were impassively reported. Eventually the RAF at very extended range were able to threaten the Luftwaffe, and Le Clerc with his brave band survived. It was just as well : the security of Wilder's Gap was the key to Freyberg's left hook, which determined the battle of Mareth.

As the start of the battle drew nearer, Freyberg set off across the desert towards Wilder's Gap with 200 tanks and 27,000 men, while Oliver Leese with his 30 Corps moved forward to make contact with the Mareth defences which blocked the Coastal Axis. None of us, at my level, felt very confident that the frontal attack through the Wadi Zigzaou would succeed. Perhaps it was to be only a diversion? Surely we would know before the battle started?

The defences of the Mareth Line, built long before by the French in Tunisia to block any Italian aggression from Libya, were formidable. The system was well-devised and included permanent fortifications as well as minefields enfiladed from flanking machine gun posts. The Matmata hills dominated the battleground, providing magnificent observation for the Afrika Korps. The attack was to be at night, and a few days earlier heavy rain had fallen adding mud and water to the other hazards in the Wadi Zigzaou.

On 20th March, the attack by 50th Division went in under a heavy barrage, but progress was slow. Brigadier Kisch, the Chief Engineer, was up with the sappers but they were in great difficulty and were not clearing the minefields as fast as had been hoped. The forward brigade hung on for forty-eight hours against strong German counter-attacks. A further night attack was ordered by Monty for the early hours of 23rd March. This never got properly started and just before 2 a.m. Brigadier Walsh, General Oliver Leese's Chief of Staff, rang me to say the attack had failed and the Army Commander must be told. My heart

Eighth Army en route to Tripoli, 'buoyed up by our irresistible advance'.

Monty with his Chief of Staff Brigadier Freddie de Guingand.

Monty's study period at Tripo[li] 'How I win my battles'. Auth[or] centre front next to Naval Liaison Officer. Monty on skyline.

The Ceremonial Parade in Tripoli: march past of 51st Highland Division.

General Le Clerc arrived fr[om] Chad and reported to Mont[y]

sank; I rang Freddie who awakened Monty. It was a moment of crisis for him and for all of us. The future seemed uncertain, and to us this was most unusual: having come so far, was it now to be 'Never glad confident morning again'?*

Early next morning I asked Freddie, 'Where do we go from here?'

The only success so far was Freyberg's unopposed advance which had taken him to the opening of the El Hamma defile, which was strongly held. He was two hundred miles away from us, and the approach to him was through soft sand. How on earth could he be supplied quickly? However by this time Monty had recovered his 'poise', and his optimism was as usual being transmitted throughout the Army. It was 'Full steam ahead with the left hook'. But there were still surprises in store.

Speed of reaction was the key because the enemy was better placed than we were to throw his weight from one threatened flank to another. He had already moved forces, released from the Wadi Zigzaou battle, to confront Freyberg. Freyberg was far from optimistic about the possibility of an early attack. He was thinking in terms of a methodical heavy bombardment by medium artillery requiring thousands of tons of ammunition. This would inevitably postpone our attack by several days: the awful prospect of Eighth Army, so near to final success, getting 'bogged down' seeped into all our minds. Freddie twisted his forelock almost to destruction: a sure sign of desperate worry. With Jock and me he groped towards the idea of a 'blitz' attack using air power in substitution of the artillery shells which could never arrive in time. We had talked of such possibilities before, but they were contrary to RAF 'Philosophy'. In this case, pilot casualties might indeed be very heavy, as the enemy had sited his 88 mm guns on both sides of the El Hamma defile for use in their dual role of anti-tank and anti-aircraft. But Freddie had the bit between his teeth and went ahead; he found the C-in-C of the Desert Air Force sympathetic and constructive. Harry Broadhurst, despite warnings from his superiors, courageously accepted the outline plan, which was then endorsed by Monty. Eighth Army's Operations Staff, with G (Air) and the RAF, worked out all the details at high speed, and on 26th March, only three days after the Wadi Zigzaou crisis, the attack went in. The scheme operated like clockwork, pilot casualties were light and the enemy was totally defeated.

* 'The Lost Leader' by Robert Browning. This phrase, used in one of his speeches by the Master of Wellington, remained for ever in my memory.

It was unusual for Monty's Chief of Staff to modify the Army Commander's plans. He had done so at Alamein over the axis of the Supercharge attack; here he did it again. In both cases, the moment was critical and the intervention was successful. By now, despite his poor health, he had established himself, not only as a superb coordinator of all the massive staff work which Monty delegated to him with total confidence, but also as a leader – but a leader who knew not only where he could intrude into the thinking of his dogmatic master, but also how he could persuade him to adopt a suggested modification as his own. Freddie, with all his intellectual brilliance and charismatic personality, was essentially a very modest man; yet increasingly his skill, loyalty and sense of duty drew him inexorably towards the centre of the stage. He had become a unique complement to his master.

CHAPTER NINE

Into Europe

After the decisive victory at Mareth, it was clear to all of us that the end of the North African Campaign was in sight. In retrospect, one must admire the sustained courage of the German soldiers and of some of the Italians. For them the writing had been on the wall since the loss of Tripoli and, despite the diminished dynamism of their great commander Rommel who had left them, and the handicaps imposed by Hitler's manic decisions, they continued to offer staunch and effective resistance to the bitter end.

For some time past, our next strategic move had been under discussion in our circle; and by now the operation was being planned in London and elsewhere. The decision to go to Sicily, transmitted confidentially to us several weeks before by Freddie, had surprised us greatly. We had never contemplated such an event, and to the extent that we looked ahead at all, we had envisaged a return to the UK, preparatory to a cross-channel assault. The barrier of the Alps, of which I had had some experience from happy days of pre-war ski-ing, loomed large in my mind. We were not equipped to assess the relative importance of 'opening up the Mediterranean sea lanes' and, as for 'knocking Italy out of the war', I mentally disparaged the Italians still with the same contempt that had prompted in India my comic, histrionic role of 'Mussolini'! Surely they were more of a liability to the Germans than an asset? In talks with Freddie we sensed that he, the erstwhile planner from GHQ who had made there such a profound impression, was much of the same mind. However, as so often before in the Monty environment, critical talk freely expressed was acceptable, but once the die was cast the 'no bellyaching' rule was universally adopted.

However, to mount in a matter of weeks the largest assault landing that had so far taken place, involving for us two new allies, the Canadians as well as the Americans, posed great problems for our commander and staff.

The immediate consequence of this situation, after the battle of the Wadi Akarit had been quickly and successfully concluded, was the problem of finishing the North African Campaign jointly with the British and American forces in Tunisia, and simultaneously preparing for the landings in Sicily, code-named 'Husky'.

The Axis forces in Tunisia were in a desperate situation corralled in the peninsulas of Bizerta and Cap Bon, with little transport and less petrol and no effective port for re-supply. Their airstrips were few, and the Desert Air Force dominated the skies above them. To their west was a force of three corps, United States, British and French, while to the south, facing Enfidaville, was 30 Corps of the Eighth Army.

After the failure at Enfidaville of an initial attack by 56th Division, which had recently arrived from the UK, Monty decided that Eighth Army's assault from the south on the strongly-held defile at Enfidaville would be too hazardous and expensive and must be abandoned. In substitution, he proposed to General Alexander that an attack from the west directed on Tunis should be carried out. For this purpose, a re-grouping of First and Eighth Armies should take place, and 4th Indian Division, 7th Armoured Division and 201 Guards Brigade should pass to First Army to carry out the Tunis attack.

Monty then persuaded General Alexander that General Horrocks, hurriedly summoned from the rear areas, should command First Army's attack.

It surprised me that Monty, keen always to be centre-stage, had offered immediately to relinquish his dominant role, and had recommended that Eighth Army in the south should play only a subsidiary part in the final attack to finish the war in North Africa, while he himself gave top priority to the preparations for Husky, which he rightly viewed with great misgivings. Not for the first or last time, professional military wisdom must have triumphed over the powerful temptations of vanity!

Confident as always in Freddie's ability to analyse the Husky problems and guide decisions in the way that he himself would approve, he sent Freddie back to Cairo. The UK planners of 'Force 141' had assembled at Algiers and Monty himself would give direction to the Husky planning, while keeping a watchful eye on the Tunis battle. Thus I was left in Tunisia as Acting Chief of Staff of Eighth Army for the final battle of the campaign. It was here that I closely observed, in his role as Army Group Commander, General Sir Harold Alexander whom

I had first met in 1937, when we were both playing polo by moonlight in Chitral. The contrast with Monty was startling. Like everyone who met General Alexander, I was instantly attracted by his easy, genuine charm; but the feeling that the firm hand of Monty had been removed from the battle was quite alarming. Eventually, after delays which, viewed against the Eighth Army yardstick, would have been outrageous, Monty's plan for the battle was adopted, demanding a very quick response from Eighth Army's staff.

It required the immediate despatch from our front of two divisions with an independent brigade on a wide outflanking move of 150 miles to a new position for attack. David Belchem, who would have taken charge of the problem, had gone back to Cairo to join in the Husky planning, leaving behind a very young major of the South African Forces, for whom I had a high regard. Late at night I threw the whole problem at him, and his eyes lit up. An hour later I asked:

'How is it going?' expecting many problems and queries.

'All finished, sir,' he said.

'Do you really mean to tell me that all the orders for the night moves and logistic support have gone out?'

'Not only gone out, but acknowledged,' he replied, and showed me the copies of the signals. Eighth Army's contribution to the final battle had developed with its usual precision!

Now that the end of the African campaign was imminent, I thought once again of my talk in Tripoli with Brigadier Kisch about reverting to major to become a sapper again. Poor Fred Kisch by this time was dead: blown up in the Wadi Akarit by a German mine. I hardly knew his South African successor. It was at this juncture that Freddie, destined because of our wider Husky responsibilities to become a major-general, was put out of action in an aeroplane crash, and I learnt to my surprise that I was to be promoted to brigadier. I accepted. The War Office in its official communication hedged its bets: 'This promotion is valid only for six months.' It lasted four years!

I wrote to my mother:

Startling news for you. I have been made a brigadier. How long it will last I don't know. My boss Freddie de Guingand has gone to Cairo as a Major-General. He remains Chief of Staff of the Army and I, as his deputy become a BGS. When he is away, as at present, I run the staff, many of whom are ten years older than me: I hope I can live up to it.

We are now in very pleasant country – olive groves with masses of flowers : poppies, white and yellow daisies and many other kinds of wild flower. I have a good mind to pick some myself, in spite of being a brigadier.

And to my sister :

I hope we can finish off this party soon. It is not much good being a 'Glamour boy' out in the Desert. The water here is vile and the French say impotence supervenes after a few months! Freddie, my boss, now looks like death, and is gulping down three medicines at once!

Eighth Army Headquarters was now split between Tunis and Cairo; our Commander was at the Cairo Embassy assessing the plan for Husky, while his Chief of Staff lay in hospital recovering from concussion. At the Tunis end, we took no part in the triumphal rejoicings after General Horrocks, overflowing with enthusiasm after a long period of inaction, achieved a brilliant and final victory. The war in North Africa was finished, and 250,000 prisoners were taken.

We had other preoccupations. For us the call was : 'Prepare for Husky'. The amphibious assault, the largest operation of its kind ever attempted, was due in two months' time, on 9th July.

Preparations for the Sicily landings under the responsible commanders then began with great urgency. Activity was spread over a wide area : United States, Canada, United Kingdom, Algiers, Tunis, Sousse, Tripoli, Benghazi, Alexandria and Haifa. Only by using the recently liberated Mediterranean ports was it possible to mount the large-scale operation successfully. General Eisenhower was in Supreme Command with General Alexander as Land Forces Commander, with Admiral Cunningham and Air Marshal Tedder commanding the Naval and Air Forces. I was sent to General Alexander's headquarters in Algiers; my role was to ensure that the overall preparations, as they developed, were reconcilable at every stage with Monty's requirements.

It was not a happy place. There were many contentious issues between nationalities and between the various Service Chiefs.

I for my part, a brigadier aged thirty-four, wearing the OBE from Alamein and the DSO from Mareth, exhibited no doubt some of the intolerable conceit, typical then of the 'Monty Man'. We had, after all, advanced successfully one thousand eight hundred and seventy-miles to Tunis, there to finish off the African Campaign, which the British and

Americans from Algeria had signally failed to do. We knew full well that it was our victorious commander who was taking a firm grip on the Husky operation, and imposing his will as usual not only on subordinates but also on his nominal superiors. Thus the original plans, conscientiously evolved by those in London, were being torn to shreds, and rightly so. In Monty's eyes, anyone associated with those plans was suspect : there were many of them at the headquarters in Algiers. To me, forty years later, the phrase : 'rivalry-ridden hot-house'* is accurately evocative of Alexander's headquarters.

As early as April 1943 Monty had examined the Husky plan, which had been worked up by 'Force 141', the special planning staff set up in London. Determined as always to achieve 'balance' and 'poise' in his forces, particularly at their most vulnerable period immediately after an assault landing, he had forcibly recommended to General Sir Alan Brooke that the proposed landing at Palermo should be omitted in the first phase, and that the two United States Divisions thus released, should land on the south coast within supporting distance of the British landings, with the objective of securing essential aerodromes in that area. Thus a firm base was to be secured, from which future offensive operations could be developed.

This fundamental modification of the plan, which had been strongly backed also by Freddie, had been put to General Alexander by cable.

On 2nd May, with Freddie in Cairo, I was summoned to accompany the Army Commander to Algiers where he was going for a conference with Eisenhower, Alexander, Cunningham and Tedder. As I sat beside him in his aeroplane he explained that he was going to get agreement to the final plan for Husky. On his millboard he started writing in his schoolboy hand with soft pencil and an indiarubber within reach, and after some minutes he turned to me : 'Charles, read that. Is it clear ? Is it clear ?'

Knowing my 'master' I knew this was no formality: he never expected his staff, or indeed his ADCs, to agree to anything if they did not.

I answered that it was quite clear. As usual he had summed up the strategic argument with great force and few words. However, knowing as I did something of the prejudices of Tedder and Cunningham who were going to be very disinclined to alter their arrangements to satisfy the 'egotistical' Monty, I felt his chances of success were small.

* *Monty*, Vol II, Nigel Hamilton (Hamish Hamilton).

But succeed he did. I was not present at the high-powered meeting, but on the return journey he was contented and relaxed.

After six months at the head of Eighth Army, however, Monty needed a rest. Before flying to England, and thinking as ever of his devoted staff, he wrote to Freddie :

My dear Freddie,

I am in Cairo checking up on HUSKY. Before coming here I visited Algiers and got various things agreed as a result of the acceptance of my plan.

I then visited Alexander and got everything I wanted agreed to. There is now no need for worry on any matter. I have had conferences here and have explained the whole business to everyone; the foundations and framework of the whole project are now firm.

I am quite happy about the Air matters.

In fact everything is going along so well that I am myself going off to England on Sunday next, 16 May; Army H.Q. pulls out of the battle that day and goes back to the Tripoli area. Oliver (Leese) will be in charge while I am away; Belchem is running everything quite excellently. Charles Richardson will be at Algiers as my representative at Force 141. I have persuaded Alex to remove Charles Gairdner; he is useless.

Now about yourself.

It is absolutely vital that you should get quite fit *before* you come back.

You are not to worry about the business, or even to think about it. It is quite unnecessary for anyone to go up and see you, and keep you in touch.

There is nothing to worry about; everything is now splendid.

You must stay where you are; amuse yourself; have a thorough good rest; and be back here on 1st June *and not before*. I will be back myself by 5 June at Tripoli (Main Army).

I shall come to Cairo about 8 June, and go off with Ramsay to the rehearsals about 11 or 12 June.

Show these orders to your wife and tell her I rely on her to see them carried out. You are far too valuable to be wasted, and I should be 'in the soup' if you came back too soon and cracked up again later.

So stay where you are and be back here by 1st June.

Good luck to you.

Yours ever
B. L. Montgomery

Monty's statements : 'I got everything I wanted' and 'no need to worry', though exaggerated perhaps to encourage Freddie, were to prove optimistic. Unhappy argument and disputation were to re-emerge all too soon. His intervention had not been popular with General Patton, who had had his eyes fixed on Palermo.

One incident in Algiers provided an element of tragi-comedy. One of the officers with me, a highly conscientious lieutenant-colonel, received a summons to Cairo to face a security investigation. As we were old friends, he told me the story and asked for my advice. In Cairo he had experienced some difficulty in keeping track of all the details of the Sicily landings. Knowing him well, I could readily understand this. There was a special security procedure under which Husky documents were marked with a codeword and had to be handled by a special procedure. This officer with the best of motives flagrantly disobeyed the security instructions, and decided to keep a small personal notebook in which he wrote down the crucial facts of the assault landings, i.e., the beaches, the units due to land, etc., timings, etc.

One evening in Cairo, exhausted no doubt by the duration and intensity of the planning sessions caused by our tight timetable, he forgot on returning to his flat to retrieve his notebook from his khaki shorts. The Egyptian bearer duly sent shorts and notebook to the laundry's *dhobi* and he, eking out a meagre existence in Cairo, was delighted to find a notebook in which the pages on one side were not used. He took the book into use, and started sending out to a large Cairo clientele his *dhobi* bills written on the unused sides of the pages. One bill was received by an officer involved in Husky planning, who was amazed to find the details of the Husky assault inscribed on the other side of his laundry bill, and reported the incident to the Security Authorities. Much later, I was glad to hear that my friend, although court-martialled, had been treated leniently. None of the information ever reached the Germans; nor indeed did they profit from another much more serious lapse : a top secret signal containing the recommended date and hour for the Sicily parachute landings was dropped in Shepheard's hotel in Cairo, and handed by an Egyptian to the General Manager, who was an Austrian. He passed it back to the British !

June passed quietly in my 'hot-house'; I found relief in an occasional duty visit to Cairo where David Belchem had taken charge most effectively during Freddie's recovery from the air crash. Freddie was lucky to be alive; at the best of times he had not got a strong constitution and this incident, although he brushed it aside, left its mark.

While Freddie had still not fully recovered and Monty was on a visit to England I was called upon to represent him at the naval rehearsal of the invasion of Sicily. This took place in the Gulf of Aqaba.

Admiral Ramsay, the miracle worker of Dunkirk, had now become very well known to us all. He was a quiet, friendly, intelligent man, who understood the amphibious business in all its ramifications. Throughout the course of our joint planning I noticed that, unlike some other senior, rank-conscious commanders, he was quite prepared to discuss problems with Army officers much junior in rank, if by so doing he could expedite our joint affairs. There was nothing of Monty's showmanship about him, but they got on splendidly together, and Monty admired him as much as we did. On board his Headquarters ship, he treated me with great courtesy, as if I were a senior general. That evening in the Red Sea, he and I and the Captain sat down to dinner at a polished mahogany table adorned with silver candlesticks and crystal goblets, ready for a five-course menu served by a smart steward.

At dawn in terrific heat, token landings were made at the head of the Gulf, while the whole of the communications drill of the ships taking part and of their Army counterparts was practised. The event, lasting two or three days, was a most enjoyable interlude; it inspired me with great confidence, and reinforced my affectionate admiration of Bertram Ramsay.

Finally, at the beginning of July, I flew to Malta to make arrangements for the headquarters of Eighth Army to control the assault from that island. We were to be squatters for some days, perhaps few in number, but difficult to forecast. I thought the Royal Navy might find this irksome, and was much relieved at my first call on Admiral Creasy, Admiral Ramsay's Chief of Staff. He received me with great courtesy and a pink gin, and said: 'It's all yours: if there are any difficulties come to see me at once.' There were no difficulties. Our signal organisation, which had proved itself so well all through the long march from Alexandria to Tunis, got quietly to work, and I set up my operations room under the battlements. Everywhere we were treated like honoured guests.

This reaction by the Navy was in their best tradition of co-operation and clear decisive action. But during those preparatory weeks, although I was partially shielded by Freddie from the acerbities, international and interservice, that were building up on all sides I had sensed an increasing malaise born of complication and compromise. The grand simplicity of Eighth Army's posture and progress in North Africa was now blunted by irrelevancies. Furthermore, the splendidly sterile theatre of the desert was about to give way to a different scene : Sicily, with its ancient hilltop villages surrounded by the ruins of antiquity, and peopled by impoverished peasants with their innumerable children. These were to be our future unintended victims.

The operations in Sicily were by past standards confused. As BGS (Ops) of Eighth Army I should doubtless have done more to overcome the muddles. One of the brighter features of the scene was Colonel Toby Low, the future Lord Aldington, who was Colonel (General Staff) of General Dempsey's 13 Corps. Aged only twenty-nine and shortly to become a brigadier he was very able and co-operative.

Many things were against us. Politics had entered in and this was not Monty's forte. The terrain was difficult : those terrible Sicilian lanes which the present day tourist, driving at speed along the Autostrada, seldom experiences. Day by day, Anglo-American feuding was growing in intensity and the only man, other than the maverick Patton, who seemed certain how the battle should unfold was Monty, and he was not as clear as usual. What of Alexander and what of Eisenhower? I thought back to March when Eisenhower had first met Monty in the desert. Freddie had flown back from Tac HQ to tell us of the encounter :

'They got on well,' he said. We asked, 'What did Monty make of him?'

With a wry smile Freddie disclosed : 'The verdict was "good chap; no soldier"!'

Now we also know what the future President of the most powerful nation in the world thought of our Monty at this first meeting : 'Of different calibre from some of the outstanding British leaders . . . unquestionably able, but very conceited . . .'

Neither, in his assessment of the other, got very near the truth!

Somehow, despite the lack of firm higher direction, we and the Americans muddled through. But few Germans were rounded up. When we reached the Straits of Messina on 17th August, there were no celebrations of victory. What next?

Carrying the war into Italy had been on the agenda for some time. Again our trio heard little of the fierce arguments on strategy being

Sicily
1 - 9 - 43

My dear Charles

Thank you for your letter.
You have been a member of our
team for a very long time and
you will be greatly missed.
But when appealed to by the
Americans we had to send our
best; and you are very much
wanted in that show. I do not
altogether like the way things are
shapeing in your "party" !!

Yrs. sincerely
B. L. Montgomery.

Monty's letter to me on joining Fifth US Army

waged at the highest level. I felt unenthusiastic about Eighth Army's role: to creep slowly up the east coast of Italy, forcing defile after defile in the depths of winter – a sapper's nightmare! So it came as a relief when I was told I was to join General Mark Clark's Fifth United States Army as Deputy Chief of Staff (British).

The landing at Salerno, 150 miles further north, seemed to me to be much more promising. From the beachhead, we could capture Naples, an invaluable port and, sustained from there, we could march on Rome. We might even be able to cut off some of the German forces in Southern Italy. I feared that my old friends would get stuck in the mud!

General Mark Clark's Army was to consist of a US Corps under General Dawley together with the British 10 Corps under General Dick McCreery, whom I had met in the Tunis battle and at Algiers. I was to have a small British staff as an increment to the US headquarters. Operationally, we were to fight as an integrated force, but the logistic and personnel functions were to be kept separate.

I said goodbye to Freddie and Bill Williams and to David Belchem who took over from me as BGS (Ops). After writing a goodbye letter to my Army Commander, I flew to Fifth Army's headquarters at Mostaganem, a coastal town about 180 miles west of Algiers.

I expected to feel a bit 'homesick' for Eighth Army; but Monty, who viewed the Salerno operation with disquiet and sent me a very encouraging letter.

At Mostaganem I met General Mark Clark, who gave me a warm and courteous welcome, his Chief of Staff Major General 'Al' Gruenther and Brigadier-General Don Brann, head of G3, the operations branch in the American Army.

General Mark Clark, a tall, slim, tough-looking figure, reminded me of those Indian Chiefs striding across the prairie in Wild West films. He certainly had courage and the personality of a leader, but I soon began to wonder whether he had a real understanding of operations at Army level. He was younger than Monty and had had only a brief experience of World War I as a captain. After many staff appointments, he had become C-in-C Ground Forces in Europe in July 1942 and, preparatory to the Allied Invasion in North Africa he had successfully led a secret mission by submarine to make contact with French leaders.

But although a four-star general, he had never commanded a division. In the British Army such experience would have been regarded as an essential qualification. Like Monty he obviously appreciated the importance of Public Relations in the art of command, but I was doubtful whether real professional knowledge lay behind the outward façade.

Major-General Al Gruenther, a thin frail-looking general with a deceptively pale face, was obviously popular and highly respected. I soon realised that he had a brilliant mind and was completely devoid of intellectual arrogance. I found also that he was totally unbiased in his approach to the British or American elements of the Army. Moreover he was highly resilient; this was fortunate in view of the strains that were to be imposed on us at Salerno. I was told that as an instructor in the rank of captain at West Point, he had become notorious for his frequent nocturnal absences from the Academy. He was known to be one of the best instructors there, but his repeated absences through long hours of the night posed a mystery. It was said that he was involved in playing bridge : could it be that this hobby was militating against superior performance of his military duties? It was decided to set a watch on his activities lest it be found that after a prolonged nocturnal absence the brilliant instructor was not at the peak of his form. No such conclusion emerged; indeed the nocturnal absence seemed if anything to improve his performance at duty.

The full story then came out. Captain Gruenther, a bridge player of international class, had decided to supplement his army pay by organising and presiding at competitive bridge tournaments, often several hundred miles from West Point. The money was good, and his requirements for sleep were minimal! Later I saw how this habit of dispensing with sleep had a military use at Salerno.

Brigadier-General Don Brann had been a contemporary of Eisenhower at West Point, and mentioned this far too frequently. I foresaw that with him the age gap, if nothing else, would create problems. Later, I was introduced to the Commander of the US Corps, Lieutenant-General Dawley : to me he seemed very old, and seemingly devoid of that dynamism which had been the hallmark of Monty's corps commanders.

Then it was suggested by Al Gruenther, the Chief of Staff, that I should call upon General Patton, although he was not immediately involved with the Salerno landing. Although I had seen him at our 'teach-in' at Tripoli and heard of his escapades in Sicily, the encounter surprised me greatly. I was led by an ADC into a large room; in one corner, flags of the Allies, very large flags at that, were erected behind an enormous desk. A slim elderly figure rose up, with pearl-handled revolver strapped to his hip, and greeted me in a movietone accent. Was I at war, or was I in Hollywood, I wondered?

I had seen him only occasionally in Sicily. I knew that having captured Palermo, which in the eyes of General Montgomery and of General Bradley, his commander, had no strategic value, he had 'seized the bit between his teeth', and decided in his obsession to win glory for America by a victory at Messina. He went ahead regardless of the operations of General Oliver Leese, Monty's corps commander on his right flank or of the ineffective instructions from General Alexander. Although Monty, held up before Catania, had ultimately to agree to this, I had gathered from Freddie that the relationship between the histrionic Patton and the legendary but increasingly egotistical Montgomery would need 'watching'.

But at Mostaganem in September he seemed to me very old and desiccated. Perhaps he was still keeping a low profile after his public disgrace in August when Eisenhower had relieved him of his command over the 'hospital incident'.

The assault landing at Salerno was only a few weeks away, and it was obvious that I was in no position to influence the plans which had already crystallised. I made it my business to weld my small band of British officers into a working team, to establish close relations with the Commander and staff of the British 10 Corps, and find out more about my American colleagues at Army headquarters.

I had much to learn about American procedures, and they had much to learn about battles. It was for me a startling change from those easy relationships within Eighth Army, cemented by disaster and by triumph, which by now had formed an indestructible matrix perfectly adapted to carry candid comment and communication in all directions. In my new surroundings I would have to remember that the British and the Americans were two nations divided by a common language.

A few days before the landing, there was a final presentation of plans by the corps commanders, with their divisional commanders at hand.

The event was in striking contrast to the many similar conferences I had attended in Eighth Army. General Mark Clark, the Army Commander, unlike Monty, did not seem to give a prominent lead. Certainly he presided, and his status demanded respect, but as far as the forthcoming battle was concerned he seemed to be too much in the hands of his staff. The scene was set, the objectives stated and the tactics explained by the head of G3, Brigadier-General Brann. This could of course be merely another way of achieving the object of informing subordinate commanders of the tasks they had to achieve. But it entirely lacked the conviction and the psychological urge that permeated Monty's performances.

The United States Corps Commander, General Dawley, took the floor : he seemed to be completely dominated by his staff. The thought 'ventriloquist's dummy' flashed through my mind.

He was followed by General Dick McCreery. Monty disparaged McCreery, in my view unjustifiably. As the British Corps Commander in Mark Clark's American Army I thought his performance was excellent. He certainly made a very good impression on his audiences, both British and American, when he followed General Dawley at the pre-Salerno briefing. We all felt that he had worked out very firmly in his own mind how his corps battle should develop after the assault landing, and clearly he was not in the hands of his staff. This impression remained with me as the battles continued.

It was not easy to get to know Dick McCreery as by temperament he was reserved, and he spoke very quietly in a strange hesitant way. When deeply concerned over some problem, he would lower his voice almost to a whisper; to his staff and to others this was a well-known warning signal. During that winter of 1943 he and I had too many whispering sessions together, when he was critical of the conduct of the Army battle.

I shall never forget an alarming scene much later in the campaign when, with Al Gruenther, I had gone to see him to discuss the Rapido river crossing operation, in which the Americans were to put in the main assault, and the British 10 Corps, fortunately, only a diversionary feint. As we left, Dick McCreery's voice, still a whisper but choked with emotion followed us to our jeep : 'It's not on! Tell your Army Commander he will have a disaster.' And for the Americans, disaster it was;

Preparing for the Landings in Sicily. Monty with Vice-Admiral Ramsay, Air Marshal Harry Broadhurst and Freddie de Guingand.

Monty's staff in Malta, July 1943. Author, now BGS (Operations) bareheaded in second row.

Victory in Sicily. Monty with Harry Broadhurst, Freddie de Guingand and Miles Graham.

(Above) General Alexander at the crisis of Salerno. A 'Glyndebourne' picnic with the Author, now Deputy Chief of Staff (British) in the US Fifth Army.

Monty, deprived of the opportunity of 'rescuing' the US Fifth Army, meets Mark Clark.

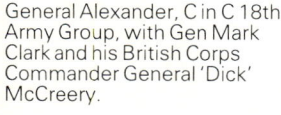

General Alexander, C in C 18th Army Group, with Gen Mark Clark and his British Corps Commander General 'Dick' McCreery.

their casualties were appalling, leading eventually to a Congressional investigation.

Meanwhile on 10th September 1943 at first light I viewed the assault landing at Salerno from the bridge of the US warship *Ancon*, which was Fifth Army's headquarters ship. The operation seemed to go more or less according to plan. It soon became clear that 10 Corps had secured its initial objectives, but that the situation on the US Corps front was unsatisfactory. Their divisions had never been in battle before, and I doubted whether they had received the vigorous and imaginative training that Eighth Army had received from Monty before Alamein. I told General Mark Clark that I would visit the beach-head at first light on D + 1, and I spent most of that day going round the various headquarters of Dick McCreery's corps. Although casualties had been heavier than expected, he was confident that his situation was under control.

Shelling was not intense, and at the headquarters of the British divisions I was told that although casualties had been high, objectives had generally been achieved. I visited the headquarters of our brigades and found this to be so. At General Dawley's headquarters there was an eerie lack of information, and I was told that the forward units were having 'a bad time'.

As dusk approached, I returned to the beach where my American landing craft was waiting with two young American sailors. *Ancon* was standing off about two miles away. After ten minutes it seemed to me that we were making no progress and, after a closer look I said to the lads, '*Ancon* is moving out and we shall never catch her'. I hadn't a toothbrush with me and my sandwiches had gone at midday. As darkness was falling we steered towards a US minesweeper. On board I told the captain of my predicament : 'We're going to get the hell outa here to avoid the bombing,' he said, 'but we can give you some chow.'

The American ration stew, with its pronounced synthetic taste, went down very well. I told them I must stay in the bay to connect with *Ancon* in the morning : how was this to be done? They advised me to try the HQ ship of Admiral Connolly who was supporting the US Corps landing. It was a dark night and lights were forbidden, but we made it. The Admiral was most welcoming : 'We've got about thirty "refugees" already,' he said, 'but we can certainly take another.'

After all, in American eyes, I was a 'Brigadier-General'!

I spent the night on a narrow shelf in their wardroom which was packed with miscellaneous bodies. The Luftwaffe bombed us repeatedly, but I slept on, despite the sensation that our destroyer appeared to become airborne every time a bomb landed nearby. The next morning *Ancon* reappeared: I had never been warned that she might leave the bay: but there were no apologies.

Soon after the assault, General Mark Clark decided that he must get a small headquarters ashore; we set up shop in some bushes about 1,000 metres from the sea, and spent an uncomfortable time there under German mortar fire. There were no 'facilities' other than a bottle of whisky which a member of my small staff had thoughtfully brought with him. As an indication of our primitive conditions, I can still recall Mark Clark's stentorian voice echoing across the bay at first light next morning: 'Chaney [his negro batman], Chaney, have you found anywhere for me to crap?'

Until that moment I had supposed that Army Commanders were decently reticent in these matters!

The situation was not only becoming distinctly uncomfortable as shells and mortar bombs fell alarmingly close, but it also indicated to my mind a loss of dignity by a senior headquarters. With one of my colonels, I spent another fitful night in a shallow scrape under a bush. The battle in the American sector was not going at all well. Dick McCreery, whom I visited frequently, started whispering: quite rightly he was alarmed. Some of the American soldiers, green as they were, were giving way under fierce German counter-attack. Al Gruenther, slightly paler in the face than usual, but with his acute brain operating at a hundred per cent despite lack of sleep, kept me fully informed of the critical situation. Suddenly there was a considerable flurry in our headquarters patch, a jeep appeared in a cloud of dust and Mark Clark with an ADC went off at high speed towards the front line, which by now was uncomfortably close. I heard the tale soon afterward. Mark Clark had driven right up to a forward battalion which had started to give way, and had personally restored the situation. A courageous feat of leadership; but Monty, I am sure, would have said: 'Such things should never happen.'

The bridgehead nevertheless still remained insecure; plans were therefore made to bring in 82nd Airborne Division, and a call was sent for heavy bombardment by warships. Al Gruenther summoned me to a late night conference with Mark Clark, at which possible evacuation was discussed. Should the headquarters ship, which had withdrawn to Palermo, be called back? Remembering Dunkirk and Auchinleck's Gazala retreat, I said 'yes'. The move could be ordered secretly, and *Ancon* could keep below the skyline, just in case. . . . The 82nd came in; huge shells from the warships whistled overhead to a road junction in the enemy area which, no doubt, the Germans avoided; we remained in our patch, and the threat seemed to diminish. The next day General Alexander, deeply concerned no doubt about the critical news, arrived to see us; I was sent to meet him on the beach. It has often been said that his mere arrival at a crisis was in some mysterious way worth an extra division, and I certainly felt it on this occasion. To my surprise he said, as we walked up the beach: 'I've had no lunch yet, so we'll have that now.' I hadn't either; so we sat down and had a picnic: it could have been Glyndebourne! After a few bites he said: 'What's the situation here?'

I replied: 'I think the crisis is over: it was very tricky yesterday.'

We discussed the fighting: I told him about Mark Clark's feat, and the arrival of 82nd Airborne Division, but had to admit I could not understand why the Germans hadn't tried harder to kick us into the sea.

After that, normality gradually took over; a proper headquarters was established with vehicles in great profusion. Our standard of living, which in the beachhead had plummeted far below anything I had ever experienced in Eighth Army, now rose to absurd heights. Our 'senior officers' mess' was accommodated in an excellent hut complete with Viennese chef; a column of heavy lorries miles long was needed to move Army HQ! In my Eighth Army caravan, primitive by American standards, I found a case of whisky 'with the compliments of the Army Commander'. This was indeed a friendly gesture, and I and my staff much enjoyed it. But how to reciprocate? A substantive major, temporary brigadier with most of his pay in London, had no great financial reserves to dig into. I consulted Al Gruenther, so sympathetic and wise, and the outcome was a NAAFI carton of Colman's mustard, which it was said the Army Commander always relished!

It was I suppose hardly surprising that the procedures to which I now had to adapt myself seemed excessively laborious. In Eighth Army's headquarters, almost everything had been done by word of mouth.

In a letter to my mother, I wrote :

It is a most interesting experience serving in an American Army. Their ways are different, but we can teach them a lot about making war. I have managed to sell them some ideas, and they have adopted some of the Eighth Army's systems. Looking back now, I can appreciate how extremely efficient and well-organised we were : things were done with the minimum of fuss or paper and in about half the time it takes here. In this job I have been able to see quite a lot of the fighting, much more than in Eighth Army . . .

[This was an understatement of the Salerno landing.]

General Montgomery sent me a little book of his called 'Higher Command in War' with the following inscription :

'To Brigadier Richardson, who has served on the staff of HQ Eighth Army during months of hard and victorious fighting and whose good work and devotion to duty have contributed largely to the victories we have gained.'

'Very nice of him,' I say.

In this pamphlet, and I have it still, he had written :

A commander must train his staff and his subordinate commanders to work and act on verbal orders or instructions.

There is far too much paper in circulation in the Army as a whole; no commander can have time to read all this paper and also to do his job properly. Much of the paper in circulation is not read; much of it is not worth reading.

This was good Monty stuff !

I found that American staff work, which I had supposed would be extremely slick, laboured under a system by which any executive instruction – and perhaps wrongly I considered myself entitled to issue such after consultation – had to be 'authenticated by the Adjutant General'. By the time this clumsy procedure could be completed, the instruction would be worthless. Perhaps the head of G3 could have helped me through this jungle, but my relations with him were difficult; so I transacted business either through Al Gruenther, a process which was always enjoyable and effective, or through the lieutenant-colonel G3, who after the war became a 'four-star' general. To overcome the 'log jam', I set up a personal radio link between myself and the Chief of Staff of 10 Corps.

My relations with the US Air Force on the other hand were very easy. The Army/Air interface had not been developed as we had in North Africa and, during the critical days after the landing, I found myself co-ordinating US Air Force plans with the Fifth Army's ground activity. Colonel Darcy, of the US Air Force, was a most effective and charming colleague, and we frequently found ourselves writing notes at midnight amongst the bushes of the Salerno beachhead.

There were some very capable British officers in the G(Air) branch at that time. I saw a lot of Major John Hare, the future Viscount Blakenham, a modest reliable officer, with whom it was a delight to work. Another quick and skilful operator was Major Jack Profumo, a future War Minister.

I did not know then that great efforts were being made by General Alexander to encourage Monty to 'rescue' us by an offensive by Eighth Army. So I was surprised when, on about 15th September, after our situation ceased to be critical, Al sent for me to show me a 'cocky' letter sent to my new Army Commander by my old chief :

'Say, Charles,' said Al, 'how am I going to handle this? The Army Commander won't like it.'

The tone of the message was very condescending : sympathy was expressed for our dire plight, and the hope that we might hang on until Eighth Army joined up with us. Monty relished the role of 'saviour' !

I said : 'I should just give him the gist of it, if I were you.' General Mark Clark too had his *amour propre* !

At the beginning of October we captured Naples, and for a time I and my American friends thought, 'We're on our way.' I took a few hours off : a close sapper friend, Henley Dowson, who had been commissioned with me in 1928 was the Deputy Director of Survey, providing maps both for the Americans and ourselves. My letter home on 5th October 1943 reveals a much more relaxed situation :

We are having an interesting time and since the crisis I have been less busy. I took a morning off with Henley Dowson. We went to Ravello in the hills above Amalfi – a most beautiful place with a lovely villa. We had a very reasonable lunch and an excellent bottle of white wine – minestrone soup, meat and peas and beans, grapes and apples and walnuts. Yesterday I went into Naples. It has been frightfully battered by the

bombing and by German demolition. On the way back I visited the ruins
of Pompeii. Unfortunately they have been damaged a bit by our bombing; some of the houses (2,000 years old) are complete with paintings,
plumbing and furniture and cooking pots, in good condition. I am getting
very tired of American food. It is frightfully synthetic and, once the
novelty has worn off, it is very monotonous. Nor can I get accustomed
to eating bacon with golden syrup, and stew with plum pudding. I have
just finished 'The Years of Endurance' by Arthur Bryant. Most excellent,
and a wonderful parallel between 1795 and now, even down to operations in Sicily and Naples. Unfortunately there is no Lady Hamilton
waiting for us in Naples !

Despite the capture of Naples it gradually became all too obvious that
we were getting bogged down; Eighth Army was doing no better.
Prominent in this boggy situation was 56th Division, commanded by
Major-General G. W. R. Templer. At that time I hardly knew him,
and on the first occasion I saw him – we were fellow passengers in a
Dakota – I didn't like the look of him at all ! But during those horrible
winter months, when his division was deployed on the tops of hills facing
the Cassino Monastery, I visited him frequently and was full of
admiration for his staunch spirit.

Conditions were appalling : in order to get ammunition up to the
infantry posts on the snowy hill-tops, a light anti-aircraft regiment had
to be re-organised as human porters to supplement the pack mules. I was
convinced that until spring came little could be achieved, and I felt sure
he knew that himself. Yet, never daunted, he was constantly looking for
means to improve his divisional position and achieve some modest
success. I learnt afterwards that he was one of Monty's young generals,
and had risen to lieutenant-general in the UK; he had reverted to
major-general to gain the experience of commanding a division. I owed
much to him in my later career.

It was to break the deadlock on the Cassino line dominated by the
Monastery, that an outflanking movement by sea with a landing at
Anzio was first conceived. We were all swept into a maelstrom of
strategic argument, with Churchill's influence from Marrakesh power-
fully at work. The Anzio landing was the only operation since Dunkirk
which I was convinced from the start would never succeed. This conviction started weeks before the assault and grew stronger and stronger
as D-day approached. At quite an early stage, the very competent

American Intelligence colonel, affectionately known to us as 'Crystal Ball', had made a study of the probable German reaction to the landing; eventually he showed me a detailed timetable of the enemy divisions that could arrive successively at Anzio. At the time I suspected it came from Ultra. I now know that it was Major-General Terence Airey, my old boss in SOE, now Alexander's Intelligence Chief, who, from Ultra messages received at Caserta, produced this remarkably accurate prediction. From this assessment, it was quite clear that the comparatively small Anglo-American force, restricted in size by the diversion of landing craft from the Mediterranean to the UK for the 'Second Front', would be bottled up after a few days unless the main German line at Cassino broke under the effect of a strong frontal attack combined with a serious threat to its rear. But why should it break? Was the amphibious threat serious enough?

But in the Fifth Army's plan for the Anzio landing there had never been any intention of our force pushing inland to threaten the main German lines of communication. General Lucas, the American corps commander who seemed to me to be very defensively minded, ruled this out because of his lack of armour, and General Mark Clark accepted it. At his presentation, he reiterated that he was going to occupy his 'goose eggs', i.e., defensive positions, on the bridgehead line, and hold them. It was quite clear to me that this was in accord with his mentality; he was no Patton! Nothing could be done to bring in sufficient armour because of the limitation of landing craft. I pressed that at least some sort of light mobile force should be organised to advance inland, create what threat it could and then withdraw into the bridgehead. This was considered impracticable.

D-day came; the landing on 22nd January 1944 was almost unopposed: enemy reinforcements arrived precisely as forecast and the bridgehead was duly bottled up. Churchill's 'wild cat hurled ashore' became a 'stranded whale'. Later Mark Clark sent me up there for a fortnight to show the interest of Army headquarters in the plight of those besieged. My visits there were indeed most uncomfortable: Constant shelling in a tight perimeter, and the nearer one was to the port the worse it became. Later, when General Truscott took over at Anzio, the situation improved greatly. To me he seemed to be a general who really understood the battle.

Two days after the Anzio landing, the first attack on Monte Cassino by II US Corps took place. It was unsuccessful. We were now hopelessly held up on the Cassino line, with the Anzio force about to be besieged and rendered impotent.

On 16th February the second attempt at Cassino, under General Freyberg, was made. I had always been doubtful about the effect of the United States strategic bombers, but General Freyberg had insisted on having them used for the initial bombardment. When with General Alexander and my Army Commander I watched them at work, with many bombs falling wide of the target, I was even less impressed. Heavy casualties were incurred and nothing decisive was achieved by the operation. Further weeks were to go by before German resistance was finally overcome.

During 1944 we had become a very international army which included Indians, New Zealanders, Brazilians, as well as the French Corps under General Juin. The latter were mostly Moroccan *Goumiers*, and they achieved notable successes in the high Apennine country on our Eastern flank. General de Gaulle came to visit them, and General Mark Clark invited ten of us to dine. Colonel Charles Saltzmann, the 'Secretary to the General Staff', who spoke good French and was a very efficient and sophisticated war-time soldier, took immense pains to make the dinner party a success : the visit was well-timed since Juin had convincingly maintained *la gloire de la France*. De Gaulle arrived, and individually we were presented. I noticed a cold damp hand and an expression of haughty disdain. Throughout the evening, brought prematurely to a close, he was the wettest blanket that I had ever experienced! Why? Surely it was an opportunity to 'make friends and influence people', and the honour of France was not at stake !

Although by now there were hopes that the Italian campaign might make some progress and we were confident that Hitler would sooner or later be defeated, it was clear that Italy would remain a secondary theatre, and that the 'Second Front' was to be the key factor in achieving victory. So I was delighted to find myself ordered at short notice in March to report to the headquarters of 21 Army Group in London and thus rejoin my old friends, who were busily planning the Normandy invasion. I was to be Brigadier (Plans).

I had made some real pals amongst the Americans, and had been greatly impressed with the speed with which they learnt from harsh experience. They had started a lap behind us, but in under a year I reckoned that they had caught us up. In efficiency we were now equally matched.

Wearing the ribbon of the United States Legion of Merit, I was flown from Casablanca to Prestwick to become a 'Monty man' once more.

CHAPTER TEN

Second Front

It was good to be back amongst old friends : Freddie, Bill and David. There was also a newcomer, 'Bert' Herbert, who had survived the purge instituted by Monty on his arrival in London to take over 21 Army Group. This was the process, now familiar to us all, by which those whom Monty designated as 'quite useless' were removed to other appointments, and those whom he called 'my own chaps' were inserted. 'Bert' left us in no doubt that those who had gone were better employed elsewhere; but the process, somewhat irregular, did not gain friends for Monty. Field Marshal Alanbrooke stopped it immediately the war ceased.

Monty always insisted quite rightly that planning for an operation must be directed by the commander responsible for carrying it out, and that he must be appointed sufficiently early to make this possible.

General Frederick Morgan of COSSAC and his staff, who, for many months, had been working in London on Overlord, had not the profound professional expertise of Montgomery and were not capable of producing a viable operational plan. Nevertheless in the perspective of history, it would be wrong not to recognise many of the great achievements of Combined Operations Headquarters and COSSAC in the logistic field, which had had to be initiated long before any possible future commander could have been appointed. Thus we, the 'Monty gang', became the immediate beneficiaries of the Mulberry harbour, the Pluto oil pipe line, the special assault equipments of General Hobart's 79th Armoured Division, the beach intelligence reports brought back by naval and marine parties, and many other aids.

I reported for duty at St Paul's School on 1st April 1944. We were housed very conveniently in the flats at Latymer Court opposite the school. Freddie told me that after a great deal of bitter argument, Monty's outline plan for the invasion, markedly different to that worked up by the COSSAC planners in London, had been finally accepted.

Already the vast invasion armies were beginning to move to their concentration areas, where they would later take part in exercises designed to test the orderliness, timings, security, and logistic arrangements for their moves to the ports of embarkation.

On 7th April Monty, with his staff, gave his first presentation of the master plan in the presence of Brooke, Portal, Cunningham and Eisenhower, with the other Allied commanders and their staffs. Monty's address, which carried me back to the talk he had given us preparatory to Alamein, was as always crystal clear and supremely confident.

The phase lines, which had in fact been drawn on the vast map not by Monty but very roughly by his Military Assistant, were shown to indicate where the Allied Forces might be by various dates. In many historical investigations into the meaning of these phase lines, and their repercussions on the credit due to Monty for the overall success of the invasion, there have been some theorists, inexperienced in the conduct of battle, who have attempted to maintain that they constituted firm guarantees that such territory would have been gained by the due dates and hence that Monty failed in his objectives. This is nonsense. They were never more than 'best guesses' on which logistic and airfield planning could be based; those plans, like others involved, were also subject to modification as operations proceeded.

Monty, in his ninety-minute talk, described how he expected Rommel to react, based on Bill Williams' intelligence estimate; then, phase by phase, he showed the build-up of our forces against the enemy. Finally he defined in very few words the tasks allocated to General Bradley's First US Army, and General Dempsey's Second British Army, fighting side by side; General Patton's Third US Army in a later phase was to pass through First US Army directed towards the Brittany and Loire ports. Though couched in his usual down-to-earth vocabulary, it was a brilliant exposition, which enormously impressed all of us who were there.

I found that I had acquired a very good team in G(Plans) Branch. It was our job to fill in all the details of the agreed outline plan, and to start examining possible future eventualties. For this purpose we had to consider the effect of our own build-up against the forecasts of enemy reinforcements, the terrain over which our advances would take place, the capability of captured ports to maintain our armies and air forces, and the likely development of the air battle.

In citing here some of the papers which we put before Freddie, many of which have now been unearthed and quoted by various historians, I am reminded of the French general who in a desperate retreat in World War I was found writing a meticulous order for an elaborate counter-attack; challenged as to his purpose, he replied: *'Mais, c'est pour l'histoire.'*

This was not the purpose of G(Plans) 21 Army Group! In our appreciations of the development of operations, we strove to anticipate and influence the course of future events beyond the prevision of our Commander-in-Chief, knowing that he, having set the immediate pattern, would necessarily have to concentrate on its rigorous implementation. From our long association with him, Freddie and I knew that he would not engage himself, even if he had the time, in hypothetical speculation; yet long-term anticipation was essential if the vast resources at his command were to be marshalled in such a way as to meet likely developments. This was our purpose.

On 8th May, four weeks before the landings, we published a strategic appreciation* of the possible development of operations, based on the outline plan we had already heard in April. After intensive discussion, my staff had produced a very thorough study. The main points which strike the reader now, forty years on, are:

The Emphasis on the Normandy 'Bocage': This terrain was a chequer board of very small fields each surrounded by tree-lined hedges on banks. The bocage had been closely studied from air photographs, and I had had many discussions on methods to overcome it with my US Deputy Colonel 'Tic' Bonesteel. Monty had drawn attention to it in the presentation of his plan at St Paul's. Nevertheless it proved very difficult for both armies; and General Collins, Commander of VII US Corps, compared it to the obstacles he had experienced in jungle warfare in the South Pacific.

The likelihood that the enemy build up would slow down our progress by D + 14, with the danger of losing the initiative: In the event, it was on D + 16 (22 June) that Monty warned us that the front was becoming 'glued up'. Our situation then had been rendered doubly dangerous by bad weather, which had severely delayed our build-up. Nevertheless Monty took immediate decisions to remove the glue!

Our ability to break through the German cordon would not occur

* PRO Ref WO205/118.

until D + 30 at the earliest: This in fact did not occur until
D + 54 (end of July). When that moment came, the effect was
overwhelming.

The document was issued to both Armies and in a covering letter I
wrote : 'With regard to the outline of action at Part IV, this represents
the Commander-in-Chief's intentions as far as they can be formulated
at this stage. Whether operations will develop on these lines must of
course depend on our own and the enemy situation, which cannot be
predicted accurately at the present moment.' This was four weeks before
the assault. The conclusions were :

The type of country immediately South of the initial bridgehead does
not favour a rapid advance. The Allied build-up relative to the estimated
German build-up indicates that a period may supervene round about
D + 14, when there will be a grave risk of operations stabilising on a line
which gives the Germans advantages in defence. The greatest energy and
initiative will be required at this period to ensure the enemy is not
allowed to stabilise his defence.

Once through the difficult bocage country, greater possibilities for
manoeuvre and for the use of armour begin to appear. Our aim during
this period should be to contain the maximum enemy forces facing the
Eastern flank of the bridgehead, and to thrust rapidly towards Rennes
(80 miles East of Quiberon Bay). [See map on page 185]

On reaching Rennes our main thrust should be towards Vannes (near
Quiberon Bay) but diversionary thrusts with the maximum use of decep-
tion should be employed to persuade the enemy that our objective is
Nantes.

If, at this time, the enemy weakens his Eastern force to oppose us
North of Redon (40 miles South West of Rennes), a strong attack should
be launched towards the Seine.

The Quiberon Bay project offers great scope for surprise. Once the
bay is captured and provided constructional estimates are fulfilled, our
build-up should be assured for some time to come, and our Southern
flank can then be rested economically on the Loire.

For administrative reasons we should aim at securing the Seine ports
as early as possible. By alternative thrust towards the East and towards
the South West, we should be able to retain the initiative, reap the benefit
of interior lines, and keep the enemy moving his reserves from one flank
to the other.

The different supply systems of the British and American forces will
restrict the flexibility of our plans. Re-allocation of air support, an
alternative to the planned build-up and a move of the inter-Army
boundary provides the most practical means of influencing the weight
behind our alternate thrusts.

In the event, the overall development of operations followed very closely Monty's master plan; but we were all far too optimistic about the timings early in the battle; nevertheless the D + 90 phase line was achieved before the estimated date, despite great anxieties in the intervening periods.

Studies complementary to ours had been undertaken by the logistic planners assessing the capacities of ports and beaches, estimating the tonnages of ammunition, petrol, stores and supplies to be brought in, and the phasing in of transport units, workshops, hospitals, etc., together with the evacuation of reparable tanks and vehicles or their replacement from UK. Estimates of casualties had been made and personnel reinforcements organised.

These aspects of planning, which necessarily had to be conducted on a national rather than Allied basis, had gone ahead smoothly as far as we British were concerned. The task was in the able hands of Major-General Miles Graham, assisted by the admirable Colonel Oliver Poole, with whom I had previously established a close and cordial relationship in North Africa. They were a remarkable pair of gifted amateurs. Miles, a scholar of Eton, had served in the First World War in the Life Guards and won a Military Cross. He then had a successful career in industry. Rejoining in 1939, he had gone out with the First Cavalry Division (and their horses) to Palestine where he became Staff Captain to a seaside transit camp. Humorously he would boast that from the deep obscurity of that appointment, he became a major-general in 1944. Amusing and blithe in every situation, he had shrewd judgement and carried great responsibilities seemingly without effort. Much of the logistic detail he left to Oliver, the future Lord Poole, another Etonian who had served in the Life Guards in 1932–33 and had arrived in the Middle East with the Warwickshire Yeomanry in 1939. He also was a very popular, amusing, and talented member of the team, and our friendship continued long after the war.

In contrast to the logistic planning, the air plans seemed to present great problems, and Freddie asked me to concentrate on this aspect; it was no longer straightforward, as in those happy days with the Desert Air Force. The air power involved, American and British, was immense and was only equalled by the magnitude of the partisan interests and national philosophies which intruded into the problem. From January until March a bitter controversy had raged in British and American circles over the part to be played by the Heavy Bomber Forces. Were they to attack targets such as railways which were directly related to the invasion plan, or were they to continue attacking strategic targets, oil installations, industrial cities, etc. – deep in Germany, which some of the protagonists still claimed would achieve victory with no need for an invasion? We had thought that this controversy, in which 'Bomber' Harris was the principal advocate of the strategic target policy, had been settled at least on paper on 17th April 1944, when we had received a directive from Eisenhower. But tag ends of the dispute continued right up to D-day. Once the invasion had taken place, strategic obsessions were for a time cast aside; and some, but not all Commanders-in-Chief concentrated on the critical actualities of the battle.

But pre-D-day, an urgent question which had greatly concerned us was the policy to be followed over the bombing of the Seine bridges. In the first phase of the land operations the Seine was to us a godsend, in that any German reinforcements that might be sent from NE France to contain our bridgehead would have to cross that river. Moreover it was a major aim of the Deception Plan, successful as it proved, to convince Hitler that a second landing would take place in the Pas de Calais. Thereby we hoped that substantial German forces would be retained there and not be launched in counter-attack against our vulnerable bridgehead in Normandy. In the event, German reinforcing divisions were retained there for more than four weeks to meet the imaginary threat.

It was obvious that the RAF's attacks on targets related to the assault must be so woven into the total air plan of bombardment as not to point conclusively to a landing in Normandy. Sporadic at first, and accompanied by attacks in the Pas de Calais area, they must be increased in severity as D-day approached. It was hoped that all the Seine bridges might be destroyed immediately before the invasion.

However, a major inter-service problem then arose. The RAF, led by Mary Coningham, uncompromisingly took the position that daylight attack by fighter bombers on railway bridges defended by anti-aircraft guns was not an acceptable task for the air forces. I was engaged in repeated sessions with the Senior Air Staff Officer of our Tactical Air Force to press home our requirement: meanwhile Freddie was exerting pressure on a higher level. It appeared to be an impasse, until eventually the RAF accepted that one of the bridges should be attacked as an experiment, to see how hazardous it might be. The attack was completely successful and the pilots survived. After that, somewhat late in the day, the comprehensive plan was launched, achieving excellent results by D − 1, and contributing greatly to the success of the armies' operations.

On 15th May, Monty gave his final briefing in St Paul's School: in addition to the previous audience there were present King George VI, and Churchill, who had come for part of the time on 7th April. It was an unforgettable experience. Soon after that we left London and moved to the Portsmouth area, adjacent to Southwick House, the Naval headquarters for the invasion.

At the end of May all the arrangements of the three armies were well in hand. The exercises in the concentration areas had gone well; they included a study of the arrangements for postponement of the assault, if bad weather supervened. It became evident that the complexity was such that there was very little latitude in the date of D-day, if security was to be maintained.

For a whole week, Monty visited the assaulting formations, British and American, 'binging up' their officers both senior and junior; the reaction even from the Americans was terrific. We too shared their confidence.

At 21 Army Group headquarters, however, there was still a most important item outstanding, the air plan for the first forty-eight hours of the assault.

In view of all the controversies which had raged for so long in Air Force circles, it was hardly surprising, but nevertheless disgraceful, that the pre-planned air bombardment in close support of the D-day landings was not decided until a dangerously late hour just before the assault. That it was finally decided was due mainly to David Belchem and a young American brigadier-general. David chaired an overlarge meeting at which every air force, British and American was represented, and he asked me to help him; I recollect over twenty officers round the table. At length after many hours of argument in which the American brigadier-general ably supported us, an agreed plan for the use of the immense air power available was finally settled in precise detail.

At Southwick House, as the fifth of June approached, the old Eighth Army team, with their communications installed and their situation maps in readiness, waited for the final decision to launch the invasion.

At Southwick House Naval HQ for the Normandy landings: the invasion chart.

Troops landing on the Normandy beaches.

Problems with the C in C Allie Expeditionary Air Force, Air-Marshal Sir Trafford Leigh-Mallory, seen here with Generals Bradley, Montgomery and Dempsey.

The Prime Minister visits the Normandy front, and observ an air battle with Generals Dempsey and O'Connor.

The Battle of Arnhem: sapp paratroops, captured at Arnhem, escape and row down the Rhine to the Nijmegen bridge to rejoin th units.

The tension was not unlike that before Alamein, but there was no relaxation : opportunities for a lunch in Alexandria were not forthcoming! Freddie, somewhat exhausted physically by ill-health and the effects of the aeroplane crash, and mentally by coping for two years with his exacting chief, was showing some signs of wear and tear. Nevertheless as always he rose to the occasion, and kept us fully in touch with the progress of decisions at the highest level, particularly over the weather. On 6th June after a 24-hour postponement, there was universal relief that the great enterprise, so long discussed, planned and prepared was to go ahead.

In Monty's veteran team at 21 Army group, confidence in the outcome was strengthened by memories of the assault on Sicily; but the successes on the British and Canadian fronts by $D + 1$ and the achievement of so great a degree of tactical surprise were beyond our expectations. Once again Rommel, as at Alamein, was absent on leave in Germany when the first assault waves landed. The Germans had estimated that no assault was likely in the sea conditions then obtaining. By nightfall 156,000 Allied troops had been put ashore. By $D + 3$, the most critical stage of the operation, when German counter-attacks could have driven us into the sea, was successfully passed. Rommel had missed his opportunity! Only at Omaha was the position critical because of serious casualties. Monty landed in France on $D + 1$ and under his direction General Bradley soon restored that situation.

On $D - 2$, Freddie had asked me to leave Southwick House and go to Bentley Priory at Stanmore, the headquarters of the Allied Expeditionary Air Forces under Air Chief Marshal Sir Trafford Leigh-Mallory, to be Monty's representative there, and to ensure as far as possible that the requirements of air support of the land forces would be met. As soon as I had set up my caravan in the grounds and established communications with HQ 21 Army Group, I found the situation very strange indeed. All the Commanders-in-Chief, both American and British, and all the Air Forces, heavy bomber, coastal, fighter and tactical were located there, and Leigh-Mallory was charged with the almost impossible task of coordinating their activities. Each one of them revelled in the near autonomy which he had so far enjoyed : the heavy bomber forces acting under the general direction of the joint chiefs of staff, and the tactical air forces acting almost independently and unaccustomed as yet to working intimately with their associated armies, except for those who had learnt these techniques in Africa and Italy. Leigh-Mallory's experience had been in Fighter Command, and in this group he was badly placed. By contrast many in this collection of 'barons' which included Spaatz, Tedder, Anderson, Vandenberg, Doolittle, Brereton, Harris, Sholto Douglas, Lloyd and Coningham were more experienced in the spheres either of tactical support or of heavy bombing.

Side by side with this incomparable collection of prima donnas, was Solly Zuckerman, whose scientific specialisation had, I understood, been the sexual habits of apes. I was unaware that he had already built up a high reputation in the previous year as an operational researcher in the use of air power, and had exerted a powerful and valuable influence on the policies of the Allied Expeditionary Air Force. In this head-quarters, he had the advantage of being personally uncommitted to any of the service prejudices which influenced his colleagues. He was scientifically objective and articulate, but could also communicate easily with laymen with tact and humour. I noticed that he was on good terms with Tedder, had established a dominant influence over Leigh-Mallory and that the prima donnas tended to listen to him. I decided that my best chance of success was to discuss Monty's requirements with him privately before the formal 11 o'clock meeting of all the 'Air Barons', at which tasks were assigned. Although controversy still abounded in the higher reaches of the air hierarchy, and were to lead to much frustration for Monty and for Leigh-Mallory in the ensuing weeks, this procedure did ensure that Monty's daily requirements of tactical air support were duly met during the time I was there.

However the atmosphere was far from congenial. Leigh-Mallory seemed genuinely keen to obtain support for the Army when needed, but he was in no position to demand compliance from those barons who controlled the resources to provide it. This imperfect arrangement was to create many difficulties thereafter, particularly with Mary Coning-ham who was determined not to permit any dimunition of his authority; moreover his relationship with Monty had for a long time been abrasive.

On D + 2 of the invasion I was called upon by Leigh-Mallory to brief King George VI, Winston Churchill and Field Marshal Smuts on the progress of the invasion. Apart from the disaster on Omaha beach in the United States sector, I was able to report that the battle was progressing satisfactorily. In a scrappy letter sent home I wrote that 'the King was silent, Winston did not say much, but Smuts was extremely inquisitive'. A lasting memory is of the extraordinarily soft, silky hand of our rugged Prime Minister as he greeted me.

On D + 5, I was able to report to the assembled barons that the build-up of the Allied armies was up to schedule, sixteen divisions having been landed. They were facing fourteen enemy divisions, three less than had been expected. British casualties were estimated at 6,600. That evening a meeting took place to consider Monty's request for 1st Airborne Division to be dropped on 13th June at Evrecy, SW of Caen behind the German lines, in order to assist 7th Armoured Division in the encirclement of German panzer troops in that area. Leigh-Mallory opposed it strongly as likely to be very expensive. It could not take place by day, as required by the Commander 1st Airborne Division, as the area was too heavily defended, and an operation by night would involve flying over the Allied fleet, who could not guarantee that they would hold their AA fire. Leigh-Mallory's refusal, conveyed to Monty by signal rather than by a personal visit, caused a deterioration in their personal relations which was not repaired for several weeks. He demanded that Leigh-Mallory should fly over to see him !

On 13th June the airborne plan was abandoned, and Monty signalled to Freddie that a visit by Leigh-Mallory was no longer necessary. Meanwhile the thrust of 7th Armoured Division towards Evrecy had failed. At Stanmore the atmosphere was tense. On the next day I reported that the enemy's resistance had 'stiffened on all fronts' and gave a sober and detailed account of the situation throughout the US and British fronts. Casualties were estimated as 12,000 British and 14,000 US. Thirteen thousand prisoners of war had been taken. However, Mary Coningham appeared to think that the situation before Caen, which Monty certainly had hoped to capture earlier, was critical, and this view was supported by Tedder who spoke of a 'dangerous crisis'. For my part, although fully aware that our operations were not as successful as we had hoped, I had full confidence in the outcome and said so. Coningham and Tedder were unconvinced.

However, this unnecessary panic, perhaps artificially created by those who had no faith in Monty, had one useful result : a visit by Leigh-Mallory to Monty's Tac HQ, bearing with him an offer to provide Bomber Command, 8th United States Air Force (heavy bombers) and all available medium bombers to support an attack on Caen by General Dempsey's Second Army. However, no sooner had a team of Staff officers been sent out to arrange the details with Second Army, than the whole project was peremptorily called off by Mary Coningham supported by Tedder. After a briefing by Monty, Leigh-Mallory returned to Stanmore where I was glad to hear him announce that my appreciation of the military situation at the conference on the previous day had been a truer picture than the more alarming appreciation given by Air Marshal Coningham.

Although the intervention of heavy bombers had aborted, the idea that such a proposition could be contemplated, even by those who still attached higher priority to attacks on oil installations and industrial targets, was to bear fruit at a later date. After some days in this strange gathering where sharp controversy could spring up at the drop of a hat, it was a relief to return to 21 Army Group's headquarters at Southwick House where the more relevant land battle was making good but not spectacular progress. After the very close contact with the battle which I had had in Eighth Army and in the Fifth US Army, it was frustrating to have to wait week after week in Southwick House and merely observe on a map the critical scene across the Channel. However we had plenty to do and on 16th June my planning staff were busily engaged on another study in which we examined the possibility of not waiting for the capture of the Brittany ports but instead of thrusting eastwards towards the Seine, with the American wing being used in the south to cut the enemy's escape route south of Paris. Freddie highly approved of this plan, named Lucky Strike, and recommended it to Monty. At that time we thought we might reach the Seine by mid-July. But all this was over-optimistic, and in the event it was not until the middle of August that Monty's strategy culminated in the encirclement of an enormous German force in the Falaise pocket and, in the south, the wide American sweep by Patton towards Paris.

Eventually 21 Army Group Headquarters moved to Normandy. Shortly afterwards to our surprise, a glut of Camembert cheeses came to hand. Bill Williams suggested that the Planning Staff should immediately publish a *Cheese Guide to NW Europe* emphasising important strategic objectives for the gourmet!

However, there were more important tasks confronting me! One of these concerned the Army/Air set-up in the headquarters of Second Army commanded by General Dempsey. There, many of the Army and Air Staff officers concerned had not had the experience of the Mediterranean campaigns: co-operation was ineffective, particularly with the controversial and unhelpful influence of Mary Coningham permeating down the line from the top. I was sent by Monty to stay at that head-quarters, and 'sort it out'. During the week I was there I found that all I had to do was to create the same system of consultation and generate the same mutual confidence that we had enjoyed with the RAF in North Africa. Forty years later, I can now confess that the idea occurred to me that if I played my cards right I might be invited to become Second Army's Chief of Staff, and thus find myself a major-general. But this was not to be for another ten years!

I would have liked working for General Dempsey. His personality was quite different to that of Horrocks. When discussing air problems with him, I felt I was in the presence of a very intelligent, much admired headmaster! He was very courteous and self-effacing, but always imperturbable.

Monty's plan for keeping the British 'Hinge' firm in the neighbour-hood of Caen, drawing the enemy's armour to that area, and then bursting through with the Americans on our western flank and sweeping the enemy forces up against the Seine, had been maintained throughout. However the slow progress in the British sector, where objectives were laid down and all too frequently were not fully achieved, worried us all. Freddie, who was a target for the persistent criticism of his master which arrived from many directions, was worried more than any of us.

Eventually a major attack on 7th July to capture Caen was planned some forty-eight hours ahead, involving the Canadians and two British divisions. RAF Bomber Command, for the first time in history, was to participate in the initial bombardment. This possibility had been under discussion at the highest levels for some time. I was sent with the Chief of Staff of the Canadian Army, Brigadier Charles Mann, to organise this unique co-operation. We reported to my old haunt at Stanmore where the barons were installed as before, with Solly in attendance. I explained the proposition to him, and we went in to the formal morn-ing meeting. I put before them Monty's case for the use of heavy bombers, and was not greatly surprised when, after some desultory discussion under Leigh-Mallory's chairmanship, the subject was dropped without any decision; the conference then turned its attention to strategic targets and broke up at midday. There were only thirty-six hours left before our battle was due to start. Solly, as always, had been helpful, but he seemed to me somewhat unenthusiastic over the plan. I spoke to Tedder: 'General Montgomery's battle will start in thirty-six hours and I must have a decision. How do I get one?'

'You had better go and see Air Marshal Harris at his headquarters.'

So off we went to High Wycombe where 'Connie' Constantine, Deputy to the senior Air Staff officer, met us. We told him the story. By this time our 'Script' which I had recited to the 'Barons' was becoming somewhat dog-eared. However he realised that we were in earnest and was determined to help. So he sent us to see the great 'Bomber' Harris himself.

A solid figure with an inscrutable expression sat behind a large desk: 'What do you want?' he said.

'We want your heavy bombers to bomb German defences, immediately before our attack is launched,' I said. I then described the area of the attack and outlined the Army plan and timings. He pressed a switch and said:

'Send me Air Vice-Marshal Bennett.'

Bennett was the commander of Bomber Command's Pathfinders; it was their task to navigate with great accuracy and drop their special bombs with coloured markings precisely on target. The other bombers following closely behind, then released their bombs on the targets illuminated by coloured flares.

'Richardson, tell Bennett your story,' said the C-in-C.

For the fourth time I repeated our well-worn script.

'Can you do it?' said the C-in-C to Bennett.

'Yes, Sir,' said Bennett.

'Right. It's on; fix up the details with Bennett and report back to me in half an hour.'

This we did; and at 5 p.m. returned to the C-in-C's office. He was in a genial mood, and asked me: 'When are you returning to 21 Army Group?'

'We are crossing at midnight by Naval launch from Portsmouth,' I said.

'Time for a decent dinner in London: take my Bentley and my chauffeur,' he said.

Thus was our business despatched: hardly a surplus word was spoken on either side. The great 'Bomber' Harris was tough, decisive, even daunting, but his final gesture showed the warm consideration with which I believe he treated all his subordinates. Years later, at the unveiling of the statue of Lord Portal, who had started his career in World War I as Lieutenant Portal, Royal Engineers, I was able as Chief Royal Engineer to remind him of his friendly gesture.

We looked in at Stanmore on our way to the 'decent dinner'. I heard from Solly that he proposed to watch the bombing. I arranged to meet him near the battlefield on the night of the attack. We positioned ourselves not very far from the target. Precisely on time, the Pathfinders arrived and dropped their flares; then wave after wave of heavy bombers flew in and the earth literally shook beneath our feet. The results however were disappointing: in daylight we walked over the churned-up area of the bombing. Dead Germans were noticeably few.

Throughout this period my planning staff was engaged in studying the likely development of operations four to six weeks ahead. These staff papers formed the basis on which the logistic staff could juggle their demands for petrol and ammunition, the Engineer planners could anticipate their requirements of bridging equipment and the whole vast organisation of staff and supporting services could anticipate events.

On 22nd August as we approached the river Seine, for which the crossing places and bridging requirements had long since been decided, we were asked for an estimate of the number of divisions that should be allotted to the Army Group which would move northwards from the Seine to strike into Germany.

As a preliminary, we examined the four possible approaches:

Route A. Via Antwerp and Holland 'across numerous rivers and through a maze of inundatable areas'.

Route B. The historic route through Maubeuge and the Aachen gap thence northwards round the Ruhr.

Route C. Through the Ardennes.

Route D. South of the Ardennes through the Metz gap (to the Saar and Frankfurt).

We recommended route B as 'the most suitable for a major thrust in autumn and winter'.

We estimated that fifteen divisions should be directed on Aachen, with eleven divisions to clear the coast and to capture ports, i.e. twenty-six in all to thrust north of the Ruhr. But this was not to be. Despite Monty's proposed thrust of forty divisions, 'so strong that they need fear nothing', and despite the SHAEF planners recommending in

September that the thrust north of the Ruhr should be twice the strength
of the Frankfurt thrust, no major thrust was ever consistently adopted
by Eisenhower, who became the Land Forces Commander from 1st
September. In default of higher direction, each Army Group virtually
decided its own strategy; Monty's 21 Army Group eventually became
bogged down in 'the inundatable areas of Belgium and Holland' of
Route A, there was no strong thrust via Aachen, and the chance of
finishing the war in 1944 was lost.

During July I was also heavily involved in planning possible operations with the headquarters of the British Airborne Corps located in
Berkshire. It was a strange experience to leave the intense operational
atmosphere of our headquarters located in a Normandy orchard, and
then sit round a polished table in England with the Airborne planners,
some of whom were calculating how to finish their duties in time to
watch the 4.30 race at Ascot! General 'Boy' Browning, elegant and
debonair, seemed to fit well into that scene. We had to take a very sober,
realistic view of the possible gains of such operations; and more particularly study the crucial question of how soon could an airborne drop be
supported by a land follow-up with armour and heavy weapons. Not
one of these operations which were linked to the crossing of the Seine,
the Somme and the Aisne, etc., was ever launched, because the land
advance moved so quickly as to negate the requirement of an air
landing. This series of aborted operations was to contribute to a
tragically wrong decision in mid-September.

Towards the end of August Eisenhower allocated to Monty the
resources of the recently formed Allied Airborne Army, commanded by
the US Major-General Brereton. This force included the British 1st
Airborne Division and the 52nd (Airportable) Division together with
the US 82nd and 101st Airborne Divisions and the Polish Parachute
Brigade. As an élite force, they were intent on getting into the battle.
They spent their time in England training intensively and planning for
various possibilities associated with 21 Army Group's advance, and in
early August Monty and 'Boy' Browning had discussed a possible
operation at Boulogne, which never took place.

On 27th August, after a conference in which I had been involved,
General Brereton issued orders to General Browning as 'Task Force
Commander' to carry out an operation at Tournai, 'to seize a firm base,
hold a bridgehead over the river Escaut and control the principal road

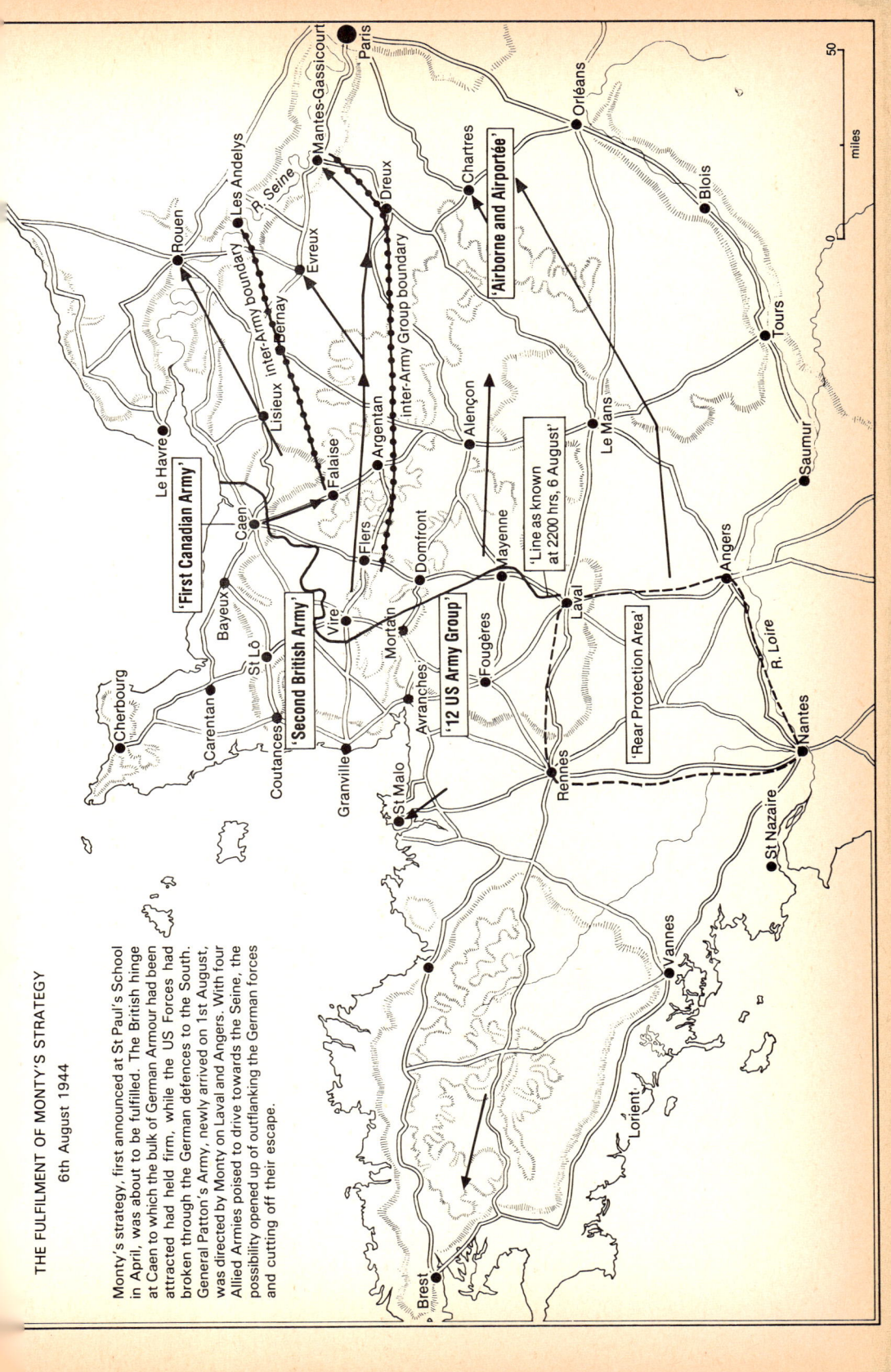

THE FULFILMENT OF MONTY'S STRATEGY

6th August 1944

Monty's strategy, first announced at St Paul's School in April, was about to be fulfilled. The British hinge at Caen to which the bulk of German Armour had been attracted had held firm, while the US Forces had broken through the German defences to the South. General Patton's Army, newly arrived on 1st August, was directed by Monty on Laval and Angers. With four Allied Armies poised to drive towards the Seine, the possibility opened up of outflanking the German forces and cutting off their escape.

Paris

Mantes-Gassicourt

Orléans

Les Andelys

R. Seine

Dreux

Chartres

'Airborne and Airporté'

Rouen

Evreux

Blois

Le Havre

Lisieux

Bernay

inter-Army boundary

Argentan

inter-Army Group boundary

Alençon

Le Mans

Tours

'First Canadian Army'

Caen

Falaise

Flers

Domfront

'Line as known at 2200 hrs, 6 August'

Angers

Saumur

Bayeux

St Lô

'Second British Army'

Vire

Mortan

Mayenne

Laval

R. Loire

Cherbourg

Carentan

Coutances

Granville

Avranches

Fougères

'12 US Army Group'

'Rear Protection Area'

Nantes

St Malo

Rennes

St Nazaire

Vannes

Lorient

Brest

50

miles

0

nets . . .' Although this operation, like many before it, never took place, an immense amount of staff planning was put into it; so much so that in terms of procedures it may have led to over-confidence. Changes in the operational situation near Tournai then took place, to which I drew Freddie's attention on 2nd September : 'The conditions of this operation have changed so much, that I feel that certain points should be emphasised to General Browning before he takes off . . . the object of the operation now seems to me to be to give added infantry strength to the Second Army right forward so that they can continue their thrust to Antwerp. The strength of Second Army's thrust is limited by maintenance and hence, to achieve our object, the Airborne Force must be independent of ground supply. This makes the securing of an airfield of first priority, and there is little doubt that it can be done provided we do not give the enemy time to blow up the runways . . .'

I went on to suggest that the Polish Brigade was no longer essential, and should be removed from the Tournai operation and used instead in Second Army's thrust to Antwerp. There, by a *coup de main* they should be able to prevent the flooding of the area.

However, on that day the weather became so bad that the Tournai operation was called off. The task force was still standing by, and I then suggested that it might be used on General Bradley's front to secure the bridges over the Meuse between Maastricht and Liège, but this was later turned down by General Bradley.

We expected then that the Airborne Divisions would be used for a Rhine crossing probably at Wesel. But Monty, after consultations with General Browning, agreed that drops at Grave, Nijmegen and Arnhem should take place to avoid the strong concentrations of German flak at Wesel. Thus the tragic Arnhem operation 'Market Garden' was set in motion.

It was hardly surprising that Monty enthusiastically adopted Browning's plan as his own. He was still intent on trying to finish the war before winter set in at the end of 1944, and to remove the threat of the V2s which was known to be imminent. He was totally frustrated at Eisenhower's vacillation over priority for the main thrust; the two commanders were 500 miles apart and had not seen each other for many days. He was clinging tenaciously to his theme of a very strong thrust north of the Ruhr, a theme which was militarily correct but politically almost impossible to adopt. He had been allocated the airborne resources by Eisenhower to augment his northern thrust, and the airborne divisions together with the Poles were 'raring to go'. Eisenhower in a letter of 24th August had emphasised that they must be used. Unlike the Tournai operation and all those that had been planned before it, Market Garden had a strategic objective which was crystal clear and of overwhelming importance. The stakes were high. Freddie, who could have inspired greater caution, was in poor health and out of touch. The potential difficulties inherent in the operation were underestimated by General Browning, and Monty in his frustrated but overconfident mood went along with him. He spoke of it to us with great confidence as 'the laying of a carpet'. Such metaphors are always dangerous : if it was a carpet, it had to straddle some dangerous gaps of which the furthest was the most critical. Those who proceeded along the carpet would gain no security until the end was reached.

There had been a surfeit of airborne planning; it was perhaps for this reason that Monty accepted this plan without the usual cautious scrutiny that he personally applied, reinforced by detailed examination by his staff. My only concern with the plan, which arrived at our headquarters ready-made and accepted by Monty for immediate implementation, was that the force to be landed at the furthest bridge was inadequate : it was stated that additional aircraft to increase his force were not available. Freddie was sick at this crucial comment, but David, Bill and I were successful in obtaining from the Americans a few more aircraft, but not in our view enough. We also recommended a postponement of the operation, while these matters of life and death were being further considered.

As was our custom, David after much discussion with Bill and myself gripped the executive handling of the operation, now only a day or two away. We were very remote from the action with an Army HQ and a Corps HQ intervening before General Horrocks's divisions were reached. The Guards Armoured Division and 43 Division were chosen for the vital follow-up by land : a follow-up in this case along one embanked road with sunken Dutch meadows on either side.

Immediately after the airborne landing, I decided to leave the fleshpots of Brussels, where the citizens had been so generous to us, and drive to Nijmegen accompanied by my friend Oliver Poole, the logistic planner. We realised that there was little we could do about the forward battle, but by short-circuiting the long complex chain of command we might make ourselves useful over any logistic emergency that might have arisen. On the way forward, we were very worried by the slow progress of the follow-up. Geographically the situation could not have been more difficult – divisions advancing on a narrow frontage of one road with no possibility of manoeuvre. We ourselves were repeatedly held up as scattered German units attempted to block the advance. Eventually we arrived at Nijmegen, where I reported to General Horrocks, who seemed less decisive than usual, and to General 'Boy' Browning and the American commanders of the 82nd and 101st US Airborne divisions, both of which had a very high reputation in combat.

Although the Nijmegen bridge was eventually taken intact, it was evident by now that disaster had occurred at Arnhem. Hopes were expressed here and there that that situation could be overcome, but I greatly doubted it. Oliver intended to return to Brussels that day, but by now the access road had been cut by German units behind us, and we spent a disturbed and frugal night in a Dutch cellar. Greatly depressed, we returned to Brussels the next day after the road had been cleared. There we heard from David that Monty had categorised the operation as 90% successful. This was for public consumption! The operation had failed. Had it succeeded, the course of history would have been radically altered.

I shall draw a veil over the frustrations that followed as winter descended and the Allied advance became 'bogged down'.

On 16th December the great German counter-offensive through the Ardennes, initiated personally by Hitler and prepared in great secrecy, took the US Forces by surprise. The situation became alarming; a large salient was driven into US First Army's positions, and there was a possibility that German Panzer divisions might get across the Meuse and drive towards Brussels, thus outflanking 21 Army Group.

Monty reacted instantly with his accustomed professional skill. Liaison officers were sent far and wide to discover what was going on in the US Sector where information was vague and scanty. Emergency defensive arrangements were organised on the Meuse bridges. On 19th December Eisenhower instructd Monty to take command of the US First and Ninth Armies north of the German Salient, since the command arrangements of 12th US Army Group had been rendered ineffective by the enemy's intrusion.

If proof were needed that an overall Land Forces Commander was essential, as Monty had repeatedly argued with the Supreme Commander, the Ardennes disaster provided it.

We viewed Monty's immediate grasp of the crisis with profound admiration; and at the time we heard that those American divisional commanders who were 'taken in hand' by Monty and directed what to do with comradely encouragement, had openly recognised a first-class commander and a friend in need.

Unfortunately, although Monty acknowledged that the battle was won primarily by the staunch fighting qualities of the American soldier, he mishandled a Press Conference and this gave rise to public bitterness between the United States and Britain.

Meanwhile my staff in conjunction with the Sappers were concentrating on the problems of bridging the Rhine, which we anticipated would take place in the early spring of 1945. Monty had decided to cross the Rhine, the greatest water obstacle in Western Europe, with Second British Army on the left and Ninth US Army on the right between Rheinberg and Rees. At low water the width was about 500 yards, increasing to 1,000 yards at high water. A major risk in the operation was flooding, and much research was undertaken to assess the likelihood and the effects of flooding during the crossing operation. Booms upstream were planned, and other measures undertaken to lessen the potential risks. Geologists analysed the Rhine's gravel and mud to determine their bearing pressures; these were important factors in relation to trestles to be built after the assault. Enormous quantities of bridging material and stores had to be brought up, amounting to 10,000 tons per day at railheads.

The techniques of the assault operation included a massive air drop, heavy concentrations of artillery and air support together with the use of smoke and of amphibious tanks and vehicles. Naval craft were transported by road from the Channel coast. Thirty-seven thousand Royal Engineers and Pioneers and twenty-two thousand US Engineers took part. The technical director of this vast enterprise was the Chief Engineer 21st Army Group, Major-General Sir J. Drummond Inglis.

After four days of fighting of varying intensity the operation was successfully concluded.

Meanwhile Freddie had returned to us: he was somewhat worn down by illness due to his frail constitution, and by the immense strain of coping with Monty's demands and shielding him where possible from the dangerous consequences of his tactless antics. David was a splendid supporter; loyal, efficient and sympathetic; he introduced into Freddie's office at this time a 'remembrancer' – an excellent cavalry officer, Major Bill Bovill, known by us as 'the Black Prince' from his dark complexion and courtly manners. It was the Prince's duty to keep Freddie up to date with current problems, and to record and disseminate the decisions taken verbally in his office. Freddie's memory was becoming unreliable, and we seemed to be losing touch with Monty who was becoming more and more despotic.

My mind was turning increasingly to the problems of controlling Germany after resistance had ceased. I was convinced that with Hitler in charge fighting would continue until the bitter end. This was not the view in London where governmental negotiations had been in train to agree with the Soviet Union the post-war division of Germany into zones of occupation. As early as September we had been given the internationally agreed boundaries with the Soviet Armies and the division of Berlin into the various national zones.

An impressive staff, including some thirteen elderly generals, had been set up to exercise control from Berlin. The concept in Whitehall seemed to be that these gentlemen, including civilian experts in the economic, transportation and financial fields, would be flown into Berlin at an appropriate moment, establish themselves alongside the relevant German ministries and issue the necessary instructions by memoranda and telephone through German civil servants. We, on the other hand, persisted in the belief that any form of German central government would be destroyed before a surrender took place, and that the control of occupied Germany must be built up parish by parish as these were reached. Much later, some form of centralised control could be superimposed on top.

Monty was eventually appraised of this controversy and, relishing no doubt the opportunity of correcting his superiors in the War Office, he sent me to see the Vice-Chief of the Imperial General Staff, Lieutenant-General Sir Archibald Nye, in Whitehall:

'Tell him, Charles, he's got it all wrong. Tell him to sack all those useless generals. We'll run the show, and when we want any help from Whitehall we'll let them know.'

Off I went to the hallowed portals of the War Office. Never having served there, I entered by the front door, not knowing that this privilege was exclusively reserved for the Secretary of State for War and the Chief of the Imperial General Staff! The doorkeeper, august in livery, smuggled me round to a side door where I was asked to declare my business: then I was led to the VCIGS's office. 'Archie' Nye greeted me with great courtesy and sat me in an exceedingly low armchair. I said my piece, omitting any reference to the sacking of generals. Provided we obtained acceptance of our concept, most of the generals would disappear through inanition. And so it came about.

The Allied advance accelerated in the spring of 1944, with the British being directed on Lübeck and the Americans on the almost mythical 'last redoubt' in Bavaria. Tragically the option of capturing Berlin was left to the Soviet Armies. German resistance in the north was beginning to collapse, and we felt the time had come to call forward from London Major-General R. H. Dewing, the British general destined to represent the Allied Supreme Commander in Copenhagen, when 'liberated'. He arrived with a very efficient female officer as his personal assistant. No sooner had I briefed them both on the likely course of events, and made arrangements for their return to London the next day, than information reached us that the German forces in Denmark proposed to surrender immediately. Thus the General's destination became Copenhagen not London. He was to fly there on 5th May the day after the German surrender at Luneberg Heath.

His personal assistant, a dynamic young lady of considerable initiative immediately came to see me:

'Of course I shall go with him,' she said.

'Quite impossible.'

'But he won't be able to function without me.'

This was an exaggeration, but it seemed to me that there might be a grain of truth in it! I gave her the reasons for my refusal:

'We have heard about the surrender only by an obscure radio link, and some of the enemy may well not observe it. Your general is being flown in by RAF bomber and there's no guarantee that his plane won't be fired at. Generals are expendable, but we can't have a woman killed.'

She continued to argue, so I produced my trump card:

'Perhaps you would like to come with me to see Field-Marshal Montgomery and give your reasons?'

Aware of Monty's reputed attitude to women, she capitulated, and packed her bags for London. A few days later, the RAF flew me into

Copenhagen for a three-day visit. On arrival I was greeted with a friendly smile by the General's female assistant.

'I've got you the best room in the best hotel,' she said.

'Very decent of you,' I said. 'I congratulate you on outwitting the bureaucrats of Whitehall.'

She was a very loyal and determined lady!

By day, Copenhagen was certainly en fête. At night there was ceaseless small arms fire: Danes of various persuasions were paying off old scores!

I flew with General Dewing over the coastal areas of Denmark where, in accordance with the directions issued by my planning staff, hundreds of thousands of Germans were 'corralled' into various peninsulas, while squadrons of British armoured cars patrolled the exit necks. Rations were dropped to them by air: the terrifying scourges of Europe were now remarkably docile and well-disciplined!

Monty, as was to be expected, staged the surrender scene at his Tactical Headquarters on Luneberg Heath as a solo performance. His Chief of Staff, Freddie, was not invited. Shortly afterwards General Kinzel, the Chief of Staff of Field-Marshal Busch the German C-in-C North-west, was ordered to report to Freddie to receive instructions, and to establish himself at our headquarters with radio communications back to the surrendered German armies. Some ten of us staff officers sat with Freddie on one side of a table in a tent when General Kinzel was announced. I could not help thinking that the scene had been extracted from some opera. He wore glistening black thigh boots and spurs, a long dark grey overcoat faultlessly pressed, a highly embellished general's hat which failed to conceal a typically teutonic head fading away vertically at the back; the final touch was a pair of mauvish grey gloves which, after a superbly formal salute, he slowly peeled from his manicured fingers.

He sat down alone on the far side of the table and as Freddie read out from his notes the innumerable orders to be carried out, the General in staccato German successively replied:

'Yes, sir, understood.'

It became our custom to invite our tame German to 'Morning prayers', when the principal staff officers were assembled, and Freddie received reports and issued verbal instructions. After some days of faultless co-operation, Freddie asked the German whether there was

(Top left) The occupation of Germany: General Sir Ronald Weeks, Deputy Military Governor, at his Headquarters Schloss Benkhausen, Lubecke (with Author on right).

(Top right) Staff officers of HQ 21 Army Group just after VE Day. Brigadier 'George' Baker tipping his chair, and Brigadier 'Bill' Williams reading in the foreground.

Schloss Benkhausen in Hitler's day: a parade of Hitler youth.

Skiing with friends from Berlin in 1946. Author in front, now Chief of the Military Division of the British Control Commission, with Captain Martin Evans RN and Lieut-Commander Nigel Browne, RNVR.

My Soviet colleague Lt. General Lukienchenko, debating the demilitarisation Germany in the Quadripartite Military Division of the Allied Control Commission.

Entertaining American, Fren and Russian colleagues, Lef to right: Maj-General Silas B Harper (USA), Brig-General Gauché (France), Maj-Gene 'Sandy' Galloway Chief of St 21 Army Group, Lt-General Lukienchenko (USSR), Capt M. Gow (Scots Guards) by door.

Monty's 80th Birthday Dinn at the Royal Hospital Chelse 17th November 1967. Left t right: Kit Dawnay, Hugh Mainwaring, Frank Simpson Johnnie Henderson, Bill Williams, Charles Richardso Llewelyn Wansborough-Jones, Harold Redman, George Cole, Richard Sharples. In front: Freddie d Guingand, Monty, Brian Robertson, Miles Graham, John Harding, Oliver Leese anything we could do to help him discharge his onerous task. Kinzel asked that a Personal Assistant might be brought to the headquarters to assist him. This request was granted, but cancelled when the PA turned out to be a beautiful blonde.

Not long afterwards, the General failed to appear at Morning Prayers. Whilst on a visit to his German headquarters he had shot his girl friend and himself. Verdi would have relished it!

CHAPTER ELEVEN

Berlin

From 'surrender' we turned to 'occupation'. Germany was totally devastated, and thousands of Germans were starving or dying of cold. The only form of government that was functioning was that which had been set up locally by our own Military Government branch under General Templer who had become Director after recovering from being wounded in Italy. Berlin was in the hands of the Soviet Army: although access to it had been politically agreed, and sectors of the city had been allocated to the Allies, we could not enter Berlin until permitted to do so by the Russians. There was talk of signing a formal treaty of surrender there, but despite repeated enquiries no one knew when this might happen. Monty went on leave to England, as did Sir William Strang, his political adviser.

On 4th June, suddenly with that arbitrariness which I learnt afterwards was typical of Soviet procedures, they announced that the treaty was to be signed in Berlin in 36 hours time. The Supreme Commander was invited together with the national representatives including the French who, by this time, had somehow established their status as victors. I was told to arrange the British part of this event, which increasingly assumed the character of *opera bouffe*.

The RAF agreed to assemble five Dakota aircraft on a wartime airstrip not very far from our headquarters. I sent off signals to Monty and Sir William Strang, and hoped these would reach them and be acknowledged. A group of cypher clerks, pressmen and Military Police with their motor cycles was assembled. I inspected them at 6 a.m. on the airstrip after a sleepless night on the telephone. We all looked to the north-west, hoping that the principals would arrive before the curtain went up. My modest aim was to arrive at Tempelhof at least ahead of the French, who to my mind had little justification for being there.

Monty and Sir William Strang arrived late, and off we set. No one had any inkling of what lay ahead. On arrival, lined up at Tempelhof, there was a massive guard of honour extending over five hundred yards or more. Monty was seized by a Russian colonel and, with his best victory smile firmly in place, disappeared towards the Guard of Honour. Another colonel seized me and placed me in his staff car.

'Where is the Field Marshal going, and where am I going?' I asked. Through an interpreter, it appeared that we were going to the same destination – unspecified as yet. I could but relax!

We drove at high speed through derelict streets lined on either side with immense piles of rubble, and arrived at a suburb (it was in fact Potsdam) where my Colonel Ivanovich (if that was his name) led me into a little villa; in the dining room was laid out a massive feast of caviar and cold delicacies, together with bottles of sweet Crimean champagne. The wing commander in charge of our Dakotas, who had accompanied me, looked pleased. His pilots were back at Tempelhof enjoying Russian hospitality.

'Will the General (that was me) please sit down, and have some refreshment?' asked Ivanovich through his interpreter.

'A little later,' I said.' First I must find Field-Marshal Montgomery and discover what is going to happen. Do you know?' I added.

'I know nothing,' Ivanovich replied. 'I am here to look after you.'

Reconnaissance seemed to be the best course for me, so I walked out into the suburban street. No sign of life anywhere. I turned a corner and there stood a reporter of the *Daily Express*!

'Do you know what's going on?' I asked.

Like every good reporter he knew quite a lot!

'Field Marshal Montgomery is in that house over there trying to get Zhukov's agreement that the British do not withdraw now from the Magdeburg bulge: not a hope, I would say! Then I believe the treaty is to be signed in the Yacht Club over there, sometime this afternoon.'

Monty's attempt to bargain with Zhukov, prompted by Churchill, was a hopeless task. The agreement on the final zones having been endorsed at Yalta on 11th February 1945, Churchill had always hoped that the Allied Armies would reach Berlin, the capital to be internationally occupied, before the Soviet armies could arrive. But Eisenhower's policy of advancing on a broad front, instead of with a concentrated thrust, combined with the lure of Hitler's last redoubt in Bavaria and Monty's failure at Arnhem had denied that chance, which had seemed within our grasp in September 1944. Nevertheless, in the British sector, we had advanced eastwards into part of the designated Soviet zone – the 'Magdeburg Bulge'. Monty's brief was to obtain Zhukov's agreement to setting up the Allied Control Council in Berlin before we withdrew from the Bulge.

Having thanked the war correspondent, I visited the Yacht Club; inside a small public room there was an immense circular table : arc lights were being erected by Russian soldiers. Then I returned to Ivanovich, and sampled his delicacies !

Later the great men smiling for the photographers assembled round the table. Diplomatic speeches were made by all the participants, who then withdrew for a private meeting. Meanwhile, as it was getting late, I thought I had better get Ivanovich to assemble some transport. Then someone said, 'We are all going to a banquet and staying the night.' I thought this might be interesting, although we were quite unprepared for it; not a toothbrush amongst us ! I understood that the Russians always enjoyed a party. But Monty, not a party man, and always early to bed, decided at 7 p.m. to leave with Eisenhower, to the dismay of Zhukov and his colleagues.

So, no banquet for us, but back to Tempelhof, where a strange sight met the eyes of the wing commander. One Dakota was unserviceable with a punctured tyre : so were two pilots stretched on the grass, over-come by Soviet hospitality ! A quick change of the loading plan, and Monty was safely airborne, though somewhat erratically. The three other Dakotas followed, leaving the last with the wing commander and myself and some passengers. Despite Crimean champagne and caviar he was competent. We flew off westwards as dusk was falling. He told me there were no established aids for night landing at our airstrip. Then in a relaxed mood he put his plane on 'George', and came back to my bucket seat and asked me to join him in the second pilot's seat. Soon he was fast asleep ! Better leave him alone, I thought, so that he can perform well at our night landing. 'George' appeared reliable. We reached the landing strip where a few improvised flares helped the wing commander to make a perfect landing. So ended for me the signing of the Treaty of Surrender at Potsdam. The history books describe it differently !

The four Allied Powers, USA, USSR, Britain and France were to govern occupied Germany through a quadripartite Control Commission, as agreed at the Yalta Conference. The Military C-in-C was ex-officio the Military Governor, and he was to be allocated a Deputy who was to handle most of the work of civil government. The first Deputy Military Governor to be appointed in the British Zone was General Sir Ronald Weeks, later to become Lord Weeks.

General Weeks had had a distinguished career as a Territorial Officer in World War I, and afterwards had been very successful in industry; he rejoined the Army for World War II, and rose to become Deputy Chief of the Imperial General Staff. I was appointed as his Military Assistant to help him get the wheels turning when Germany was still reeling from defeat. We set up our headquarters in Schloss Benkhausen near Lübbecke. General Weeks was an immensely able and very likable man – very quiet in his dealings, as so many high executives often are. There was so much to be done under Monty's broad direction that he had to select his priority objectives with great care : transportation, food, economic development on a democratic basis, currency reform, denazification, prisons, educational reform, trade unions, reparations . . . the list was endless. Transportation was a top priority and the railways with full German co-operation started to revive quickly. We flew together from meeting to meeting, and I watched with admiration how he sparked off initiative after initiative, and then soundly delegated the ensuing implementation to others. He had excellent personal relations with Monty, whose lucid thinking even in the unfamiliar worlds of economics and high finance he much admired.

Monty had assailed the task in Germany with his usual mixture of leadership and foresight. To the civilian heads of the Control Commissions' 'Divisions' he had explained his military method of working: General Weeks would be his 'Chief of Staff'. He invited direct contact between the heads of the divisions and himself, but this seldom occurred. He identified the problems of food, coal and transport, which must be tackled with great vigour before the onset of winter, and later he forecast an increasingly liberal policy towards the defeated Germans, to whom he had no inclination to be charitable, having had to fight them twice in his own lifetime. Yet his dictatorial rule over the ruins of Germany did contain a strong element of Christian charity and a vision of a better Europe at peace. His policies to the Germans were promulgated by a series of 'Messages', some of which, in advocating political activity and an uncensored Press, were in 1945 ahead of time and became highly controversial with the Americans.

Unfortunately General Weeks, after a few months, had to retire on grounds of health; but meanwhile I was appointed to Berlin as Chief of the British Military Division of the Quadripartite Control Commission. After a long delay the Soviet Authorities had agreed to admit us; there I set up shop in July 1945.

I was allotted a superb house, architect designed, in a fine residential area close to the Grünewald, with our offices in the centre of the British Sector of Berlin. The house had previously been occupied by the Soviet Army. An armour-piercing shell had penetrated one corner leaving two neat holes, but there was nothing neat about the bedrooms where the Russian soldiers with axes had removed every available mirror, never having seen such things before. In those early days, the Russian soldiers in Berlin were very primitive; they appeared to have come from the outlying Asiatic provinces of the USSR, and their crude conduct did nothing to sustain the reputation of our Soviet Ally. Stalin's directives matched the barbarity of his soldiers: the punitive and wholesale removal of industrial machinery, plant and stores, and an order to his armies that they should live off the German economy now in ruins were typical of his policies.

My house had five bedrooms and three bathrooms as well as staff quarters and stabling. I acquired a splendid English-speaking German butler, 'Albert', an ardent Anglophile from his days with a catering firm in India; he still retained vivid recollections of the Delhi Durbar of 1912! A cook, two housemaids and a Polish lieutenant-colonel from a prisoner-of-war camp to act as groom completed my entourage. My horse of 17 hands came from a Polish remount depot and, like the groom, cost me nothing.

Our task in conjunction with our allies was to draft laws for the demilitarisation of Germany; on the face of it this appeared to be simple. Our proceedings, which had virtually to be unanimous, were passed upwards to the Allied Control Council for endorsement. The Council consisted of Eisenhower, Zhukov, Montgomery and Koenig (for the French).

My colleagues were an interesting assortment: the Russian was an enormous Lieutenant-General Lukienchenko, originally, I understood, a peasant from the Caucusus; the American was a Major-General Harper of the US Air Force whom I found very congenial; the Frenchman was an elderly, cynical Brigadier-General Gauché. At our first formal meeting, we agreed that the chairmanship should 'rotate' monthly, and that our American should first take the chair. He set an awkward precedent by deciding to have a dinner party for his colleagues – a stag party, since there were no wives in Berlin. On a fine evening we assembled with our interpreters at the American General's sumptuous house by the Havel lake. Martinis 'on the rocks' were handed round by his ADC, as we stood on the lawn admiring the sailing boats.

'Do you have sailing boats like this in Russia?' I asked Lukienchenko in desperation. After a lengthy translation the answer came back:

'The General says that the boats in Russia are much bigger.'

So, diplomatic tittle-tattle proceeded laboriously for three-quarters of an hour: there was no sign of dinner, the martinis were getting stronger and the General's ADC was looking increasingly worried. Then the truth came out: our dinner was to be cooked by electricity and the Russians, who controlled Berlin's electricity, had turned it off at 7 p.m. Finally we sat down, emotionally and physically exhausted, at 10.30 p.m. After dinner, to enliven the sombre proceedings, my American colleague put Churchill's war speeches on his gramophone. 'Luke', as we called him, was not amused!

I was to be the next chairman. Profiting from my friends' mistakes, I had a generator installed in the garden. Next I clearly needed an ADC, and so sent a request to the War Office. The reply came back immediately 'ADC's are not authorised for Brigadiers'. I countered with: 'Amendment: for ADC read GSO III (operations)'. The war had ceased and there were no 'operations', but Michael Gow, aged 21, arrived. How fortunate I was! Subsequently in 1954, he was my brigade major, and we have remained close friends ever since. Now as General Sir Michael Gow he is about to retire after a most distinguished career. In Berlin he entered at once with enthusiasm into our 'Alice in Wonderland' existence, organising our social diary, keeping our colleagues and our Germans happy, and spurring Albert on to further 'distinguished services' at our frequent parties.

With Michael's support, I decided that we would try to avoid the *longueurs* of a stag party by having a dance after dinner in my superb L-shaped drawing room. I approached various 'military and diplomatic' ladies including Gill Gambier-Parry, a general's daughter, who was soon to marry Bill Williams, and persuaded them to accept my invitation in sacrificial vein in the cause of inter-allied solidarity. Personally, I had great hopes of our 'Chairman's Party', and thought I might begin to understand Luke's thought processes. The Russians after all, were our allies, I said to myself : as yet we had not been briefed by Sir Christopher Steel on their sinister intentions. Indeed we still had a vision of a united Germany!

The menu for our stag dinner at 8 p.m. was arranged; excellent wines were acquired and a German band was hired for the night. Luke had neither answered my formal invitation nor told me who would accompany him, ADC or Commissar or both. However I was confident that he would come. At 7 p.m. as I was relaxing in a hot bath, Michael tapped on the door :

'Sir, the Russians have come an hour early, I gather on Moscow time, not Berlin time!'

'All right, keep them in play with lots of drink while I put on some clothes.'

When I arrived in the drawing room Luke, in full regimentals, was warming his backside in front of our baronial fireplace. I noticed that the Commissar with his shaven head, not one of our favourites, stood by him. But Luke was not drinking : this boded disaster. I took Michael aside. In a worried whisper he told me :

'He doesn't like whisky, vodka, gin or brandy.' (This restraint may have been due to the Commissar's presence.)

'I'm going to try him on our Mosel.'

The Mosel was very special : ordered for the first course, I had been rather mean; there were only six bottles and Luke took to it in a big way. Thereafter Michael and I had to work hard until the other *chers collègues* arrived : they all played up splendidly, but the dinner party was stilted and dreary. My interpreter, Captain Freddie Dub of the Royal Pioneer Corps, whose family had come to England in 1938 from Czechoslovakia, skilfully lubricated the diplomatic scene : I am glad to say that we still meet regularly forty years later.

At 9.30 p.m. the ladies arrived and the band struck up. Luke continued to warm his backside. With shiny black riding boots up to his thighs, it seemed that incapacity as well as unwillingness prevented him from taking the floor. Michael was tactfully urging the colleagues and the girls to get going. I was called away by Albert, and when I returned I was overjoyed to see Luke and Gill waltzing enthusiastically round the room engaged apparently in animated conversation. She spoke no Russian and he no English!

From that moment onwards, the party went splendidly. By 4 a.m. when the sacrificial girls had retired to a well-earned rest, the four 'principals' sat round a small table for a final gossip. Luke had not drunk much, but the American had greatly enjoyed himself. The conversation, as I dimly recall it after forty years, went something like this:

General Harper: 'If we four can understand each other and stick together like tonight, the peace of the world is assured' – perhaps then there was a hiccup!

Luke (giving nothing away): '*Saglassna.*'

This, the Russian for 'I agree' and, more frequently, '*Niet*' (no) were the two words of Russian that I learnt in my ten months in Berlin.

French Brigadier (cynically): '*Ceux sont des affaires pour les politiciens.*'

Myself: 'Perhaps it's time to go to bed!'

Luke on leaving seemed happy and relaxed. Yet at our next formal meeting he was more stubborn and frustrating than ever before. I came to the conclusion that his thought processes were set in some Asiatic mould.

At our monthly meetings, our task as military dictators was straightforward. Yet in July 1945 a draft law prohibiting the carrying of firearms by German citizens was not agreed until after nine hours' debate. Luke suddenly went 'all soft'. 'Should not German farmers have shotguns to shoot rabbits?' he persisted. We could not visualise such a situation in the Russian Zone, where we already knew that draconian treatment was being handed out to the German population by their ruthless conquerors.

With the help of a political briefing from Christopher Steel whose advice, spiced with humour, was always well received, the scales fell from our eyes, and we realised that our Russian allies were playing quite a different game. Their intention seemed to be to try to create disagreement between me and my American colleague: in such an event a minority recommendation had to be submitted to the Allied Control Council, and this would doubtless provide useful opportunities for propaganda. Once the rules of the game emerged, it became much more interesting.

The true nature of the Soviet Government's policy became startlingly clear at a meeting of the Control Council which we all used to attend as observers. Marshal Zhukov, suddenly and without warning, launched a bitter attack against Monty and the British for 'perpetuating the Wehrmacht' in the British Zone. Their intelligence organisation had doubtless reported back the existence of hundreds of thousands of ex-Wehrmacht personnel not as yet in prisoner of war camps but disarmed in concentration areas, and of our *Dienstgruppen* (Service units). These units, mostly from engineer, transport and pioneer personnel, had been formed by discharging German soldiers and then reforming them dressed in dark blue battle dress under the command of British officers. The *Dienstgruppen* were then employed on high priority tasks of reconstruction in order to minimise starvation, disease and death amongst the German population.

Zhukov ended his harangue, delivered somewhat shamefacedly, by demanding a quadripartite commission of enquiry into the British Zone. Monty, caught unawares, played it well :

'I am greatly surprised that my comrade-in-arms, Marshal Zhukov, has thought fit to level these extraordinary accusations against the British occupying power. Since he has not had the courtesy to give me notice of his request, I must inform the Council that I reserve my position, and will reply at our next meeting.'

By this time, Lieutenant-General Sir Brian Robertson had become the Deputy Military Governor and he summoned me to his house for a lengthy discussion of this problem. What should Monty say in a month's time? Obviously the Russians could make embarrassing propaganda out of our *Dienstgruppen*. Our activities could not be concealed, nor could the *Dienstgruppen* be disbanded immediately as their role at that juncture was vital. The solution finally adopted by Brian Robertson for his brief to Monty was to brazen it out. We should say that we would welcome a quadripartite commission of enquiry into the British Zone, but there was one proviso : this precedent must be accepted by all and a similar commission should enter the Russian Zone to enquire into certain matters which gave the British some concern.

I was present at the Council when Monty delivered this rejoinder with his usual verve. Poor Zhukov, with Stalin on his tail, looked nonplussed and miserable : the subject was allowed to drop. In due course when their work was done, we disbanded the *Dienstgruppen*.

My task, though interesting, was not over-demanding, particularly when, uninvited by me, an excellent Deputy arrived in 1946. For a few months we really did enjoy the fruits of victory. Our international social life was highly entertaining. The concert hall used by the Berlin Symphony Orchestra, which had rapidly been reformed, despite having had its first conductor shot in error by American sentries, was in the British Sector of Berlin, and I had a call on the 'Royal' Box. I shall never forget entering there in 1945 with my colleagues all in uniform, while the vast German audience rose to its feet for 'God Save the King'!

My life was sweetened by a most attractive and intelligent French girl who was working in the French delegation, and I made many friends amongst the members of the Foreign Service who shared a mess with us, and with two naval officers, Captain Martin Evans and Lieutenant-Commander Nigel Browne. We used to go on leave together, with skiing in Bavaria or Austria as the prime objective. For one such trip, Martin through his Russian opposite number obtained permission for us to drive from Berlin to Munich straight through the Soviet-occupied zone.

The journey was hilarious and fully in keeping with other experiences with our 'gallant ally'. They kindly provided us with an impressive pass, which stated that we were on military business of the highest priority; this was emphasised by an enormous seal and the signature of Zhukov's deputy, General Sokolovsky. I could not help wondering what Brian Robertson's reaction would have been if invited to sign a pass for a brigadier and naval captain going on holiday!

In our military staff car, bespattered with Union Jacks and with skis on the roof, we left Berlin at 6 a.m.; after forking south from the Helmstedt Autobahn into the Russian Zone we expected to be challenged. Nothing happened. All went well until 3 p.m. when we came to a demolition on the Leipzig Autobahn with a Russian soldier on guard. We showed him the pass, which he turned upside down and roundabout but obviously could not read. Between the three of us, we had four words of Russian and a few hundred of German, and with these we enquired how to get to Munich. The Russian with a broad sweep of his hand indicated we should go east, so off we set on a cobbled road. Later we arrived at a farmouse close to a stream complete with Bailey bridge. To our surprise an American Top Sergeant appeared on the far side :

'Hullo, folks. Are you limeys?' he called out.

'Yes,' said Martin. 'This is General Richardson,' hoping to impress!

'Where are you from?'

'Berlin, and we want to get to Munich.'

'Jeez, that's strange: they won't let you over here.'

Meanwhile the Russian sentry at our end of the bridge was becoming increasingly alarmed, despite having been shown General Sokolovsky's signature.

I conferred in undertones with Martin. Time was passing; should we not chance our arm and rush the bridge? The Russian sentry, sensing our irregular intentions, blew his whistle and thirty soldiers under a captain tumbled out of the farmhouse with tommy guns at the ready. We parleyed with the captain, who was able to read the pass, but he decided that a policy of bureaucratic obstinacy was the safest course for him:

'This is not an official crossing place,' he said in German.

'But our military business is of the highest importance and it's getting late,' we countered.

The soldiers took up tactical positions and fingered their triggers. Then, adopting the well-known British technique of 'shouting at the natives', I roared, *'Wo ist Ihre Kommandant?'*

He was not prepared to say. Snow had started, dusk was falling and I had visions of the Kommandant in bed with his girl friend. Eventually we obtained directions to his headquarters five miles away. We set off cross-country in the snow and darkness, and were eventually challenged by another sentry. This one was amiable and seemed much more intelligent. He indicated that his headquarters was in the village; so off I set with him. No sign of life in the little village! But we came to a house, where the sentry opened the door and led me up a dark narrow staircase to the top floor. There I opened the door, and immediately stumbled on a large collection of empty wine bottles scattered over the floor.

The room was lit by one candle and there were nine Russians present, all seemingly intoxicated. This did not seem propitious; however I advanced on the Captain at the head of the table, produced the pass with a smile, and said 'Munich'. There was some discussion as to where Munich was, but eventually to my surprise the Captain, who was not drunk, started to give me directions. I indicated that he should come downstairs to the road to make all things clear, which to my surprise he did.

It was now 8 p.m. and we had hoped to be in Munich by 7 p.m. We set off once again across the snow, and arrived at another post on an Autobahn with indications that this crossing place was in use. Out of the post jumped a young officer of the NKVD, very efficient: he read the pass, understood it, called for two sentries and had the car searched by torch from top to bottom. We thought we were in the clear; but no, there were problems of identification! We all carried Allied Commission identity cards in two languages, English and Russia, but our driver Corporal Chalk of the Royal Marines appeared in Sokolovsky's pass as Corporal 'Cheek'. Pandemonium ensued, but just after midnight we were permitted to cross into the US Zone. Almost immediately we encountered a unit of the US Army on the move. Their friendly Colonel was surprised to see us; after hearing our tale he said he was sorry he could not offer us beds for the night as they were moving to another location, but would we like some hot chow? Despite my distaste for US Army food, I remember it as one of the best meals I have ever had. We reached Munich at 8 a.m., and were skiing that afternoon.

On our return journey to Berlin, we had arranged to attend two days of the Nuremberg trials. It was a strange experience to look down from the visitors' gallery on the Nazi ogres, whose names had been execrated for so many years: the obese Goering whose Luftwaffe had nearly brought Britain to her knees; the mysterious Rudolf Hess who had flown to Scotland; the pornographer Streicher, Hitler's intimate and arch Jew-baiter; Baldur von Shirach, the Youth Leader who escaped the death sentence and died in 1974; Rosenberg, the Nazi philosopher whose department for the Occupied Eastern Regions was nicknamed by Goebbels 'the Ministry of Chaos'; Frank Funk, the lawyer who was Governor-General of Poland and received a life sentence; Frank, the financial journalist who became Plenipotentiary of the war economy responsible for terrible crimes against the Jews; William Frick, another lawyer who had helped Hitler to power and as Minister of the Interior was responsible for countless acts of massacre and torture; Kalten-brunner, with the spirit and appearance of an ogre who as head of the Reich Main Security Office was responsible for the extermination

programme; Dr Ley, alcoholic and leader of the German Labour Front
who hanged himself in his cell; Sauckel, accused of hideous crimes
against foreign workers, and his boss the talented Speer, Minister of
Armaments at the age of 36, who escaped the noose; Baron von Neurath,
well known in London but responsible for brutal crimes against the
Czechs, sentenced to fifteen years' imprisonment; Fritz von Papen,
charged with conspiracy to wage aggressive war but acquitted; Seyss-
Inquart, the Austrian Quisling responsible as Reichs Kommisar in
Holland for 'liquidating' about 120,000 Jews; Dr Schacht, President
of the Reichsbank, a devious intellectual who was acquitted; General
Jodl, a very correct and competent German officer responsible for shoot-
ing without trial captured British Commandos and countless civilians;
Ribbentrop, the champagne salesman and one time ambassador in
London who, found guilty of war crimes, went to the gallows with
courage; Fritzsche, who was acquitted; Keitel, Chief of the German
Armed Forces who disowned all responsibility for carrying out Hitler's
criminal orders; and finally Admiral Raeder and Admiral Doenitz,
Hitler's successor, accused of war crimes at sea, but sentenced only to
imprisonment.

The accused, as they entered the court, looked a very sad, disillusioned and frightened group, with one exception: Goering. He,
surprisingly, had obtained the Court's permission to bring a blanket in
with him; he claimed that he felt the cold! He used to emerge last from
the small door leading from the cells and then, glancing round in a
leisurely fashion, he would grin a greeting to the other prisoners, while
sweeping his blanket over his shoulder like a Roman Emperor! Goering's
defence was in progress during our two-day visit: a senior Luftwaffe
general had been led by the German defence counsel through Goering's
activities in the inter-war years, his 'constant search for peace', etc., etc.
The witness trotted all this out with the greatest confidence. David
Maxwell Fyffe, the British Deputy to Sir Hartley Shawcross, then got
to work on him. Maxwell Fyffe, with his back to us, had a strange
habit of stroking his buttocks while in a very quiet voice he posed his
deadly questions. After half an hour, the Luftwaffe general who was
sitting facing us in a gothic style chair, became incoherent almost to
the point of insanity. It was a brilliant cross-examination, but not a
pleasant sight. Mr 'Khaki' Roberts, QC, who kindly gave us lunch, told
us that Maxwell Fyffe had repeatedly demolished witnesses in this

manner. It was not surprising that he later became Lord Chancellor, as Lord Kilmuir.

Although I felt justified in our decision to witness a small part of this extraordinary event, I left the devastated city of Nuremberg with relief. The trials left many ethical questions unanswered in our minds. Did the Allies have the moral right to hold such trials, bearing in mind that their own hands, though not stained with the innocent blood of millions, could not be regarded as scrupulously clean? Was there any alternative?

The only alternative that had been given serious consideration was Churchill's proposal that a number of prominent Nazi leaders should be summarily executed. Wisely, the British Cabinet and our Allies opposed this suggestion; it could so easily have created martyrs to be revered by succeeding generations; moreover the evidence of the worst Nazi atrocities, such as the extermination programme, would never have been so fully established.

Certainly the trials revealed in lurid detail the extent to which a great and cultured nation could be totally subverted by a manic leader who assumed dictatorial power by manipulating the political machine out-side the bounds of genuine democracy, and thereafter imposed his will through a group of despicable confederates. The lesson to be drawn is perhaps of more than transient value : mini-Hitlers can still arise in unlikely places !

It was natural and inevitable that those of us who had been campaign-ing without a break for seven years should make the most of the fruits of victory, which were ready for the taking in Berlin in 1946. Superb concerts, free membership of the Blue-White Club the Wimbledon of Berlin with a professional coach on hand, riding in the Grünewald, excellent accommodation with a staff to match, skiing in the Hartz Mountains or further afield in Bavaria, excellent wine at cheap prices, and a social round with charming and intelligent people of both sexes.

Yet this hedonistic atmosphere could be dissipated instantly by walking down the Kurfurstendamm : pinched pale faces would look upwards from the basement windows where whole families cold and hungry, were attempting to survive. My complacency was regularly shattered on the frequent occasions when I flew to London for con-ferences. From the air the spectacle of bombed and desolate Berlin, particularly in the Soviet Sector, was a forcible reminder of the grim reality of the situation.

The appalling task facing the Control Commission was to restore the social, political and economic life of the heartland of a great country, which had been completely destroyed by the bombing of its cities, and utterly demoralised by Nazi rule, total defeat and the collapse of any form of German Government. But some of those in the Control Commission who, like me, had enjoyed their fruits of victory, carried back to the United Kingdom a false picture of whisky-sodden bureaucrats 'living it up' in luxury, while the German population, prostrate under the victor's jackboot, was left to starve. In fact an enormous, urgent and successful effort was made by the British and United States Occupying Forces to rehabilitate their zones as quickly as possible, to minimise hardship and loss of life.

General Sir Brian Robertson, the Deputy Military Governor, was well supported by some brilliant civilian administrators, such as Sir Percy Mills, head of the Economic Division, later to become Lord Mills, Sir Robert Birley, Education, and Sir Paul Chambers of the Finance Division, a future chairman of ICI, whose early devaluation of the Deutschmark provided a remarkable stimulus to the German economy.

In the zone, executive action was in the able hands of General Templer whose dynamism was recognised on all sides. As at a later date, the Communist terrorists in Malaya were to find that he could be hard and ruthless in removing obstacles in his path; but if one knew him well, one could discount his occasional brusqueness and picturesque language!

The Deputy Military Governor himself, who later was to become Military Governor and Commander-in-Chief of BAOR, soon dominated the proceedings of the Allied Commission and earned the respect not only of his British and American Allies but also of the Soviet representatives. Strongly supported by Ernest Bevin, the Foreign Secretary, he exerted a profound and lasting influence on the evolution of the post-war German political system, on the structure and philosophy of their Trade Unions, and on the revival of education purged of Nazi influence. Thereby he earned the admiration not only of the Foreign Secretary, but also of Dr Adenauer. He was fortunate to be guiding and helping a people whose spirited determination and energy, once released from the Nazi yoke, was to produce a national revival, which in its speed and magnitude astonished the world.

By the beginning of 1946 I started to become restive in my job. The atmosphere of 'Congress Dances' amidst the appalling ruins of Berlin was beginning to pall. It was obvious that we could achieve little with the Russians. I had hoped that I might find some means of establishing a personal understanding with Luke and remove some of his suspicions, and had arranged to have him invited into the British Zone for a visit, with some game shooting. Not only did he not accept, but he never gave me a straight answer to my invitation.

I wrote home: 'The Field-Marshal's future is unsettled . . . I dined with him here in Berlin the other night (9th January 1946). He has great ideas on the future of the Army: I hope he is allowed to put them into effect.'

Monty, now in the running for CIGS, but not yet confirmed despite Field-Marshal Allanbrooke's recommendation, was as usual studying the major military problems that loomed ahead. Three months before, in a lecture to the Staff College, he had identified 'six fundamental points round which we should now plan the post-war Army. . . . They were:

'The structure and organisation of the Army of occupation; Organisation for command and control; The peace-time strength of the Army; Selection and training of officers; The standard of life of the soldiers; Research and development establishments.'

He had prefaced his six points with the statement: 'It is not practicable to start planning now the organisation and equipment of the Army on the basis of what will be required in the next war; if only because the full effects of developments such as the atomic bomb cannot yet be properly assessed.'

At the dinner party in Berlin, amongst the topics which Monty discussed with us were some which were to influence our futures. He argued that selected officers of Arms other than Royal Armoured Corps and Infantry should serve for two years with Armour or Infantry, to fit themselves for higher command. He emphasised also the need for proper organisations for studying the research and development of armour. Another point was the need for a high-level Director of Military Training in the rank of lieutenant-general.

These and many others of his 'great ideas on the future of the Army' were in several cases supported by Field-Marshal Alanbrooke before leaving the appointment of CIGS. But I was not to know this.

Four days later, uncertain of the future, I wrote home: 'The job here will tend to peter out in April . . . I shall then have to decide to take some longish leave, and trust to getting some sort of job at the end of it.' (I had had no leave, other than a few days, for nine years.)

The Monty team was breaking up. Soon Freddie, who was physically in poor shape and by now deprived of an appropriate niche in the post-war Army hierarchy, decided to retire. He went off to South Africa to make a fortune. Later he asked me to join him, but I declined. His life-style – big business allied to a powerful gambling urge – did not match my idea of happiness. This view was reinforced years later in Salisbury, Rhodesia, when I was the guest of Bob Long, by then the Major-General commanding the Federation Army of Rhodesia and Nyasaland. He recalled a visit to Freddie in Johannesburg: 'It was just like your Eighth Army Ops Room in battle. Four telephones ringing day and night, with Freddie responding instantly with, "right, sell gold, buy copper" or "put the lot on Happy Warrior in the 3.30".'

My debt to Freddie was enormous. At Haifa when we had first met each other, I had been struck immediately by his lively but profound intelligence; his imagination was as fertile as Chink Dorman-Smith's and like him he would never accept a conventional solution just because it was obvious. But unlike Chink, he disciplined himself to produce invariably a sound and practical conclusion. He had a strong critical judgement, but brought this to bear with such a wealth of tact and humour that the greatest personalities of the war had opened their doors to him. To us, his apprentices, he was the wisest and kindest of masters, instantly aware of all the intricacies of the complex military and political scenes, warmly approachable and a never-failing source of generous and objective counsel.

From time to time he returned to England and we met. Sadly his relationship with Monty went sour. I never fully understood the cause of this; but years later I was delighted when Brian Robertson assured me that the breach had been healed. 'I told them,' he said to me, wearing that daunting magisterial expression that I knew so well, 'you are old men now. You must not go on behaving like children.'

By now, others of Monty's team were moving to new opportunities. Oliver Poole had been demobilised so rapidly to stand for the Conservative seat at Oswestry that we missed the chance of dining him out, and had to be satisfied with a lunch party. We demanded from him a sample of his electioneering speech which, as a comic satire, was superb!

Bill Williams went off to New York to work for the United Nations. David Belchem after serving Monty faithfully for a few more years decided to leave the Army and enter industry. It was sad that with all his services to Britain in her darkest hour, real happiness seemed always to have escaped him. Miles Graham returned to his directorships, one of which was *The Times*. Without telling me, he put my name forward for the job of General Manager, but after an interview with the directors in the historic precincts of Printing House Square, I decided to 'stick to my last'. I had just got married and it was not the moment to gamble.

Peacetime soldiering was far from dull. A ruptured Achilles tendon removed me from Berlin and after too long a period in hospital, I emerged late in 1946 ready to contribute to the assessment, referred to in Monty's preface: the plan for a peacetime Army, taking account of the atomic bomb. I was fortunate to have as colleagues Rear-Admiral Charles Lamb, soon to be First Sea Lord, and Air Vice-Marshal 'Ted' Hudleston; our task was to forecast 'British Strategy 1946–61' and recommend the size and shape of Naval, Army, and Air Forces to be maintained in the light of nuclear weapons, intercontinental missiles, etc. At the end of ten months' research, including a session with our US friends, where I was glad to find Brigadier-General 'Tic' Bonesteel as a Defence Planner in Washington, our military crystal ball was still dim, but not as murky as that of our political adviser, who had assured us that Italy in 1946 was lost to communism, and France so nearly so as to be discounted as an ally. Yet Ernest Bevin's Western European Union, strongly supported by Monty, was only just around the corner.

After a year of high-level 'hot air', I was glad to relinquish my temporary rank of brigadier to command an Engineer Regiment in BAOR as a lieutenant-colonel. This lasted only a year and was followed by further staff jobs as a brigadier.

For my next critical assignment, which was in 1953, I was fortunate to command the infantry brigade of 6th Armoured Division. This opportunity seemed to follow the pattern of Monty's thinking and indeed of others. My sapper friend of Quetta, Major-General 'Splosh' Jones, was already commanding a division. I was very lucky to have as my principal staff officer (brigade major) and adviser, Major Ian Gill, who had commanded an armoured squadron in battle in his early twenties. Ian with his experience, clear brain and generous personality, steered his commander, too far removed since Eighth Army days from the battlefield, well clear of innumerable pitfalls. I owe a great deal to him. He was followed, much to my approval, by Michael Gow, my erstwhile ADC from Berlin days. Both had distinguished careers in the post-war Army.

Then, owing to the death of the incumbent in 1955 I was sent to become Commandant of the Royal Military College of Science as a major-general. I had never heard of the place! For six months it had been without a Dean (he had been promoted to the meteorological office), and of a Commandant.

I acquired a Dean, part-time to start with, Professor S. J. Davies of Kings College, London : he was an admirable colleague. Field Marshal Sir John Harding, by now CIGS, told me he was sending me there 'to make Science fashionable in the Army'. As usual he had put his finger on the nub. Those officers in the Army who knew of the College, and they were not the leaders of fashion, seemed to me to be in two minds: either as soldiers they despised it as being too academic, or as mathematicians they lauded it at the expense of the Staff College, where the emphasis was on the qualities for successful command.

Since those days, I have maintained that any general aspiring to the top should at some stage command professors. It is a daunting but enlightening experience! However I was given time to brood, and came to certain conclusions :

First, the immense speed of technological advance, which must be applied urgently to the military arts.

Secondly, that many of the future leaders of the Army were not only ignorant of this, but some of them rejoiced in shutting their eyes to it.

Thirdly, for the task of marrying these technological advances to weapon development it would be wrong to rely exclusively on the 'Scientific Civil Service' who, though many were dedicated, could not command the salaries available in industry, with the inevitable result that brilliant men could seldom be attracted.

Fourthly, that the officers made available by the system of staff training to take part in weapon development were by that very system drawn from the 'second eleven', and were destined for diminished careers, never leading to the top. This seemed too great a risk to accept in peacetime.

Fifthly, that the study of technological advances which were moving well beyond the capabilities of the Army to exploit them, must be put on a professional and permanent basis and not left to *ad hoc* study groups assembled without careful terms of reference or technological forecasts.

Lastly, that the appointment of the Master General of the Ordnance, the Army's weapons man, should not be given to any good general without technological experience of any sort, but to a good general, though not a specialist, who at some stage of his career had been in contact with these problems. Moreover he must not be frequently changed, but must remain in the appointment for a minimum of four years, bearing in mind that the development period of a major armament was ten to fifteen years.

I acquainted the War Office with these conclusions and there was a deafening silence! Nevertheless 'the elephant never forgets', and three years later I was required to establish in the War Office, in which I had never served, a new directorate of Combat Development, the 'think tank' of the future army. A year later as Director General of Military Training I was able to introduce changes in staff training to overcome many of the disabilities to which I had drawn attention. After eighteen months as QMG, in 1967 I was invited to become Master General of the Ordnance for four years, taking me to the age of 63.

When with hindsight of my six years on the Army Board I now look back to Monty in 1946, I can see why the role of CIGS did not suit him. As a commander on the battlefield, secure in the knowledge that he knew more about the business than anyone else, except perhaps Alanbrooke, he could be dogmatically simplistic and expect that his views would prevail. In the new environment where political factors forcibly intruded, the CIGS, despite enormous personal prestige, had to lobby, persuade and even negotiate. This was not his style.

Some of his great assets as a commander were irrelevant. The jungle of Whitehall, not very different from today's scenarios in *Yes, Minister*, was unfamiliar and, I suspect, distasteful to the master of the battlefield. He was not a Commander-in-Chief, but a government official whose best services to the Army might well be derived from skilful negotiations with his Naval and Air Force colleagues and with Ministers. His technique of simplifying the conflicting issues of battle, if applied without modification to the problems of the Army Council, might well be unproductive and even dangerous; he would have to master briefs which would necessarily involve more detail than he liked. He used his skilful, tactful Vice-CIGS General Sir Frank Simpson as a Chief of Staff, but even this created difficulties since, in the Army Council, the CIGS in theory is only *primus inter pares*. His colleagues expected to see a lot of him, and they didn't.

However, those of us who knew him well, and remembered how he had galvanised an Army 'baffled and bewildered' to fight and win as never before, still regarded him with abiding admiration and even affection. Years later in 1967 we assembled at his 80th Birthday Party in the Royal Hospital at Chelsea, and on a subsequent birthday I wrote to him suggesting I might call. A telegram flashed back : 'Delighted to see you. Letter follows.' The letter instructed me to arrive at 4.15 p.m. *and leave at 5.30 p.m.* 'Master' had not greatly changed ! We spent a lively afternoon dissecting his fellow members of the House of Lords. If my memory has not faltered, all were 'useless', 'quite useless', except Shinwell, Carrington and Shackleton.

As I prepared to leave at 6 p.m., he said :

'Charles, are you married ?'

I admitted that I was.

'Any children ?' he enquired.

I acknowledged there were three.

'Bring them with your wife for tea on the lawn. We'll have tea on the lawn.'

With a heavy hand, I mobilised two of the three teenagers, who showed little keenness to meet this survivor from a remote past. We were taken round the garden, where I noticed that his 'Rhus Cotinus' had been shorn 'back and sides'; it was clear that discipline ruled in the garden as elsewhere ! At the tea table, within ten minutes, the children were captivated. Two days later in answer to my 'bread and butter' letter I received a reply :

'I much enjoyed meeting your wife and children. Martin is a good lad, but needs a hair cut.'

My last visit to Monty, suggested by David, his son, was to his bedroom where he lay in pain a few weeks before he died.

His lieutenants, two of whom were to follow him as CIGS, I am sure retained their admiration for him as a leader on the battlefield : John Harding, Gerald Templer, Brian Robertson, Sidney Kirkman – to name a few. They were all very helpful to me; and I like to think I was as useful to the post-war Army as I had been to 'Master'. Certainly I was given every opportunity.

Now at the age of 77, I also look back. When I ask myself what sustained us nearly fifty years ago in those terrible times of impotence and disaster, I believe it was the conviction that the British Army would in the end prove superior to the Wehrmacht, not because of a greater talent for killing but for the qualities that lay much deeper : its long tradition of civilised duty, of incorruptibility and self-sacrifice, driven by that powerful impetus, genuine comradeship at all levels – the mainspring of the Army's successful evolution down the centuries.

Index